The
Dynamics
of
Group Behavior

© American Management Association, Inc., 1970. All rights reserved. Printed in the United States of America.

This book may not be reproduced in whole or in part without the express permission of the Association.

Standard book number: 8144-5204-3

Library of Congress catalog card number: 72-108179

First printing

The
Dynamics
of
Group Behavior

Elton T. Reeves

American Management Association, Inc.

HM
131
.R39

To my wife, Elsie,
who has seen me through this effort
and who knows I love her

Foreword

This volume has been inspired by a feeling that each person has a right to the knowledge and understanding that will help him in living with others. An attempt has been made to use terminology that is completely understandable to laymen in any walk of life. Controversial areas of theory have been labeled as to author and origin, but not every minute particle of behavior input has been referenced.

It is to be hoped that a reading of this material will clarify the ways in which people work together in groups.

ELTON T. REEVES

Table of Contents

	An Introduction to Group Dynamics	11
1	Individual Motivation	25
2	Group Motivation	49
3	Different Kinds of Groups	77
4	Properties of Groups	107
5	Effects of the Group on the Individual	135
6	Effects of the Individual on the Group	161
7	Leadership	183
8	Followership	211
9	Multigroup Membership	237
10	Role Conflict	263
11	The Deviant	286
12	The Isolate	309
13	Group Effectiveness	331
14	Group Dynamics and the Family	352
	Conclusion	378
	Glossary	380
	Index	387

An Introduction to Group Dynamics

*I*F THERE has ever been a time when it was important that people understand each other, that time is now. Mental blocks, stereotypes, and intellectual and physical violence are so rampant as to make necessary a rationale for better understanding. It is the purpose of this book to provide a basis whereby any individual can better understand how *he* fits into the social scene and how *he* can better adjust to a terrifyingly complex milieu. Before this can be accomplished, three basic concepts should be defined.

1. *Group.* For the purpose of this book, a group consists of two or more people with common objectives. These objectives may be religious, philosophical, economic, recreational, or intellectual, or they may include all these areas.

2. *Dynamics.* This word assumes a vectorial field—that is, forces active in any direction whose sums reinforce or negate each other. There may be a state of stable equilibrium if all forces add up to zero; or, if they reinforce one another,

there will be motion in some direction, and this motion will accelerate in proportion to the magnitude of the forces.

3. *Group dynamics.* Group dynamics is the study of the forces exerted by the group on the individual or by the individual on the group. We are thus concerned with group dynamics literally in almost every moment of our lives. At no time in history has it been truer that man is a social being and that it is impossible for him to exist as an independent entity.

Do human beings really change? Implicit in every educational and training activity of our society is the belief that a person's behavior can be changed by concentrated external effort. This belief is so ingrained in our national consciousness that we no longer debate it. The only controversy remaining is about the most viable and economical methods of achieving a desired behavioral mutation. There are too many documentations in daily life of radical shifts in thought and actions for us to doubt this truism of change. We have set valid and replicable patterns and procedures for alteration of an individual's personality configuration and adopted primary conditioning as a basic modus operandi for our national educational systems. People do change, and this change should be in the direction of growth and greater ability to utilize natural or acquired skills. One of the most pertinent duties of education is to enable a person to adapt to a changing environment. The mastodon was a giant of his era, but the only record we now have of his presence on earth is encased in ice. He was a victim of his own inability to adapt to a changing scene.

On the other hand, man's educational efforts can effect differences in the responses of mind, body, or spirit—changes that can be salutary or horrible beyond belief.

We must remember, however, that changes in the lifetime of one individual or of millions of individuals are no evidence of any alterations of fundamental human nature. It is the job of the historian to keep on reminding us of the cyclical nature of civilization. Group reactions under a given stimulus were as predictable in the days of Moses as they will be in A.D. 20,000. The immutability of human nature is the only solid rock upon which we can build hope for the future of mankind. It is on this rock that the entire structure of group dynamics rests its hope for utility.

The serious student of group dynamics, and the one who will benefit personally from that study, constantly keeps this dichotomy in balance. He must make intuitive evaluations many times a day as to what is generic in nature and what are those elements of change which are so important in his daily life. A generation ago, a young man borrowed the family car; today, every member of the family must have some insurance of personal mobility through the wildly different strata of his own particular megalopolis. A generation ago, a young man needed the price of a movie and a bag of popcorn for his big date. Today, a young man's serious date entails an expense approximately equal to his father's monthly income when he was married. We should not forget the exponential increase in the group memberships which today's young people enjoy as compared to those the preceding generation participated in.

At this point, no value judgment can be made as to whether the changes occurring are good or bad. The problem is to adjust to this kaleidoscopic world and maintain a near-to-normal attitude. There would be no purpose to a study of group dynamics unless it kept us on a smoother track in our everyday life. The man of the future is the one who can make these adjustments and keep a sane outlook with the least possible trauma.

Generalizations over a statistical population. Few principles in the behavioral sciences are so universal as to be called laws. There is usually no more than a high level of statistical probability that an event will take place within certain conditions. This is confusing to the average citizen, who is unfamiliar with the research methods of behavioral scientists. Workers in the "hard" sciences have established a research routine which is relatively simple and easy to follow, both theoretically and in practice. The research worker starts by simply gathering all available data, without attempting to interpret it. Hypotheses and theories are formulated only after intensive sorting and classification have been applied to the ascertained facts. More work is then done to validate or refute the working theories. If the results can be replicated independently, credence will be given to the hypothesis, which eventually can emerge as a "law" of the hard science.

The behavioral scientist works in a completely different way. He evolves theories of varying complexity and then devises experimental situations aimed at proving or disproving his theories. When working with human beings and special aspects of their behavior, the scientist finds too many independent variables to be certain of the universal applicability of his findings.

Useful applications of the behavioral scientist's findings are dependent on careful use of the normal bell curve which will develop when the statistical population has been properly chosen. Predictions can then be made in any area of the distribution curve with a high degree of accuracy. It is on this basis that certain predictive tests have been evolved which do give insight into the tester's chances of success in a given field. A good example is the complex battery of tests given by New York Life Insurance Company to prospective salesmen. The firm's experience has led management to believe that it can choose or reject sales applicants on the basis of results from this battery of tests.

There are few broad principles which can be applied to human behavior. In everyday life, we must make many judgments purely on the basis of intuition, without the backing of "laws" to assure us in advance of the validity of our decisions. In the area of group dynamics, however, there has been much experimental activity during the past several years. We are not concerned here with a minute documentation of either the scientists or the experimental methods involved, since these have been described voluminously elsewhere. Rather, we are concerned with the ways in which the individual layman can adapt these findings to his own advantage in his daily living. For instance, an awareness of the characteristics of groups will make his orientation to and assimilation into a new work group much easier. If he is the leader of a group, either formal or informal, his leadership will be stronger if he understands the theory of leadership and is sensitive to some of the forces at work within the group. Is the deviant in his group simply out of touch with the common group objectives, or is his deviance the result of thwarted aspirations to higher status within the group? Does the leader know under what circumstances group sanctions can be evoked to change the behavior of one or more members of the group? Is he sensitive to the verbal and nonverbal cues that are indicative of a change in group consensus? Is he making advantageous use of one or more of the informal leaders within his group to attain his objectives more easily?

A knowledge of certain behavioral science principles will make it possible for a group leader to predict more accurately the responses of his group to a particular set of circumstances. By ordering his own activities with care, he can avoid a threat to the safety of his group. The application of fundamental tenets of individual motivation, combined with accurate knowledge of his individual group membership, will make easier the achievement of the group's goals.

An understanding of group dynamics should not be limited to the leaders of the group. All members will find their group living more comfortable when they are aware of the forces that operate within a group. Their own effectiveness can be multiplied many times if they know some of the effects the individual can exert upon the group.

The biggest danger is that one's confidence may be shaken if a particular prediction does not materialize. The laws of probability tell us that we must expect a certain percentage of failures when we try to predict or control the behavior of group members. An occasional failure does *not* invalidate the essential usefulness of an understanding of the principles of group dynamics.

Why be concerned with group dynamics? Each of us may have his own reasons for being interested in the field of group dynamics, but, generally speaking, there are five principal reasons why an alert adult should study this area.

The first reason is that this study will increase his self-knowledge. In all the years since Plato first said, "Know thyself," no progress has been made in resolving the universal human difficulty: understanding oneself. How many times does a man say, "Now, why did I do such a thing?" His curiosity is real; he is not aware of what motivated a particular action he has just taken. Introspection, like any other action, can be overdone, but most of us do very little of it on a planned basis.

The basis for comfortable group living is adequate self-knowledge. Before we can understand others, we must first understand ourselves. That most useful attribute, *empathy*, is a measure of how well a man knows himself as well as others. How can we understand the thoughts and feelings of others unless we first relate them to our own consciousness?

The study of group dynamics forces us into introspection. In striving to be a more effective member of the groups to which we belong, our first objective is to increase our sensitivity to the impact of our own personality on others. Since the world we live in becomes more complex each year, group membership also becomes more important to us. In today's world, the old-fashioned rugged individualist has a more difficult time with each passing day. The person who has a clear understanding of what makes him tick can, if he wishes, adjust more positively and more quickly to changes in a group situation. However, it may be that the change in the group is so great that he will lose his identification with it.

Self-knowledge is closely related to intellectual and emotional maturity. The more a person studies group dynamics, the more easily he will increase his own self-knowledge. And this will in turn make quicker and easier the necessary decisions about groups in which he wants to seek or maintain membership. It is embarrassing for all concerned when an individual aspires to and finally gains entry into a group, only to discover immediately that it is not one with which he can identify. Each year, for example, young people join college fraternities and sororities and then find they cannot possibly identify with them. Nor is this unfortunate situation limited to the young. Many adults spend time, energy, and money affiliating with groups whose objectives they later discover to be far from their own.

The second major benefit of understanding group dynamics is a better ability to anticipate the actions and reactions of others. Any person whose batting average is high in this area goes through life with a tremendous edge over his fellows. If he knows with reasonable certainty how others will react to a given stimulus, he can plan his actions advantageously. Nowhere is this better illustrated in the business world than in labor relations. Both union officials and management labor relations people are successful in direct ratio to their ability to predict the actions of others with accuracy. The entire ritual of labor negotiations is based on a series of predictions as to how the opponents will react.

A more important use of this ability to predict the behavior of others is in family life. It has become fashionable to say that parents can no longer understand their children. Why can't they? This generation's young people are psychologically no different from their parents. Any normal adult who takes the trouble to do a little work in the area of teenage psychology will have a reasonable chance of bridging the generation gap in his family relationships.

An ability to predict others' actions can be put to other than salutary uses. The Chinese Communists and the North Koreans showed some years ago that they were masters at predicting human behavior when they had control of the physical surroundings of their victims. However, it is assumed for the purposes of this book that most of us are men of goodwill.

To repeat, no one should expect to maintain a perfect record in predicting the reactions of others, no matter how deep his knowledge of the principles of group dynamics. It is as certain as tomorrow's sunrise that he will meet an atypical reaction every once in a while. Further study of the situation will usually reveal a major variable which he had not considered. (The general area of atypical behavior is considered at greater length in Chapters 11 and 12.)

One interesting fact should be remembered. A deep knowledge of human motivation does not mean that we will *necessarily* alter our behavior under a given stimulus. We shall probably react in the same way we always have, but without puzzling over our reactions. One university course in the T-group, for example, was made up entirely of graduate students in psychology. The infuriating thing was that all the participants knew why they behaved as they did but still did not change their actions and reactions. If anything, the anxieties, frustrations, and hostilities which developed early in the experience seemed to be intensified.

From the standpoint of personal motivation, an ability to predict the actions of others would stand high on the list of reasons for studying group dynamics. The usefulness of this ability is immediately apparent to everyone, if only for selfish reasons.

The third advantage to be derived from a study of group dynamics is smoother interpersonal relationships. Once a man knows himself better and has learned enough about his neighbors to be able to predict how they will behave, his interpersonal relationships should be significantly improved. This is another iteration of the old adage that we tend to like people we know well and to distrust those we do not know. All this presupposes a positive attitude on the part of the parties concerned. Even if it were possible for Americans to know everything about the Communists, they would probably not be able to get along together. A harmonious social existence requires the commonality of major objectives which we included in our definition of a group.

Let us examine for a moment the present-day obsession with good interpersonal relationships on the part of a great section of the American citizenry. If we normally have good relationships with most of those around us, we can expect several things to happen. The general tenor of our life will flow more smoothly, with a resultant saving in our expenditure of energy. Our general physical health will be better, and fewer ulcers and cardiacs will occur among the populace. We will all get our work done more easily, for a true spirit of cooperation can exist only where there is goodwill among the interacting people. Our absorption in getting along with our peers is a fallout from the fact that our life today is immensely more complicated than it was when we were children. An attempt to better our relations with others can thus be seen as a pure defense mechanism.

Up to this point, a directive assumption has been made that a study of group dynamics will automatically result in better interpersonal relationships. This assumption should be tempered with one caution: If any man is having trouble with social living and wants to correct the situation, he has to be prepared to make some major changes in his own behavior. It is childish to expect the whole world to adapt itself to his desires. It is in this area that the trauma, if any, associated with a study of group dynamics will appear. We are the products of so many conditioning processes and reflexive reactions that our nervous systems recoil when we make a serious effort to change our behavior in any major way.

It all comes back to the fact that this facet of social living, like so many others, is a matter of attitude. If our mental set is such that we are consciously trying to elicit cooperation and goodwill from others, we can minimize the shock to our organism from the change projected in our general behavior.

At this point, we might note a widely held fallacious belief—that a mature human being cannot basically change his personality. Under a strong enough stimulus, any person can make major alterations in his personality at any time in life. Actually, we see this happening every day of our lives. Alcoholics Anonymous is living proof of this fact. Each of us has known one or more persons who have changed their careers in middle age, a move which often requires a great deal of expertise in the area of interpersonal relationships.

The fourth reason for studying group dynamics is the almost certain increase in satisfaction of what Abraham Maslow calls the self-actualization needs. The term refers to the constant need to grow into a larger and better self. In many people, this need is not articulated but remains as a vague sensation of uneasiness never expressed in words. The entire area of group dynamics lends itself to both a conscious realization of this basic need and a methodology for helping a person to satisfy it. Structured as it is today, life can be most fulfilling and most rewarding through success in group living. In order for any personal growth to take place, successive templates must be drawn as bases for comparison in the groups in which we have membership. As each criterion is met, we can then proceed naturally to higher goals and expend our energies in an orderly way toward their achievement.

The prototype of this activity is the growth and development of a person in his business career. At today's pace, any person whose major goals are the same today as they were five or even three years ago is a failure. Again, personal attitude is important. If the entire field is seen as a challenge to be accepted, we can organize our response in a way that will not be harmful to us.

Never have well-rounded growth and development been so important. It is impossible for any person to master one of the modern disciplines completely. Survival will result from the ability to become a generalist in the truest sense of the word. A person must be literate in a variety of fields and, most important, must understand fully how these fields mesh and interrelate. The one vehicle designed to effect this kind of integration is group dynamics. By virtue of its dual role of attention to both the individual and the group, it can be a most cogent change agent in the life of any individual.

The fifth reason for examining the field of group dynamics is really a summary of the other four. Both spiritual and economic benefits can accrue to the man or woman sensitive to the forces active in the groups in which he has membership. By being more effective in his interpersonal relationships, he can expect to be more successful in his business enterprise. The self-confidence generated by his greater expertise in group living will add to his poise and appearance. It should be apparent that this is not a field for casual approach; it involves too much of the whole man's activity. Considerable time will be needed for anyone to develop this greater understanding of how people live and work together. Personal attitudes will also demand much time, for the attitudes of adults are not easily changed. The biggest step, however, is the decision to devote time and energy to this area. Once that has been done, the necessary patience will be forthcoming.

What price emotional maturity? Many of our modern tragedies arise from the fact that chronological maturity and emotional maturity do not have a one-to-one relationship. All of us have known many adults who were children emotionally. The resultant abrasiveness in interpersonal relationships can retard such people's progress throughout their entire lives. Emotional maturity is a recognized base for successful living and is in part a measure of skill in making adjustments. Pure knowledge alone does not mean skill: Knowledge must be acted upon before a person can become skilled in any field. A great majority of criminals *know* how they should live; they are unskillful members of the social group because they do not put this knowledge into action in their daily living.

The field of scrutiny. This book takes a look at a microcosm of social psychology. Before getting into the actual forces at work within the group, however, it is vital to understand a little about the motivation of both individuals and the group (Chapters 1 and 2). Also, we need to identify the different kinds of groups and something of their similarities and differences (Chapter 3). The unique properties of groups are brought into focus in Chapter 4 because these group properties make it possible for us to make many predictions as to the outcome of group situations as they arise.

It is important, also, to know both the effects of the group on the individual (Chapter 5) and the effects of the individual on the group (Chapter 6). These are not necessarily mirror images of each other. The leadership of the group (Chapter 7) is of prime importance, and much has been written, particularly recently, on leadership. Less has been said about the equally important matter of followership—the position occupied by most members of the group (Chapter 8). Today each of us has many memberships, and our roles in the various groups vary widely. A little understanding of the implications of these different roles can make us more effective in each of them (Chapter 9).

Because of our multigroup memberships, we frequently find ourselves in role conflict (Chapter 10), the cause of many neuroses attendant upon modern living. For pure self-protection we should know the best means of resolving such conflict. For example, much of the generation gap arises from the severe role conflict coming from the teenager's need to reconcile two or more widely divergent roles. The deviant (Chapter 11) and the isolate (Chapter 12) also present their own special problems in terms of the success of the group, and they deserve special attention.

There would be little purpose to any study of group dynamics unless one of the major objectives were increased group effectiveness. Chapter 13 therefore takes a look at how we may achieve that end. Finally, this book would be remiss if it neglected the most important item in the whole picture: Chapter 14 shows how proper application of our knowledge of group dynamics can increase the pleasures and rewards of family living.

From these bits and pieces, it then becomes necessary that the individual synthesize a perspective of the entire area. If this is done properly, our lives can be incalculably better.

Chapter 1

Individual Motivation

𝓑ᴇꜰᴏʀᴇ we can understand the interactions of a group, it is necessary to look at the individual and understand what makes him tick. Essentially, we are interested in his basic motivations, whether they are within his conscious thought processes or whether they are so deeply buried as to be instinctive. Man's behavior is so complex and is subject to forces from so many independent variables that, at first, the prospect of trying to reduce individual motivation to a ponderable condition is terrifying. However, some important work has been done recently in this area, and a much more orderly picture is evolving.

What Is Motivation?

There are many definitions of the word "motivation," depending on the training and the frame of reference of the persons concerned. To include as wide a definition as possible and yet retain an understandable simplicity, this book considers motivation a *goal-seeking drive*. That is, a person feels impelled from within to take action to achieve a particular end which seems attractive to him or to evade a situation which seems unattractive. If we look at it in this way, there is no such thing as an unmotivated act in the life of a normal person. Even those acts which we call "aimless" or "random" will, if we push far enough, be found to be clearly motivated.

Another point should be clarified before we proceed any further. *No one ever motivates anyone else.* There is a tremendous amount of loose talk about our responsibility for motivating others. This is nonsense. The only person who can ever make a man perform in a given way is the man himself. Others can, of course, give him a great deal of help in accomplishing his purpose, but the actual goal determination and the action necessary to achieve the goal must come from within the man. Wasted effort would be avoided, as well as much abrasive interpersonal reaction, if this point were thoroughly understood by everyone. One of the principal objectives of the study of group dynamics is a working understanding of the basics of individual motivation. Once this is accomplished, relationships with others become much smoother.

What Can Motivation Do for Us?

There are an infinite number of degrees of motivation, from the slightest, almost imperceptible urge to the deepest and overpowering drive which consumes all our available energy and dominates our thinking until the goal is achieved. People of tremendous potential may fail to achieve what they should because they are not sufficiently motivated. On the other hand, people of mediocre endowments can go far beyond their apparent potential under the pressure of a consuming motivation.

Good motivation will show itself in the quality and quantity of a person's performance in whatever field. The greatest damage done to the individual by our modern assembly-line production techniques is the destruction of his identification with the product, and it is this identification that is so necessary for the pride of craftsmanship which was a hallmark of the artisan. For example, it is impossible for a worker in an aluminum reduction plant to go into the courtyard, point to a particular ingot of aluminum, and say, "I made that pig." Industry's own efficiency has thus largely destroyed strong personal motivation on the part of the worker. If the individual can or does succeed in motivating himself on the job, the results are immediately apparent in increased production and better quality. It is not even necessary that the workman's personal goals be identical to the objectives of the enterprise.

We should not for a moment think that this phenomenon is limited to the work situation. Every area of a man's life is subject to the same constraint—motivation must be present if any significant activity is to take place. The major Christian sects are becoming aware of this and are concentrating their efforts on providing a climate sympathetic to deeper religious motivation on the part of their members.

Our social life is more directly motivation-centered than are some other aspects of our lives. That is to say, we make the effort to socialize only when we are positively motivated to act. Furthermore, we usually are more consciously selective about our social groups than we are about some other aspects of our existence.

Since motivation is so important in our daily living, the more recent major theories concerning the nature and "laws" of individual motivation will now be considered. Because it is so fundamental, motivation is one of the most controversial subjects in the whole field of psychology. Feelings run high, and clashes between proponents of the various theories are many and bitter. However, although the terminology varies widely, there are threads of strong similarity running through the works of all the major motivation theorists.

Four Important Modern Treatments

Theory X and Theory Y—McGregor. The late Professor Douglas McGregor of M.I.T. gave impetus to much reflection among businessmen when he propounded his Theory X and Theory Y regarding managerial attitudes toward employees. By describing the two archetypal supervisors at the two end points of a spectrum, he emphasized the oppositeness of the two postures and showed the results which are logically to be expected from both kinds of supervision. Professor McGregor's position as an influential teacher in an influential school magnified his impact on managerial thinking throughout the country. It must be admitted that the two diametrically opposed positions have caused a significant amount of managerial conflict—especially when a young subordinate operating under Theory Y works for an older superior who has been a devout Theory X man for his whole business life. The one vulnerable of McGregor's theory is his failure to recognize the large number of pragmatic managers. These are the ones who assume an attitude toward their employees about halfway between the two extremes. That is, they hold that people are neither all good nor all bad; rather, everyone is his own individual mixture of good and bad.

McGregor did as much as any other writer to upset the stereotypes of the American businessman which had existed up to his time. Even more than that of the businessman, the stereotype of the manager—the boss—was hard to dispel. He was supposed to be hard-driving, single-purposed, and completely without concern for those who worked for him, except as they could help him achieve his objectives of production, quality, and costs. It is possible that this conceptualization was a fairly accurate description of large numbers of bosses during the eighteenth, nineteenth, and early twentieth centuries.

Professor McGregor emphasized that there is indeed a manager who fits this template closely—the manager who operates under Theory X. This manager has a consistent attitude toward people. He believes that they are essentially lazy; they don't like to work, and they will go to much trouble to avoid working whenever possible; they have to get jobs in order to eat, but, because they hate work so much, they must be supervised very closely all the way to get "eight for eight" out of them. The Theory X boss is certain that his employees will deliberately sabotage his efforts whenever they can. They will band together to keep him from achieving his goals and will automatically be antipathetic to these goals. They will join together in unions to present a united front against the efforts of management and as such will exhibit great ingenuity in subverting the enterprise's goals. If you ask the Theory X manager to encapsulate his attitude toward his subordinates in one sentence, he will say, "People are no damn good."

What does the Theory X man discover during his managerial career? That he is right. His people do dislike and distrust him. Close supervision of their activities is mandatory. They do flock to the ranks of the unions in large numbers, and the unions assume a militant attitude in their meetings with management. The slowdown against company-instituted production standards is common; deliberate sabotage of company property is not unheard of. Any proposed management change is met with attitudes ranging from sullen distrust to open hostility. The threat of a strike is present in any serious negotiations between workmen and management. Any real progress on the part of the enterprise is agonizingly slow and arduous.

Professor McGregor then contrasts this managerial attitude and its attendant difficulties with one 180° out of phase with it. The Theory Y manager's attitude is that people *are* good. He postulates that people find their inherent *need* to work one of the better means of self-expression. Their need for achievement is most easily realized in their work environment since they spend most of their lives there. Given half a chance by their leaders, employees will work hard and intelligently, will not need close supervision, and will even resent it if it is present. They will make significant progress toward the company's goals in the form of intelligent and perceptive suggestions. They will participate actively and will be happy to cooperate with management in a continuing search for better methods that will culminate in greater profitability. They will identify with the concern they consider good enough to spend their working lifetimes in.

What does the Theory Y manager discover when he maintains this attitude toward his people? He finds out that he is right. His postulates are proved correct over and over again. The relationship between him and his people is rich and productive. The employees may unionize for a number of reasons, but the relationship between management and the union is a working partnership; both parties tacitly agree that their ultimate goals are identical. Progress is relatively easy in this sort of atmosphere; mutual trust makes it easier to introduce changes and thus improve the position of the enterprise.

How can these two completely opposite situations exist when the elements of both are normal human beings? According to Professor McGregor, a person tends to respond in character to the kind of attitude exhibited by his employer. Distrust is met with distrust; esteem is matched with esteem; close supervision is met by evasive tactics; participative management elicits participation by the employees.

Douglas McGregor was *not* an ivory tower thinker. He appreciated what the manager faced in his job situation, and he knew that *both* Theory X and Theory Y described extremes on a spectrum of managerial attitudes and thinking. Many modern managers fit one or another of these descriptions, but many, many more do not. McGregor died before he could complete the trilogy by refining and describing Theory Z. This theory no doubt would have encompassed the majority of modern managers by recognizing that man must not be stereotyped. No one is wholly good or wholly bad. Everyone is a human mixture of good *and* bad, with variations in the daily mix of these characteristics. (A Theory Z would have to take this fact into account.) The manager has to accept each of his employees as an individual and respond to each in kind. He must know that some of his employees will be X's and some will be Y's, but that the majority of them will lie somewhere in between. *Sometimes*—in certain situations— they need close supervision; at other times they perform best when given a reasonable delegation of authority to get the job done and then left alone. *Sometimes* they participate willingly in planning for change; at other times the leader has to show the way. The employee's private life presents many challenges and crises that could have an adverse effect on his job attitude. The manager must be aware of this and be ready to change his approach to that person when such things happen. A crisis does not mean the man is going to the dogs; it means he is under extra pressure temporarily, and allowances must be made for him until he can recover his balance.

This revised attitude presents the biggest challenge of them all. It means the manager must go to extra lengths to learn all he can about each of his employees, short of an invasion of their privacy. He must meet each employee as an individual; essentially, he should ignore the old saw that the manager "must treat all his employees alike." They are *not* all alike—why, then, think of treating them all exactly the same? Different levels of emotional maturity will demand different approaches. Some people are happiest under firm, continuous leadership; the more adventurous prefer to think of the boss as available in times of trouble or stress.

Douglas McGregor's concept of the relationship of workman to boss is grounded in basic human characteristics. He looks at the whole man, fits him into the job situation, and attempts to predict his behavior. In his view, every boss must do the same thing—and govern his managerial attitude and behavior accordingly.

The effects of McGregor's theorizing have been broad and deep in the American business world. He almost, but not quite, popularized the Theory Y side of the picture. His biggest achievement has been to make large numbers of businessmen examine their own thinking more critically in order to develop a rational defense of their attitudes toward their people. In addition, McGregor's work has influenced other present-day investigators of human motivation. His concepts present many questions which beg for scientific investigation. Are his precepts susceptible to verification or rejection? Can the effects of Theory Y operation be quantified at all? How far can the manager safely carry participative management? Is the present-day socioeconomic situation such that the manager *must* change his orientation and develop a more permissive attitude?

Professor McGregor's philosophizing has been a rich mine for social and industrial psychologists. His main contribution has been this sharp stimulus to others' thinking.

Maslow's hierarchy. Abraham H. Maslow has achieved sufficient eminence in the field of psychology to have been elected the president of the American Psychological Association. His motivational theory has one great advantage over that of other writers in the field: He extends his concepts to all areas of man's life instead of limiting them to his work. Because Maslow attempts to explain motivation in all phases of life, his theories are useful to teachers, ministers, and any others in positions of leadership.

Maslow assumes that human motivation is accomplished through at least five levels of needs. He postulates that all normal human beings have these needs at some time or another and that most of these needs are present to some extent at all times. He ascribes an ascending order to these five levels, beginning with the fundamental and ongoing physiological needs and culminating with self-actualization needs which have strongly spiritual overtones.

Maslow's ordering of these human needs facilitates the task of explaining much of man's social behavior. His theory gives the supervisor a fine tool for working with his subordinates, provided that he knows his people thoroughly.

Whether we think of it as a shortcoming or not, the one thing Maslow's theory does *not* offer is any cookbook of "how to's." The person attempting to use Maslow as a guideline is left strictly to his own ingenuity while working with others and their motivation.

Terminology in the reporting of Maslow's hierarchy of needs varies. However, the five families of needs most commonly talked about are the ones with which we are concerned here. The base of the hierarchy—the all-pervading, ongoing group of needs—is made up of physiological needs. Then comes the group of safety needs, only a little less broad in their inclusiveness. Above them lie the social needs to which man is subject. Still higher are his ego needs, and, sitting atop of the pyramid, we find the need for self-actualization or self-realization.

When one level of needs is satisfied, it ceases to act as a motivator, and a person moves up one step in the hierarchy and looks to satisfying the needs of that level. But if, while one is striving to satisfy higher groups of needs, a more basic group is threatened, the individual's concerns revert to the more fundamental level until that threat is allayed. For example, if a man who is chiefly concerned with satisfying social and ego needs discovers that his job is being threatened, all his thought and action at once revert to the physiological and safety needs levels. Social, ego, or self-actualization needs cannot be meaningful until he is reasonably certain that his physiological and safety needs are no longer in danger.

On the lowest level, the *physiological* needs include man's universal and continuing requirements of food, clothing, shelter, and sexual gratification. We come into this life howling with hunger; and every few hours thereafter, as long as we live, our body demands more food. Body covering and shelter from inclement surroundings are essential everywhere on earth. The strength of an individual's sexual drive varies more than the first three needs mentioned, but everyone is subject to sexual feelings through at least a part of his lifetime.

In the United States, our increasing awareness of social

duty to all citizens has had an effect on this most basic level of needs. It is difficult for an American to starve to death or die from exposure in our country today. If he becomes totally unemployable and dependent upon others, he will be kept alive by other individuals or a governmental agency. Notwithstanding this, the average American citizen feels deeply threatened and panics if he finds himself in danger of losing his job.

Maslow says that the most of us average about 85 percent satisfaction of our physiological needs along a time continuum. Those great numbers of people who find it necessary to work for a living can always expect to spend the greater part of their income for food, rent or housing, and enough clothing to be decently presentable on most occasions. In addition, many sociologists now include transportation under the physiological needs. They say that our sprawling cities, plus our recent tendency to live in suburbs many miles from our jobs, have made the keeping of a car a necessity rather than a luxury.

As an individual becomes more successful in the economic struggle and his income rises, a blurring may occur in the assuagement of physiological needs. There comes a time, generally after a particularly hefty raise in pay, when steak starts to appear on the family menu where hamburger was before. The family home seems crowded—even perhaps a little shabby—and the house-hunting cycle begins again, this time for a "better" place. Steak is really no more nutritious than hamburger, and the $15,000 house probably shelters the family as adequately as will the one costing $25,000. Actually, these changes in the family's situation are steps toward the satisfaction of social rather than physiological needs. Even the ego needs may be involved.

In an affluent society such as ours, less and less of total income will be spent in the satisfaction of physiological needs, and more will remain for discretionary spending on social, ego, and self-actualization needs. But the physiological needs will always be the basic ones.

Safety needs are today centered in our quest for pure air, unpolluted water, and general freedom from dangers to our physical and emotional well-being. Three generations ago, our ancestors would have found it difficult to distinguish between their physiological and safety needs. The struggle for food and shelter was dangerous in itself; but, as our society matured, the physical dangers attendant upon procuring food and shelter subsided.

In the present scene, man is emotionally involved in attacks upon his safety needs. This accounts for the savage battles joined in many communities over the question of fluoridation of the water supply. People who perceive fluorine to be a "poison" (irrespective of its concentration in the water supply) will of course react in a violently negative manner to proposals to fluoridate their water supply.

Legislation on air and water pollution has been pushed to successively higher strata of government because of our involvement with these basic necessities. In some states, a manufacturing plant can be summarily closed if it is even *accused* of polluting the surrounding air or water with its effluvium. The widely read research of one man has largely been responsible for major safety changes in the design and manufacture of automobiles.

The complex demands of our transportation systems have presented an interesting problem in regard to our safety needs. The mass of freeway systems that has been constructed across the country to facilitate the flow of millions of cars has resulted in an overt threat to our physical safety. Many people find it a terrifying experience to drive their cars on freeways. The speed at which traffic moves, the closeness of other vehicles at this high speed, the need to keep a sharp lookout for signs and directions as well as the lane-hopper and the careless driver—all exert severe pressure on our physical and emotional states. More and more, people are actively looking for routes to their destinations which do not include freeways.

Our safety needs are involved when we perceive a threat to any major part of our existence. Economic pressures (such as those generated in times of inflation) ring our safety alarm. Man's unending search for security is filled with trauma; he responds both physically and emotionally when threatened in these areas. For example, when a business must retrench and it is obvious that personnel cuts are imminent, some of the first to feel threatened are the best employees, who would be the very last to lose their jobs. Managers are aware that from the moment it is known that a reduction in force may be necessary their most valuable employees will be updating and circulating their résumés. The less valuable employees will respond with frantic efforts to intrench themselves in their present jobs rather than try to find work elsewhere.

Physical dangers are different today than they were in our grandfathers' times, but they are no less real. In some parts of our larger cities, we have regressed to the point where we can no longer safely be on the streets after dark. This particular knowledge, plus the presence of less well defined fears, has spiraled the number of threats to our emotional safety.

Maslow makes allowance for this fact by recognizing that our safety needs are consistently less well satisfied than our physiological needs. Here, in fact, our struggles are greater now than in the past, and the trend is continuing in that direction.

Maslow defines *social* needs as those which refer to man's

desire to belong. Many of our saddest memories of childhood are feelings of not being accepted by the group. This was sheer tragedy. And, in fact, social groups make up a significant part of our lives at any age. Because we spend so much time at work, for example, the social structure of our work group is of great importance to us. This is what makes our introduction to it and our assimilation into it an event full of excitement or fear. The acceptance of a new member by the informal work group is subject to a rite of its own. The group will take whatever time it needs to reach a decision on the new member; and, until that decision has been made, the stranger will remain in limbo.

The search for identity has been going on ever since there was a man; it is individually repeated in the life of every person. Our identity is substantiated by recognition from others. We can reinforce our self-image by belonging to the kinds of groups that will give us recognition and acceptance. In a country such as ours, with unlimited social mobility, a man's progress can be traced by the increasingly more important groups into which he is accepted. Even one's church membership may be actuated by felt social needs rather than by deeply religious instincts. There is a recognizable stratification of social prestige among the various sects of the Christian religion which can be traced by the migration of large numbers of families from one sect to another as they move to a new area. This movement has progressed so far as to have created an unwritten—but clearly understandable—policy in some business organizations. The alert young employee doesn't need much time to discover that the company "wheels" all belong to a particular sect.

It is on the level of social needs that we note a phenomenon called "elaboration." If a person is having great difficulty in satisfying his ego or self-actualization needs, he attempts to substitute endless acceptance for those higher needs. His billfold bulges with membership cards, and he is quick to let you know that he can "get you in anywhere."

Although the original reason for union formation (group protection from a predatory employer) has largely disappeared, unions continue to flourish because, for one reason, they help satisfy social needs. Some workers find it possible to sublimate their lack of success on the job by working hard in a union and thus getting many signs of acceptance from their fellow workmen.

American society is organized in a way that is especially kind to social groups. Because of the absence of strong caste lines, a person can have memberships across a wide spectrum of social groups. This is especially illustrated in the catholicity of hobby groups, in which bank presidents associate under conditions of complete equality with truck drivers or store clerks.

Man's continuing need for the approbation of his peers is less pressing but more difficult to satisfy than are his physiological and safety needs. In our society, he expends more energy on this stratum of the hierarchy than on the two below it.

Again, if man is concerned about being accepted by others, he is even more deeply absorbed in having others recognize his worth and achievements—the *ego* needs. A person may put much more effort into a feat than necessary in order to insure acclamation for a superior performance. Those who have a marked craving for outstanding success in the business world work as much for the satisfaction of their ego needs as they do for the money and power to be found at the top. Most people have an accurate picture of their own capabilites. They know better than others do whether they are operating at full capacity or at half power. Full-throttle activity is often elicited by the individual's need to be recognized by others for what he really is. On the industrial scene, the smart manager can turn this need to his advantage if he knows that one of his people has especially strong ego needs. He can structure the work situation so that this employee can satisfy his ego needs only by realizing his full potential. In this case, Adam Smith's carrot is imaginary: The employee will do his best work to receive public recognition from his peers or his superiors.

Strong ego drive is a recognizable part of the makeup of those who seek leadership. From a position of influence and power, it is easy for a person to reassure himself that he is receiving just recognition for his true worth. This does not mean, of course, that his followers are necessarily lacking in strong ego needs.

Excessively strong ego needs also are present in that driven man we call the "perfectionist." Because he is fearful of being responsible for any performance which would impair his image, he spends an inordinate amount of time on details. He is incapable of delegating to subordinates since he feels that their abilities do not match his own. As a result, he is both a miserable supervisor and an underproducer.

Professor Maslow says that *self-actualization* needs are usually only about 10 percent satisfied. Many people are never consciously aware of the need for growing into a bigger and finer self. They are quite satisfied with what they see in the bathroom mirror every morning. Their world is complete if the first four levels of needs are reasonably satisfied most of the time. Other people have a drive toward self-improvement which gradually becomes the strongest of all the needs. There are cases of people who have subsisted for years in a garret to the total exclusion of all other needs in order to write a book, paint a picture, or compose music. It is sad that these people are not always endowed with the talents necessary to achieve as much as they demand, but many of mankind's better achievements are produced under the drive for self-actualization. Man can create that which he can conceptualize. If he builds a better product, he grows significantly in the process. And it should not be inferred that self-actualization can occur only in the arts. Many people satisfy their needs in this area by creative activity within their job sphere. This is one of the reasons why America has taken and held a preeminent position in world trade. Self-actualization needs are largely spiritual and nonverbalized, but this does not mean that they are not some of the strongest motivators we have.

Abraham Maslow gives us a broad-spectrum theoretical matrix of individual motivation. The fact that this matrix encompasses the whole of our existence does not lessen its usefulness in the business world. If the manager is aware that not much leverage can be had from physiological and safety needs in a mobile society undergoing steady economic growth, he still has a broad field of operation with his people in the social, ego, and self-actualization needs. This does necessitate a deep knowledge and understanding of people working for him, their personality traits as well as their work habits. Once this knowledge is attained, he has a fine tool for helping him (and his subordinates) achieve personal and organizational goals.

Herzberg's two-factor theory. Frederick Herzberg is today the most controversial figure in the field of motivation. Students have a way of being violently for or violently against Herzbergian theory. Much experimental work has been done in both camps. Professor Herzberg propounds a disarmingly simple thesis—that man has relatively few motivators, but can be *de*motivated by a large number of conditions. The basic concept of the two-factor theory is one which would have seemed a truism to our grandfathers, but which is thought of as revolutionary by the present generation: The best motivator of all is the work itself.

Professor Herzberg keeps his theory within the scope of the working situation and thereby limits its applications. Moreover, the diversity of the terms he uses to designate demotivators is often confusing. Take "hygiene factors" and "dissatisfiers," for instance. Dissimilar as these words are, Herzberg appears to use them as entirely synonymous. It must be admitted, however, that he does give a satisfying explanation for the fact that increased pay or improved working conditions do not pay off in strong motivation for better work.

Professor Herzberg has attracted articulate and influential colleagues—among them Saul W. Gellerman and F. Scott Myers. Myers's work at Texas Instruments assumes the correctness of Herzberg's postulates and builds on them. The writings of both Gellerman and Myers have reached large audiences.

Professor Herzberg's theory has caused a cautious, but widespread, reevaluation of management's thinking about the whole structure of compensation, especially fringe benefits. If more money, more insurance, longer vacations, more holidays, and a subsidized cafeteria are not going to result in greater motivation, just where is the carrousel going to come to a halt?

Frederick Herzberg's approach is simplicity itself—on the surface. A person finds the challenge, excitement, and activity of a meaningful job to be the best incentive to perform at his optimum capacity. Directly associated with the work itself are such motivators as a sense of achievement, recognition from peers and superiors, and the opportunity for advancement. So long as these elements are present in reasonable quantity, we have a motivated worker.

On the other side of the coin there is the more numerous

collection of factors which Professor Herzberg calls demotivators, dissatisfiers, and maintenance or hygiene factors. All of these latter terms are essentially cognitively identical. An employee can be demotivated by bad working conditions. If, say, he has to walk half a mile from the parking lot in all kinds of weather in order to reach his work area, the employee will be demotivated. If his work area is poorly lighted or ventilated, he will be dissatisfied. In the same way, supervisory attitude and company philosophy can be strong demotivators.

Some of Professor Herzberg's opposition comes from those who consider his classification of money as a hygiene factor to be a mistake. Herzberg says that no raise in pay is ever a motivator for more than one payday. After that, it is quickly assimilated into a budget automatically expanded to include it, with the result that by the second payday the employee recognizes new wants and needs which he is not able to satisfy. On the other hand, if the workman feels—rightly or wrongly—that he is not being paid equitably for the contribution he is making, he will be *actively dissatisfied* until the situation is corrected. Herzberg's thesis is that money and fringe benefits are hygiene factors—they can be used to *prevent* serious unhappiness, but they do not act as positive motivators. The best they can achieve is a "zero" state. Raises and benefits are necessary just as daily meals are: They satisfy hunger as it occurs.

One large manufacturing company had for years maintained a strict "No Smoking" policy within the work area. Since it was traditional, there was no overt rebellion against the policy until the company took on a contract which required its employees to work with those from other companies in a joint effort. There was immediate trouble when it was discovered that the other employees could smoke on the line, and the company was forced to change its policy. The relaxing of the rule did *not* act as a motivator; all it did was to remove a source of irritation and dissatisfaction.

Failure to recognize that this sort of thing can happen has led many management people into bewilderment and frustration. After granting large concessions in money and fringe benefits, they are amazed not to find their people motivated and ready to charge. "We give them the whole plant," say the managers, "and they don't show even basic gratitude." Why should they? As far as they are concerned, all they are getting is what has been owed to them for a long time.

Professor Herzberg holds controversial positions on some other managerial fetishes as well. For the past several years, for example, it has been a common "development" practice to rotate a manager through a series of jobs in various disciplines under the theory that this will broaden his perspective and increase his motivation. This does not work, says Herzberg, for a number of reasons. For one thing, everyone knows that the situation is artificial in the extreme. The manager's tenure in these jobs is purely temporary. It is difficult for him to accept real responsibility for a position he knows he will occupy for only a few months. There is no invitation to creativity or to the innovation which has been the hallmark of this promising manager in his own jobs. The subordinates in the line are also aware that this is a stopgap situation; they will not respond to this manager in the same way they would to a permanent boss.

Herzberg's two-factor theory is especially applicable to the management of engineers and technical people. F. Scott Myers has published the results of his investigations at Texas Instruments, and his conclusions support Herzbergian theory. Both Herzberg and Myers maintain that technical people are motivated by their work so strongly that nothing else is of any real import to them. Their situation is complicated, however, by status relationships and the "colleague" syndrome. The latter can be very disruptive to the line organization. In one case, a light metals company maintained a rather large research and development group in a Southern plant. The group was headed by an extremely competent manager capable of giving excellent leadership to his engineers and scientists. Six of the section leaders under him were young Ph.D.'s. The organization was torn apart because these men completely refused to recognize their manager as a colleague. He didn't have the terminal degree; therefore, he was not given the necessary recognition as a line manager. After working with the problem for more than a year, the company management finally gave up and replaced the Ph.D.'s with other scientists who did not have the terminal degree. In other cases, because their personal motivation is so closely meshed with their professional standing, it is possible for engineers and scientists to develop a supracompany attitude. They may feel that it is beneath them to identify closely with a given enterprise; their allegiance is to the profession at large.

As has been stated, the removal of dissatisfiers from the working scene will *not* result in increased motivation. Many managers have learned this to their sorrow after spending large sums on improved parking lots, better lighting, air conditioning, or better service in the cafeteria. The most that can be hoped is that the workforce will not be actively unhappy after the installation of these improvements.

In his article "One More Time—How Do You Motivate Employees?"[1] Herzberg gives a detailed outline for job

[1] *Harvard Business Review*, January–February 1968.

enrichment. He distinguishes job enrichment from job enlargement by describing what he calls lateral loading and vertical loading of the job. Lateral loading is quite useless; the only effective way to enrich a job is to load it vertically and so motivate the worker by means of greater achievement, responsibility, and recognition from peers and superiors. In developing his step-by-step procedure for job enrichment, Herzberg warns his readers that there will be a drop in both production and quality before improvement is seen. He also points out that the supervisor may feel threatened because his people will now be performing many of his former tasks. However, the supervisor should soon realize that he now has time to be a real supervisor and manager.

The approaches of McGregor, Maslow, and Herzberg appear to be quite different. If the student looks further, however, it will be seen that there are several points of tangency among all three. Herzberg's motivator "recognition" is identical in concept to Maslow's ego needs. Herzbergian motivation by opportunity for advancement is equatable to Maslow's need for self-actualization. McGregor's emphasis on the attitude of the supervisor is reflected in both Maslow and Herzberg, but they do not see it as having quite the same importance as did McGregor.

Vroom's reportage. The contribution of Victor H. Vroom has been a meticulous and scholarly reportage, in depth, of all the major work in the field of human motivation. Maintaining a nice objectivity, he has given exposure to some lesser known experimentation as well as to supportive and critical writings about the major theorists. This generalized coverage is much needed in one of the most active areas of psychology.

Professor Vroom, in an American Foundation for Management Research study entitled *Motivation in Manage-*

ment,[2] has given us an excellent review of recent research in managerial motivation. This book analyzes the study of motivation, the motives of managers, the role of motivation in management and managerial satisfaction. Vroom concludes that managers in general report themselves highly satisfied by their jobs; they are second only to professionals in this matter. There is a direct correlation among job satisfaction, level in management, and salary as compared to that of others at the same level. This substantiates the work of Herzberg and Myers. Staff managers as a group are less satisfied than are line managers with their opportunities for self-actualization. Compared to managers in other countries, American managers report high satisfaction of security and social needs and low satisfaction of esteem, autonomy, and self-actualization needs under Maslow's classification.

Professor Vroom's specific contribution has been a good outline of the necessary research in the management field. He indicates gaps in our understanding of managerial motivation which it would be well to close.

* * *

In spite of the deceptively simple definition given here of motivation, it can be seen that many approaches are possible. The complicating factor is man's infinite variability. Not only is this variability evidenced from person to person, but the same individual can change his basic motivation overnight. Take the case of the family man who has been motivated for his entire married life to provide for his children and their education. The day after his last child either marries or accepts a job, father's basic work motivation is entirely different from what it has been for perhaps 25 years. In fact, he may not have a strong motivation to continue his work until his values are restructured and he starts

[2] American Foundation for Management Research Inc., 1965.

to think of himself and his wife rather than the needs of the children.

Any number of things can cause a similar change in a person's motivation. His group memberships will undergo radical changes as these motivational changes take place. Therefore, it is of great importance for any group leader to understand the basic concepts of motivation. If he does not, his group may be destroyed.

It is equally important that the individual himself understand what is happening to him. The sudden loss of the drives under which he has been operating for years is upsetting. The disturbance which ensues must be minimized in strength and duration. All group interactions are the result of individual motivation. All progress comes from someone's having been motivated to become a change agent. Understanding in this area is an absolute prerequisite to any further knowledge of the group and how it operates.

Chapter 2

Group Motivation

$\mathcal{W}$E HAVE seen how motivation plays an important part in the life of an individual—and why. For the same reasons, the group must be motivated before it can be effective. But we oversimplify the situation by implying that the group's motivation consists of the objectives which caused its formation. This is not the entire story.

How Does the Group Differ from the Individual?

The saying that the whole is greater than the sum of its parts is nowhere better exemplified than by a group. No matter what its size, there will be elements in the group not directly traceable to any of its individual members. In the blending of the members' contributions, transformations take place which result in new personality facets.

The time needed by a group to react to a given stimulus is always noticeably greater than that of any individual member. While rapport may be perfect among the membership, time is still necessary for communication to be effected and consensus reached before group reaction can occur.

Repeated similar stimuli will elicit more uniform responses from a group than from any of its individual members. Individual variations in mood or the posture of the moment are lost in the inertia of the group. Changes in group orientation will exhibit the same time lag. This is why careful planning for change is essential to group leadership. Even though the change contemplated is a natural one, completely in consonance with the group's objectives, time will be necessary to implement the change.

A group also has greater sensitivity to the various elements of its environment than does any one individual in its membership. This is a function of the greater number of contact points capable of inputs. However, there is an optimal group size for the greatest sensitivity to surroundings. Too small a group will not give sufficient data, while too large a group will require too much time for processing the data and reconciling apparent contradictions.

The group further differs from an individual by displaying a more complex personality to its environment than does any one of its individual members. Group member contacts with the outside world are on a one-to-one basis; there is no such thing as contact with a group. The nearest we come to this is in negotiations between two groups in which selected members communicate after each group has caucused. Labor contract negotiations are the most familiar example. Indeed, one of the commonest reasons for breakdown in labor negotiations is improvisation on the part of such spokesmen. The danger is always there that one or both of the spokesmen feel it advantageous to make a unilateral decision without waiting for group consensus. Groups have a way of becoming deeply disturbed if they discover a designated spokesman undertaking action they have not sanctioned.

The group will differ from the individual in both its perception of and its reaction to a threat. This is again a function of the time lag involved in processing the data. The group cannot react from instinct or reflex as does the individual. First there must be a collective value judgment that the threat exists. Then a deliberative time is necessary, no matter of what length, which is not required in the case of the individual. This is the theoretical basis for the success of guerrilla warfare. The small commando group resembles the individual in possessing greater speed in decision making and greater mobility than the army it is attacking. The army, larger and slower, is similar to the group.

The group is also more vulnerable than an individual to changes in leadership. There is a greater chance that a group will be significantly changed under a new leader than that an individual will undergo a major personality or character change. For example, when a change of managers occurs in a department, the new boss can produce a work group that is entirely different in appearance, action, and effectiveness without any change in personnel. Group leadership is more of an *outside* stimulus to a group, not the *inner* direction the individual maintains over his own personality and actions. The behavior of the parties at the Vietnam peace talks is illustrative of the importance given to group leadership. Hanoi's hatred and distrust of President Johnson led to stalled proceedings until after the inauguration of President Nixon. Putting aside personalities, one could expect changes in the course of negotiations even if the teams were the same.

It could be argued that some of the differences enumerated here between the individual and the group are really ones of degree rather than of kind, but this does not alter the fact that they are differences. The rational person allows for this dichotomy in his interactions with both individuals and groups. His approaches in the two cases will be different; his situational analyses will differ; his courses of action will not be the same. The major factor he must never lose sight of is the time lag he faces when working with groups. This is what frustrates the "direct action" businessman who attempts to work with a company which practices management by committee action.

How Is the Group Similar to the Individual?

There are also several ways in which the group resembles an individual. The most obvious similarity is that both are human, and so the group is subject to all the variability of human traits contained in its membership. If an individual responds to a given stimulus in a given way, it is reasonable to suppose that a group may do the same. Depending upon the ascendant leadership of the moment, the response of a group can show all the variability of response we are familiar with in individuals. One of the easier ways for an observer to trace the leadership struggle within a group is to chart responses to various stimuli, in both magnitude and frequency.

The group will have a personality just as surely as does any person. Groups can be stodgy and dull, ebullient, purely purposeful and work-centered, or conscious of their goals but light-hearted—in a word, there is the same variety of personalities we see in any normal human population. We could expect that the leader of the group would have a marked influence on the personality displayed by the group. This is true to a certain extent. In the informal group, leadership rotation can produce quick changes in personality when the group is threatened, when it is socializing, and again when it is going about its business.

A major point of similarity between the individual and the group is in mode of response to a threat. Typically, an external threat will cause a large increase in group cohesiveness, as well as a greater response to communications of its leadership. In many cases, group response to threat is indistinguishable from the response of its leader. To the student of group dynamics, this fact is advantageous in a situation of direct confrontation between two groups. If the student is familiar with the leadership of the other group, he will be able, with good statistical probability of success, to predict in advance how that group is going to react.

Groups as well as individuals go through recognizable life cycles (even when group membership is constantly changing). There are young, middle-aged, and old groups. The age of a group in this context is governed by its objectives. There are objectives which become outdated—even anachronistic: The productive middle age of a group will be indefinitely prolonged if group objectives remain in general consonance with the group's environment.

Groups have a way of developing work habits in exactly the same manner as do individuals. The division of labor behind these habits may be either planned or developed fortuitously. This is the reason why work groups should be visited regularly by methods and systems people to be sure that their work habits are good. It is easy to allow wheel spinning and duplication of effort unless attention is given at regular intervals to possible problems. Moreover, if work habits are comfortable and well received by the membership, inertia will be exhibited upon introduction of new methods, even though they may result in the saving of labor and cost. Inherent in the overall responsibility of group leadership, in short, is a continuous careful monitoring of the group's work habits.

Exactly as individuals can, groups can become neurotic or even psychotic. Group neurosis most frequently results from pressures exerted upon the group over which it has no control. This is one of the commoner causes of individual neurosis. Paradoxically, group neurosis frequently occurs when internal communications in the group are good. Common recognition of a common problem can escalate the pressures on the members and hasten the appearance of emotional disorder. Group neurosis is, in the main, an indication of weak leadership, which may or may not be recognized by the group membership. In fact, just as is the case with an individual, the group will not be likely to recognize its own neurotic behavior. Similarly, if the group leadership is popular, weakness may not be recognized. (The greatest contribution of the behavioral scientist to management consultant work is its assistance in the diagnosis and treatment of neurotic groups.) It would be unfair to infer that group neuroticism occurs only under weak leadership; it can develop under the strongest and most able of leaders. But, in the latter case, the good leader will recognize the syndrome and take corrective action on his own.

What Commonalities Exist for Group Motivation?

This chapter has attempted to establish points of difference and similarity between the group and the individual so as to put into proper perspective the common motivators of group activity. Since motivation has been defined as a goal-seeking drive, any study of group motivation will entail constant surveillance of the group's objectives. It is vital to determine the basic commonalities which will allow generalization in the field of group motivation. There are at least six general motivators for the group. The rest of this chapter will be devoted to a discussion of them.

Economic goals. These are as important to the group as they are to the individuals in it. In a work group, they are inextricably bound together. Unless the work group continues to make a profit, the economic goals of the members will be disturbed by the loss of their jobs. The nonsupervisory members' role is complicated by the fact that they are often not informed of the real economic implications of their work. More often, they are not told the economic goals of the enterprise in detail. Management defends this lack of communication by saying that complete openness about financial affairs would put them at the mercy of their competition. Theoretically, any publicly owned enterprise is subject to having its books examined minutely by an interested stockholder. But, as a matter of actuality, the stockholder finds the difficulties in his way to the pertinent financial data insuperable. Annual statements are customarily doctored to the point where no one can really tell what the situation is.

The membership of the group must accept on faith that the economic goals of the company are feasible and attainable. This works no little hardship on the group members when they try to do their personal long-term financial planning. When to buy a house and when to trade the car become matters of pure guesswork.

With few exceptions, economic goals are a part of a group's reason for being. The formal work group's economic goals supersede all others in importance. Semiformal groups find the acquisition of money necessary to their continued existence, or they may have a major philanthropic goal, which necessitates the acquisition of some money. The informal group which bowls together on Tuesdays must levy dues to pay for the time on the lanes and provide trophies at the end of the season. For the work group, other goals cannot be more than one step removed from the economic targets. The modern manager finds little reason to insist on high quality unless he knows that poor quality means returned merchandise, loss of customers, and eventual failure. Constant concern about rate of production is directly related to economic goals, since customers will continue to buy only where they can get reasonable delivery dates. The interest of management in the welfare of the employee is more than humanitarian. A well and happy employee is more likely to be a productive and profitable one.

The economic goal of the group is broader than that of any of its members. The individual thinks only of his welfare and that of his family. In order to be successful, the group must have economic goals at least $1.00 greater than the sum of its membership. Economic goals thus carry an overriding importance into any other objectives the group may have.

The delicate balance of our society is well illustrated by the intermeshing of the economic goals of two or more groups. The vendor–customer relationship is symbiotic. The good health of the one is directly proportionate to the economic soundness of the other. Even competing businesses have a selfish interest in the state of health of their competition. It is to everyone's advantage to have the industry as a whole in sound economic condition. America's industrial strength is founded on the profit motive.

Because it is so basic, the economic objective of an enterprise colors every action of the work group. Long-range planning is eventually stated in terms of dollars. These dollars are then apportioned to men, machinery, and materials according to the best judgments of management.

Success or failure in achieving the economic goals of the group is more closely bound to the team activity than are any other objectives. The chain must remain intact. There is no feasible way of distinguishing among the contributions of the individual members, since every one is necessary to final success. This is true no matter what the size of the group, but it is more cogently illustrated in small groups where individual contributions can be more easily compared. In some of the modern industrial giants, the size of the enterprise may allow for the existence of one or more groups which are losing money rather than making a contribution to economic goals. This is sometimes done from sheer snobbery, as a boast to the rest of the industry that the giant can afford this luxury. It is this sort of snobbery which causes a rich man ostentatiously to support indigent relatives who make no contribution to society. But it remains the definitive duty of management to keep the organization clean and healthy, with constant control and monitoring of the profitability of each component. It is incredible, in the light of the facts just examined, that great numbers of American businessmen still look with distrust or derision at the work of the economist. The study of basic economics is the most widely neglected area of education for a majority of managers.

To understand how other motivating factors of group performance fit into the picture, keep the importance of economic goals in mind at all times. They are the foundation on which the superstructure is set.

Developmental goals. Groups have well-defined developmental goals even as the individuals who comprise the group do. A young group under good leadership will be aware of its shortcomings; developmental planning is an essential and important part of an effective group. As a motivator, group development is in Maslow's area of self-actualization needs. Members of the group will be subjected to group pressures to grow and become more proficient in their activity so the group as a whole will function more efficiently. Much individual development is undertaken out of desire for the approbation of the group—perhaps more than is spontaneously generated by the individual himself.

A phenomenon born in this country and still nearly unique to the American scene is group developmental effort. Women's clubs, study groups, Great Books courses, and many other similar endeavors attest to how much people want to better themselves. Granted that many of these groups work in esoteric areas and will never directly contribute to the members' jobs, the fact still remains that developmental goals are strong motivators in groups.

Work groups will see a big increase in developmental activity as our technology becomes more complex and jobs require longer preparation for entry and great effort to prevent obsolescence once a person is employed. The classic illustration of this is the professional life of the engineer. He knows that five years after graduation he will be seriously behind in his specialty unless he makes a real effort to keep himself updated. On-the-job training, company-sponsored off-hours study, subsidized advanced work at universities, the sabbatical for getting an advanced degree—all are obvious recognition by industry of the necessity for both group and individual development in order to remain competitive. Many companies are now setting up their own internal advanced development programs for their people. Groups of employees with high potential are exposed to these programs rather than sent away to outside seminars. These programs have the advantage of being totally directed toward the company's interests, which is not the case when a young manager is sent to a university course.

"For the good of the order" activities on a group basis

will be found in all sorts of situations. Motivation to institute and pursue them arises on a random basis. The idea may be generated either by the rank and file or by the group leadership. It is interesting to note that these projects often receive unanimous support from the group; the work involved in them comes near to equaling the regular work output of the group. We all remember how a class of high school seniors labors on something to leave to their school or how a junior chamber of commerce undertakes the decoration of the downtown streets at Christmas.

However, not all group development is undertaken for altruistic reasons. The greater part of it is self-centered and competitive. The well-publicized American will to win surfaces time and again in group developmental work. The athlete who trains for years to participate in the Olympic Games does not do so for the sake of a small piece of gold, worth at the most a few dollars. His drive is to win—to be publicly acknowledged as "the best." Groups, too, enjoy some of their finest moments when they are acclaimed as the best of their kind.

The formulation of developmental goals requires a significant amount of the planning done by groups. They must be aware of the immense amount of coordination necessary to improve the performance of the group as a unit. The individuals' parts must be fitted together carefully to achieve the desired effect for all; frequently the labor of members must be redivided. It is natural that personal development rates will vary. If one or two members better their performance more quickly than the rest, they will be able to take on added responsibilities and a heavier share of the effort. Much of human development is in the form of "plateaus"—that is, a sudden marked improvement in performance will be followed by a fairly long period of little or no progress, in turn succeeded by another sudden spurt of improvement coming later. The group seriously interested in its development and growth will recognize this fact and adjust its work assignments to individually differing growth rates.

From the standpoint of growth and development motivation, the most difficult position for a group to occupy is one of preeminence. If it is recognized generally as being the best, its leadership knows it will be hard to maintain that position. No one sees this more clearly than an athletic coach. He knows that, the minute his team becomes the champions, he will start to have trouble in keeping the members "up" mentally. Their question will be: "Where do we go from the top?"

In general, however, the membership of the group will not need to be convinced of the advantages of growth. The status, power, increased pay, and other perquisites which accrue to better performance resulting from development are well known to everyone. The constant challenge and the continuous stretching required for development are pleasant to most people unless they overdo it. Developmental goals must of course be carefully tailored to a realistic appraisal of both the individual and the group in order to provide a climate that is strongly conducive to continued motivation of the group.

Group protection. This goal is only a little less of a motivator than economic goals. Self-perpetuation is reflexive and appears in many forms. Any group is motivated to action when it is threatened from without. A cycle of activity is touched off whenever a group sees itself about to be attacked: Group cohesiveness increases strongly; group leadership gains in status and power; alternatives are considered; and protective action is undertaken. There are two possibilities for action—the group may counterattack or, like the turtle, withdraw into a protective shell.

Protective counterattack is one of the better testing grounds for group leadership. The situation will evoke whatever latent creativity the leader has in delimiting the alternatives available to the group. The leader must sharpen his decision-making power to shorten the time lag before a decision is made. He must also intensify his efforts at communication with the group membership. It is preferable to pass on bad news rather than leave group members in a vacuum, knowing nothing about what is going to happen. In industry, this is especially true when the workforce must be reduced. If the group's continued existence is under question, the leader does well to inform his people of this fact and give them regular progress reports, even if nothing new has been learned. It is when they receive no communication at all in this situation that group morale is totally shattered.

Most groups prefer to counterattack when under threat because they dislike anxious inactivity. Motivation for self-protection will elicit a greater level of group activity than is normal. This hyperactivity will be sustained for an indefinite period if the external threat continues. One method of counterattack for a threatened group is to sharpen group performance noticeably. Increased production, improved quality, and lowered costs are the best weapons in any group's arsenal.

The "turtle" reaction to outside threat is a neurotic one. Inactivity in the face of danger is not a natural response, and most followers resent leadership which takes them in this direction. It is an admission of assumed or actual inferiority in a direct confrontation, and it is galling to any person of normal intelligence. Lack of response to the threat will also be reflected in a lowered rate of normal group activity. Production and quality will be the first casualties. In the working situation, it is difficult to tell whether the line or the staff suffers more under inactivity when threatened. The nod may go to the staff people, since their work is not done under such imminent deadlines as are the daily activities of line people. If a staff group is threatened and responds like the turtle, the battle is lost. The group will die from attrition even if the enemy makes no overt move.

The other threat to a group is internal. Deviance from group norms is always perceived as a threat by both leader and group members. Group norms are established to further the achievement of either primary or secondary goals, and the member who does not conform is naturally perceived as a threat. The sanctions which can be immediately used by the group cover a broad spectrum of severity. The popularity of the member as well as the grossness of his deviance will temper the selection of the sanction. Groups are ultraconservative in regard to those who differ. Smart leadership frequently uses the indirect approach to the control of deviance. The group graybeard, or someone else held in high esteem by the members, will be enlisted to make the persuasive approach to the deviant. The appeal will be to his group pride and will point out how his example is harmful because of his influence on other members.

If this action is not sufficient to restore conformity by the deviant, a series of successively more severe sanctions will be employed. The final and irrevocable action is isolation. The deviant is amputated from the group. If it is not possible to remove him physically, the rest of the group will seal him off by means of a total cutoff of communication. As far as they are concerned, the erring member might as well not be there.

Total consensus will not always be achieved within the group regarding isolation. If the deviant is strongly influential, a splinter group may break off. The emergence of hundreds of small sects since the time of Luther in the Protestant church is a common example of this.

Power struggles within a group represent the other great internal threat. This is observed commonly in union structures. More than one powerful international union has been eviscerated by a struggle for power at the top. When the followers find it impossible to determine whom they owe their allegiance to, the group becomes ineffective and may even die.

The self-protective instinct of groups is universal and never dies. The group will take whatever actions it thinks necessary, no matter how drastic, to preserve its integrity. The fact that all progress is the result of deviance is not germane to group leadership when it considers itself threatened. The reactions will be predictable, immediate, and as drastic as deemed necessary. A great danger is for a group leader to overestimate a threat and, in overreacting to this perceived threat, thereby precipitate a situation which will get out of control. Herein lies another of the handy little tests of leadership.

The prospect of attainable power. Power is a strong motivator to many people and to groups. It is true that the desire for power is widely variable throughout a normal population, but the mix of group membership will usually turn up a percentage of people who rank power high among their personal motivators. Human history has been made by those whose desire to manipulate others was their strongest drive. Analysis shows that many groups are formed with the objective of attaining power in their sphere of action. Lobbies and unions are the commonest examples.

When the search for power is a prominent motivator in the group, the behavioral patterns of the group membership show some interesting changes. Many case studies are available of the changes that took place in the personalities and characters of German youth who joined the Hitler Jugend groups in Germany prior to and during World War II. The fascination of a uniform for some is traceable to the symbolism of power inherent in it. When desire for power is active as a group motivator, economic motivators are reinforced because of the obvious connection between the possession of large amounts of money and the achievement of power.

We tend to forget that the word *power* has two connotations. To most people most of the time, power has a sinister meaning—that is, it denotes a negative effect on those over whom it is wielded. Unfortunately, this misuse of power is too frequently apparent throughout the world. But there is a positive, benign use of power which works to the benefit of those affected. We have only to remember the good things achieved through the powerful use of money by philanthropic foundations to realize this.

The power-motivated group will be limited mainly to two methods of achieving satisfaction. The first and oldest is the use of naked force. The imposition of our will on others gives every appearance of being an instinctive trait, as every parent knows. Some of our earliest training of our children has to do with curbing this tendency to dominate others. When this characteristic appears as a group drive, we should expect it to cause conflict most of the time. This is why the protest group will wind up in trouble sooner or later in its existence—protest can be effective only when the group attains enough power to implement the desired change. Most of the devastation perpetrated by man on man has been a result of power struggles between two nearly equal groups.

The second method open to a group seeking power is the political approach, as described by Machiavelli in *The Prince*. This approach is characterized by the manipulation of people, with or without their consent, by means other than violent. In spite of our recent national absorption with violence on the American scene, we still are and always will be in more danger from subversive groups which attempt to gain power over our minds. As a nation, we are at a disadvantage in our contacts with our enemies because we have never studied or utilized propaganda and mental subversion as a primary weapon. The Communists boast to our faces that they will beat us through this medium.

Some interesting changes occur if individuals or groups suddenly acquire power without actively seeking it. An example of such acquisition would be the unexpected elevation of an obscure underling into the top position in the hierarchy. Our personal contacts, as well as world history, are full of illustrations of the complete changes in personalities that occur in this kind of situation. One of the more famous examples is the transformation of Nero from a lovable youth to a tyrant of the worst sort after his accession to power. It is possible for the whole group to undergo this same kind of personality change after gaining dominance.

The adoption of power as a motivating objective ordinarily is a conscious group decision. It becomes a matter of policy. This means that the entire group will reach consensus on this subject and that a planned course of action toward the achievement of that objective will be adopted. When this happens, other objectives will be subordinated to power, which is a demanding mistress. In the first place, the group will automatically become the target for all other groups in contact with it as soon as its drive for power is recognized. This is a natural self-protective reaction on the part of the other groups. The power-seeking group is properly recognized as a threat. A power-seeking group should be able to recognize this fact. They must be ready to pay for their prize. The drive for power will demand more singleness of purpose and concentrated effort than other objectives.

Once this course has been decided upon, there is small chance to retreat or change direction without fatal consequences. The enmity of other groups will not be lightly abandoned after engagement has been made. Power as an objective is attractive to many groups as much for the excitement and danger of the chase as for its realization. Because of the headiness of the rewards, it is unlikely that this human characteristic will disappear in our evolutionary progress.

Status. The older a civilization is, the more important status becomes to its citizens. There are those people who make status a primary objective of their adult lives, even at the sacrifice of things which others feel to be much more important. Some groups have taken on a status symbolism as their principal reason for being. Every city has its one or two clubs which make admission to their ranks a fantastically difficult problem. From region to region within our country, churches have a pecking order in their status rank. Status as a group motivator will usually loom larger as group's membership grows older and achieves other major objectives. Maneuvering becomes intricate when status is high on the roster of group objectives. Members of this sort of group find themselves subjected to new pressures simply because of the fact that they *are* members. A high-status group becomes critical of its members' cars, clothes, homes, and a long list of other material possessions. Groups have been known to attempt to dictate a small list of acceptable schools members' children may attend.

This sort of extreme emphasis on outward appearance is an illustration of the elaboration of social and ego needs under Maslow's hierarchy. It is a form of compensation for the basic insecurity of the group membership.

Status seeking by members of work groups ordinarily has a different connotation. In the business world, status symbols have come to be directly associated with a person's or group's upward progress in the organization. The group may be seeking status, not out of pride or snobbery, but purely for public recognition of its organizational worth.

Status seeking by a group is as ritualistic and stylized as a game of chess. Most of the gambits are well known and immediately recognized, but this does not prevent their use by the group. When moving to new quarters, the infighting for the larger offices and the better locations will become fierce beyond belief. Elaborate plans are made to capture the choice spots on the parking lot.

One of the more blatant and ridiculous of the status symbols is the executive dining room, into which entry is gained either by position title or by salary bracket. Warfare among secretaries is unending. The cliques are rock-ribbed and set in concrete. Just let a department head's secretary attempt to usurp that corner of the women's lounge usually occupied by the vice-presidents' secretarial group, and everyone around will do well to take cover.

The accumulation of such minor antics of status seeking is beginning to form a caste system in a country which used to be vocally proud of the absence of one. There is a deep difference between the aristocracy of achievement and that of position. The former is earned; the latter may be quite accidental. False values attached to status symbols will warp other, more important value judgments by the individual and the group. Status, like esteem, should be earned. When status becomes a major motivator, more important objectives are bound to suffer.

The situation has become so bad that even identification badges in industrial firms have become status symbols. The color or number of the badge will automatically give its wearer a rigidly controlled status or lack of it. The ultimate snobbery is evidenced when only company executives are allowed to go without an identification badge. Some firms have had remarkably good results from removing *all* badges. The reduction of status seeking can be measured directly in increased productivity and improved interpersonal relationships. This does not mean that authority should not be earned and honored. The difficulty is putting into proper perspective both earned authority and the empty forms of meaningless status.

It would be easier if there were less difference in the significance of the words "esteem" and "status." Esteem is never bought or captured; it is always earned. Status is too frequently an automatic requisite of a position, irrespective of the actual abilities of the incumbent. The confusion between these two words is the result of fuzzy thinking. A little concentration should resolve the misperception of the value of status quickly and finally.

Both the leader and the members of a group should give frequent consideration to the values attached to status. Our native intelligence, along with minimal common sense, can serve to keep us in line. If it becomes apparent that a group's status objective is becoming more and more important, it is time for a thorough overhauling of the whole list of group objectives. Prioritization of objectives, as has already been noted, should be on a regular fixed cycle for any healthy group. As group achievements mount, a proper status and esteem will accrue naturally in the thinking of others about the group. It is not necessary for it to be excessively concerned about its own status.

Excessive concentration on status can be traced to Old

World involvement with personal honor. If honor is too easily affronted, it may be too fragile for good health. One thing, of course, which makes it harder for us to keep a healthy balance in our thinking about status is the absence of an easily accessible frontier in our civilization. The old pioneer communities were capable of thinking clearly about status because of their more urgent involvement with the real facts of life.

Ego involvement. The motivation of the group is enhanced in direct proportion to the ego involvement of the membership. Identification of the individual with the group is a must for effective action. Each of us has "membership" in many groups. In some cases, this membership is purely nominal, with little resultant activity on our part. Informed leadership is aware of this and gives ego involvement a high priority as a group goal of every member.

The increasing use of "participative" management is based on the theory that the surest way to achieve ego involvement is to get the person into the action arena. By assuming his share of responsibility and by contributing to goal setting, planning, coordinating, and the day-to-day work, a member becomes tied in a personal way to the success of the group. Business enterprises which adopt this attitude after years of authority-centered, directive leadership observe some interesting changes in personnel who were not involved before. At first, there is an inertial drag against the implementation of the change. People who have never been given significant responsibility in the job before find it frightening at first, but, once they are assured that the new environment is not dangerous, enthusiasm is generated rapidly. For the first time in their working lives, the achievement of group goals is personalized, with a concomitant feeling of reward to the contributor.

Group leadership also has its difficulties with the change

to participative management from the traditional directive type of management. At first glance, it appears that the position of the leader is under threat. The membership is now undertaking individually part of what the leader formerly had sole responsibility for. However, according to Herzberg, the leader's job will grow, rather than be attenuated. His image among his followers will take on the flavor of a coach and resource person rather than an omniscient father figure. The growth and development possibilities for both leader and followers will generate an exciting environment for the entire group.

The quality of group objectives will be closely tied to the ego involvement of the membership. If goals are too easy, humdrum and unimaginative, or too unobtainable and dreamlike for reality, the members of the group will not be interested deeply in what goes on. Goal setting for the group demands the highest creative activity on the part of both leadership and membership.

It is difficult for the social observer to evaluate the real effect of the better education, training, and increased sophistication of each new generation on group living. Do these factors lead to a clearer understanding of the responsibilities and rewards of effective group living, or do they tend to make the individual hypercritical of both group membership and its leadership? One could expect either reaction, depending upon the natures of the individuals concerned. As a protest group becomes more articulate, it will receive more attention, regardless of its size. The mobility and ubiquity of a few black militants give the illusion that they have vast numbers of followers. Actually, repeated surveys have shown that the radical blacks are *not* supported by a majority of their own people.

Ego involvement of group members will insure a con-

GROUP MOTIVATION 71

tinuity of action hard to come by from any other source. Ego and self-actualization needs are on the highest level of the pyramid, and their satisfaction is more rewarding than the satisfaction of lower-level needs. When ego involvement is not only present but perceived by others, a synergism occurs which leads to greater group effectivity. The entire group will work harder when all its members know that the others have identified with the group and its goals.

When ego involvement is universal throughout the group, developmental activity for individuals will be high. The resultant growth will necessitate closer attention to the quality of the group's goals but will reduce the need for the close control which was formerly necessary. When a man takes an objective for his own, there is less need to monitor his activity in the group.

At this point, the heterogeneity of the group is emphasized. As individual contributions become greater through studied effort, personality variations will show through more clearly. This does not have to be bad for the group, so long as goals are clearly defined and similarly perceived by all members. It only seems to be a paradox that man's best individual efforts are often his contribution to the group.

However, a leader cannot set up a group with the *sole* purpose of ego involvement: There must be an involvement with a definite object or goal. Identification with the group is a strong motivator, but it will always be subordinated to and intermeshed with one or more objectives of a more tangible nature. Seldom does only one objective operate within a group; two, three, or more are the usual quota. Effective group leadership will continuously monitor those motivators which are making the group tick. The good leader will make this activity as unobtrusive as possible, because group motivation is a tender flower and too much exposure to public view can cause it to wilt.

The area of group motivation is long overdue for deeper study and comparative quantification of the major motivators. There is too great a tendency to think that all are equal among a group of peers. This is not the case.

Demotivation of the Group

There are three ways by which a group can be demotivated. First, an individual member (or members) can demotivate themselves. For example, a member may undergo a change in his own personal goals: A man may find himself able to work for prestige reasons rather than solely under financial pressures.

On the positive side, personal development can cause a significant change in personal objectives. They will be less tangible and harder to attain than were the old ones, and it will require more intense motivation to achieve them.

Personal problems (not necessarily associated with an individual's goals) can result in strong demotivation. Domestic difficulties, abrasive interpersonal relationships, revaluations of personal value judgments, religious conflicts—the list of demotivating factors is capable of infinite extension. Man being what he is, it is ridiculous for others to command him not to take his problems with him into group situations. He will. The amount of disruption his problems cause in his personal motivation will be a function of his personality and strength of character, but there will always be some trouble as a result of severe personal problems. People often want to seek competent counsel from some quarter when such problems become too heavy for them.

And there is a reverse to this situation. Severe work problems are carried back to the home if they continue over a period of time. Many a man's castle has been gutted by fires brought in from outside. It is difficult to decide which of these two problem situations will be more destructive to individual motivation.

Second, a group can be demotivated by its own leadership. A major point has been made of the fact that one person can never motivate another; motivation is always accomplished by the individual himself. However, a group leader can be directly responsible for reduced motivation among his followers. One of the common trouble factors is faulty leader–group communication. This is ordinarily the result not so much of passing incorrect information as of either over- or undercommunicating. An uninterrupted stream of trivia will be frustrating to the members, since they will have to handle the job of prioritization and make the decisions as to which items are important. Overcommunication is less frustrating than the lack of *necessary* communication from the leader. In the latter case, group membership will be working from a bank of assumptions, either individual or collective, and the insecurity developing from this situation can be fatal to motivation.

The leader can destroy the motivation of his followers by his misinterpretation of group goals. Whether the objectives of the group are superimposed from above or arrived at by participative action, the leadership function still includes responsibility for interpretation and clarification of group objectives. The assumption on the part of the leader that his group has a thorough understanding of its objectives is never valid until it has been rigorously tested. Moreover, this testing must include more than a regurgitation of official statements of goals; these must be paraphrased before the leader can be assured that his group does indeed have a clear understanding of them.

The leader can also demotivate his group by failing to perceive group consensus correctly. If his position is strong, he will not always *accede* to group consensus, but a demonstrated misunderstanding of the wishes of the group indicates a grave error on his part. His followers will demand that he be sensitive to their wishes whether he follows them or not. The tendency toward misperception of consensus is one of the penalties of the isolated position occupied by the leader. He must make a particularly strong effort to read the cues given to him by the group.

Third, a group can be demotivated by outside variables. If the economy of an industry is undergoing severe stress, a normally intelligent group may be demotivated by what its members judge to be a hopeless fight. Before committing their full effort, they will demand a reasonable chance of achieving their objectives. An overly competitive mental set generated by strong competition has much the same effect. A shifting of effort toward the scuttling of an enemy group will demotivate the primary concern for achieving major goals.

It is unfortunately true that a group's motivation is easier to destroy than it is to build in the first place. Commonality of objective, commitment to the group, smooth interpersonal relationships, and responsiveness to leadership comprise a set of independent variables. They are individually and collectively associated with group motivation; but, if any one of them is disturbed, the result may be complete demotivation on the part of the group. In the case of formal groups, the results of this demotivation may be hidden for extensive periods of time. They will be manifested in a rash of apparently unrelated symptoms recognizable only to the trained observer. Seldom will the group members run around proclaiming themselves to be strongly demotivated. In fact, when this does happen, the formal group is already moribund.

* * *

The past two chapters have created an artificial dichotomy of human motivation. Technically speaking, we cannot seperate the motivation of the individual from that of the group, since they are both concerned with human beings. It is only when we start to treat a group as an individual that we discover differences unaccounted for under the unitary approach.

McGregor, Maslow, and Herzberg can be considered the leaders in the field of human motivation. From their writings can be synthesized a matrix which comes closer to explaining things as they are than does any single approach to this fundamental aspect of human behavior.

Implicit in the study of human motivation is the question, "What use will be made of the knowledge gained in interpersonal relations, either laterally or vertically within the structure of the group?" This will depend on the character and motivation of the possessor of this knowledge. Throughout the entire span of recorded history, there have been people who knew intuitively those things which we now lump under motivational theory. The behavioral scientist makes available to all a functional body of knowledge for group living of any sort.

It is unfortunate that those who have made the greatest use of their knowledge of human motivation are not men of goodwill. The Communists—Russian, Chinese, Korean, and Vietnamese—have used motivation as a weapon of warfare, both offensive and defensive. The Western world is lagging far behind them in putting motivational theory to pragmatic use—yet it can be just as useful as a benign, constructive tool. As believers in democracy and the human dignity of the individual, we should strive to utilize our increasing knowledge of human motivation on "the side of the angels."

The impact of the behavioral scientist has scarcely begun to be felt in our daily life, even though it has increased many times in the past 10 or 15 years. Our children and their children will be immensely more sophisticated in this area of knowledge than we have been—if only because human curiosity concerning why we behave as we do is one of the earliest traits to develop in a growing child and is one which diminishes only a little as we mature.

No matter what theory is espoused, the important thing is the emphasis placed on rational use of continued introspection. Self-knowledge is indispensable to the knowledge of others.

A good knowledge of human motivation is an excellent buttress to overall mental health. Unexplained human behavior can be directly threatening simply because it represents the unknown. If the reason for the behavior is known, this fear is minimized and eventually will disappear entirely. Also, knowledge of human motivation can contribute to a person's speed of adaptability. If we recognize clearly the limits of our field of operation, it is easier to choose a method of behavior compatible with those surroundings.

Charting the projected activities of a group becomes more akin to a routine activity if we are familiar with the motivation of the various members of the group. Leadership skills can be multiplied, or at least more easily developed, on the basis of an understanding of motivation. The life of the follower is made more understandable and more satisfying if he is aware of the motivational drives of his peers and his leader.

Chapter 3

Different Kinds of Groups

*T*HERE are so many groups in everyone's life today, and so much of our living takes place within these groups, that it is necessary to classify the various kinds of groups before we can even begin to study their properties and the ways in which they affect us. There are many methods of classifying them. In this book, they will be classified by their structure and by some of the more salient attributes of each type of group.

Formal Groups

The best example of the formal group is the work organization. It is, in the lives of most citizens, the most important group, since a major part of their waking hours is spent here. The spiraling economy has increased the mobility of the American workman to the point where he can and will change his work situation for a variety of reasons, some of them quite trivial. He becomes familiar with several different formal work groups during his lifetime and finds that they differ widely in many characteristics. In addition, he discovers that in other aspects, all work groups are identical. He becomes so used to these similarities that he accepts them without question and bases his value judgments of his current job on the differences from the preceding one.

Herzberg's two-factor theory has fastened upon some of these differences as the leading dissatisfiers in the work situation—working conditions, supervisory styles, and fringe benefits. The increased discrimination developed by a migratory working class has had noticeable effects on formal groups in America. Labor negotiations have become sharper and more sophisticated, with labor's gains rising on an exponential curve during the past generation. Concurrently, management has come to regard the workforce as a collection of individuals rather than as an amorphous mass. Most working people, on the other hand, realize that their gains must be balanced by increased productivity in order to avoid the death of the goose that lays the golden eggs. Paradoxically, this increasing sensitivity on both sides of the bargaining table has in no sense reduced the tensions which arise during negotiations. If anything, it has increased them, as evidenced by the bitterness engendered in some recent strikes.

These socioeconomic factors have influenced the structure of contemporary working organizations. Some of the newer forms of organization on trial presently are innovative and full of promise. For example, the "matrix" types used in large organizations are a combination of line and functional structures. This new sort of operation requires greater expertise and sophistication on the part of the manager, but notable economies of time and money can be achieved with it. An ambivalence is arising between the easier working conditions on the one hand and the greater emotional stresses generated on the other. It would be difficult to prove that it is easier to live in the formal group than it was a generation ago. The trend toward more complex and more delicately balanced formal groups must continue if there is to be eventual improvement in the structure of our most important group.

One of the features that formal groups have in common is leader selection by fiat. Whether the organization is an entrepreneurship, a small family concern, or one of the modern industrial giants, those in control do designate—and will continue to designate—those who are to be in charge. So long as this one element of control is rigidly maintained, the ownership of the business knows that he holds the reins. Other aspects of the formal group may be handled permissively so long as the manager is installed by the owners and remains under their control. This fundamental of modern management is recognized in the raids made by one company on another. The first and ultimate goal is to control the management of the company that is to be taken over. When this has been accomplished, mere possession of stock in the company loses much of its importance.

The increasing awareness of labor is recognized by the modern manager when he attempts a smoother and more palatable imposition of the authority figure. In other words, public relations are becoming daily more important. If management cannot be made popular, at least it must not be allowed to become the object of labor's hatred. It is for this reason that many companies are playing down the more blatant outward symbols of power and authority among their managers. The shirt-sleeved company president and the slightly smaller and less opulent executive office just may smooth some feathers among the workers. There is greater recognition of the importance of proper timing and wording of the announcement of important company matters. One of the more sensitive staff jobs is that of the communications expert who reports in complete anonymity to the executive and writes his statements and speeches. What is said is of less importance than the manner in which it is said. The fact that these announcements are seen as necessary is in itself evidence of a fundamental change in managerial thinking.

The imposition of authority from above is antithetical to the concept of democracy. It is ironic that our country developed the strongest form of democratic government the world has ever seen while riding on the strong back of a business system based on authoritarian practices. Upon examination, this is not as contradictory as it appears at first. The most democratic families employ many authoritarian practices while the children are small and wait for the proper stage of maturation before introducing a more permissive climate. It remains to be seen whether the American workforce is mature enough to accept the responsibilities of the greater democratic freedoms they now possess. In the eighteenth and nineteenth centuries, English businessmen and—to a lesser degree—their American counterparts operated under a set of beliefs similar to the theory of the divine right of kings. There could be no questioning of the intent, judgment, or actions of The Boss. How far we have come from this position as we approach the twenty-first century we have only to look about us to see.

In spite of the totally different frame of mind in which we now regard a business organization, there has been no basic change in the method by which leadership is assigned from above in our formal groups. The time is still far away when formal groups will choose their leadership on anything like a democratic basis. Owners and investors are still too vitally concerned about the safety of their capital to allow this to come about. Most of the ferment on today's business scene is due to the conflict between a more sophisticated workforce and this seemingly indestructible concept of how leadership shall be chosen. It is more than possible that another generation may see the passing of the formal group as we know it today.

The goals of a formal group are normally imposed at a much higher level than the direct leadership of the group. We have held for generations to the genial fiction that the boss is the author and executor of the goals of a formal group. This is done so that the supervisor can maintain face and the self-respect of the working group will be preserved. If the real truth were to be admitted, it would be humiliating for all concerned. Factually, there is eminently good reason for the determination of goals at a higher level than first-line supervision. There is no one segment of a modern business large enough to see the whole picture. Tunnel vision at the working level is automatic because of the constriction of the horizon. However, the goals of the enterprise are composed of many fragments welded into a unified entity.

Goal setting at a distance is the natural parent of many difficulties. It may be completely impossible for the workman to accept as his own a goal whose reason for being he does not understand. Unless, however, the goals of the group are accepted by the workman and he is able to identify himself with them, motivation is notable for its absence. Overall group morale will suffer in direct ratio to this lack of understanding and identification, and the job of direct supervision will be unnecessarily complicated. Behavioral scientists have recently attempted to resolve these difficulties by opening clean channels of communication in both directions. Though they may not be appreciative of the full implications of company goals, members of a formal group will have a better attitude toward those goals as they gain knowledge of the manner in which they are derived.

Fiscal goals, though fundamental, have little meaning to members of a formal group unless they have a direct stake in them as investors in the enterprise. Therefore, management usually attempts to circumvent this difficulty by paraphrasing fiscal goals in words more appealing to the workmen. Varying degrees of success have been achieved with this gambit. One of the more successful aliases for fiscal goals has been the term "competition." There is enough of the unreconstructed savage in most of us to bristle at a corporeal enemy who can be made to seem, in Maslow's terms, a threat to our security needs.

Executive management is endangered by its aloofness from the members of the work group. Their derivation of goals may be impeccable, from both a business and a logical standpoint, but lack of communication can be fatal to them. The one thing that makes top management completely vulnerable is failure to achieve the goals of the formal group, which points up an inherent weakness of increasingly complex organization in the formal group. Every added layer of structure presents new possibilities of breakdown in communications and a warping of goals through partial misunderstandings. Those purists who maintain that no organization can survive with more than seven layers of authority (from the worker on the floor to the president of the company) are properly shocked when faced with structures having as many as *seventeen* levels in the same span. The real wonder is that any goal ever survives the handicaps created by this sort of stifling. All of us will grant the basic logic supporting the view that goals must be formulated at the top; all of us recognize the dangers to goal achievement within the structure of the formal group. Again, we are reminded that the attention presently being given to the invention of new organizational structures is both necessary and long overdue.

In the formal group, norms are usually superimposed. "Company rules" are a formalization of those minimal norms which leadership feels comprise a social structure. The amount of rigidity specified for group behavior is an accurate barometer of company philosophy, even though the latter may not be set out in policy or otherwise verbalized. The most universally established norms in the work group are standards of production and quality. These two items are intimately associated with the achievement of the enterprise's economic goals and serve as two effective controls.

The paternalistic superimposition of social norms is rapidly disappearing. One of the last bastions of this fort to remain manned appears to be the Canadian banking system. Young men who go to work for a Canadian bank reportedly know that they will not be allowed to marry until they have achieved a stated level in the hierarchy and a minimal salary specified by the bank. This incredible anachronism would seem the last of its kind in our society.

In work groups where high turnover is common, there is a tendency for greater structuring of the norms. The intent here is to provide conduct guidelines for the new employee, and this *is* achieved, although such structuring is an irritant to many people. Industrial orientation of new employees is traditionally too short, too crammed with unrelated data, and presented in a deadening and suppressive atmosphere. When group norms are both numerous and presented helter-skelter with a mass of other information, there is little chance that the new employee will remember or even notice a significant number of them.

As a result, when he unwittingly fails to conform to a written company rule, he is fiercely upset by the sanctions imposed.

A more permissive atmosphere (for example, under a Theory Y manager) allows for the formation of natural social groups within the larger formal group. The lack of numerous constraints on the individual will encourage innovation and creativity in the work environment, but this may be somewhat vitiated by rivalries engendered among the informal social groups growing in the larger structure. As a point of reference, McGregor's Theory X supervisor believes it mandatory to specify a long list of regulations and work rules for his people. The Theory Y man will keep such a list at the barest of minimums if he has one at all. The presence of formal rules of conduct provides a visible target for labor unions in their negotiations with the company. Work-rule grievances in the steel and automotive industries have given rise to some of the bitterest conflicts between labor and management.

It is possible for rigid group norms to be superimposed by management without being reduced to writing. Verbal transmittal of such norms by the supervisor requires more finesse in communication, but can be made real and binding on the group.

If the atmosphere of an enterprise is so restrictive that no one will take an action until he is sure that it is supported by either company policy or stated departmental procedure, the normative life within the group assumes shape much more quickly, but spontaneous change is next to impossible. A good case can be made for the argument that such a conservative approach is the only viable one for certain businesses, such as banking and insurance. These businesses feel that public trust can be gained and held only when the formal group has clearly specified and rigidly policed behavioral norms for its members. The few exceptions to this dictum are the products of extremely strong personalities at the highest level of management. Once in a while, these people can project their own deviance down the line and still retain customer confidence.

Membership in a formal group is only partly voluntary. Since most of us do have to work for a living, once a person is established in his formal work group, he will go to great lengths to avoid having to change his membership. Even though mobility of the working public has greatly increased over the past two decades, it is still a traumatic experience for a workman to leave one job and be reoriented into another. The inertial forces which tend to maintain the integrity of the formal group can work strongly against the general economic trend. Even in times of inflation and expanding economy, work groups will have less than predictable turnover because of individual reluctance to pull up stakes and start afresh elsewhere.

What happens when management decides to sever the undesirable members from the group? If their performance is submarginal but their identification with and loyalty to the group are unquestionable, these members will be extremely upset. This emotion and the concomitant inertial drag can have a visible effect on the economy at large. Thus, if business is on the decline, a humanitarian management may keep members of its workforce on the payroll past the point of good judgment. If business is booming, many workers will fail to avail themselves of opportunities for advancement elsewhere because of the upset attendant upon changing jobs. And, when an entire industry is undergoing economic change, either upward or downward, adjustments to these changes will be slowed down by this human characteristic.

In a community dominated by one business enterprise,

large numbers of its employees may only maintain their membership in this formal group because there is no other place in the area in which they can find suitable employment. "Company towns" develop a unique personality. Control is exercised over the citizens to such an extent that their personal liberties are severely circumscribed. Permission may have to be received from the company before a merchant starts a new business or a family buys a home. Company dominance of the city government and the local school district produces many odd situations that are not encountered in a more normal community. It is true that many of these dominant industries are strongly paternalistic —they are the last of the benevolent despots—and their continuing dominance of the citizenry is reflected in lowered self-reliance on the part of many individuals.

Voluntary membership in a group is the biggest single determinant of group morale. A captive audience has a mental set which militates against identification and adoption of group goals. Even if there is no overt rebellion against the situation, group membership will not create a climate conducive to the mental and spiritual good health of the members.

Self-determinism, in the last analysis, is a goal for most people rather than an actuality. We have too many constraints to be free agents. But, if we can make some of our fundamental decisions for ourselves, we are much happier than when we are obviously captives of the system.

Rigidity is a necessity for the protection of the formal group. There must be inflexibilities in the pursuit of basic objectives; group leadership must be strictly supported and under the complete control of top management; group membership must conform to whatever norms are established and imposed from above. This rigidity of purpose is especially hard for the chronologically younger members of a formal group to understand and accept; the constriction of personal freedom of thought and action is especially galling to the young. But inculcation of the discipline of rigidity is the first responsibility of formal group leadership. This is the only way in which the formal group can maintain its safety and have a reasonable chance of perpetuation. Still, unless it is tempered by a broader intellectual understanding of society at large, group rigidity will operate as a strong deterrent to progress. The maintenance of the status quo becomes an icon with hypnotic powers over the members of the group.

Reconciling the needs of the formal group with the demands of society will be a continuing test of the caliber of group leadership. The leader must be aware that at a given point group rigidity should be relaxed to accommodate an observed change in the outside world. Those formal groups which insist on running against the current of the rest of the world will lose out in the end.

On the good side of the coin is the fact that the imposition of rigid controls in some areas by the formal group may possibly be the only real discipline to which some of the members will ever be subjected. Permissive attitudes at home and school make it possible for a young person to arrive at his first job without having known any real curbing of his wishes. The formal work group can serve a useful purpose by being the vehicle for insuring some measure of emotional maturity to its members.

Semiformal Groups

The differentiation between the formal and the semiformal group is slight but definitive. Some examples of semiformal groups that come to mind are lodges, churches, social clubs, and P-TA's. A large part of our social living is embodied in these groups. In Maslow's terms, many of our social needs—and a considerable part of our ego needs—find their satisfaction in the interaction they provide. It is true that membership in some of these semiformal groups is conditioned by our formal groups; that is, membership in a particular lodge may be tacitly expected of a person who occupies a certain position in the company hierarchy. This does not necessarily denigrate the actual worth of that membership, which is above and beyond that expected by the leaders of the formal group.

Elaboration occurs principally in the semiformal group. Multiple semiformal memberships may be meaningful on a diminishing plane if a person is attempting to satisfy his ego needs by elaborating on the social-needs level. However, the values accruing from the greater number of contacts in a larger number of groups may be counterbalanced by a more superficial participation in each one. Man can spread himself only so thin. Each of us has his own self-limiting ability to support a certain number of memberships in semiformal groups. Each of us will determine the point of diminishing returns for his efforts.

Semiformal groups have the same *form* as the formal group. The hierarchy is carefully delineated, the structure is formal, and membership gives the appearance of careful selectivity. Many lodges predicate their whole existence on the appearance of high snobbery. Membership is difficult to achieve and is usually attained only after a long waiting period. The societal life of a community revolves about a few of these semiformal groups. Prestige and status in the community accruing from memberships in these groups may exceed prestige and status of the formal group. Thus an individual may achieve a spurious community level that is not substantiated by the real contribution made by his activities in his formal group. In essence, two values are then assigned to his position, and he becomes an enigma to his peers.

Form is of extreme importance in the semiformal group. It is the strongest weapon for self-perpetuation. When form breaks down, the whole structure collapses. If attacked in its structure, the semiformal group will respond with its strongest defense; its existence depends upon a successful repelling of the invader.

Pro forma deliberative activities take up a large part of the semiformal group's meeting time. It confers lengthily over the manner of public exposure and the predicted reactions from the outside public. Protocol assumes momentous importance; the pecking order of opposite numbers is a matter of frustration or triumph. An individual's multiple membership positions become harrowing to him if he holds significantly different positions in the various groups. His own self-image is affected by the way in which his peers see him in his varying attempts at social- and ego-need satisfaction.

Of course, the structure of the semiformal group is one of the main attractions for everyone who covets membership in it. In his own growth and development, he will change his value judgments many times. He will seek and discard memberships more or less rapidly, depending upon the rate of his evolution, and the plotting of his progress will be most illuminating as to the degree of his maturity.

The fact that the semiformal group has the same form as the formal group has nothing to do with voluntary membership, group objectives, group leadership, or group norms. Whether they are similar or quite different is not germane. Structure has carried the Roman Catholic church for two thousand years; it is only during the cataclysmic struggles of the latter part of this century that it has felt threatened to any great degree. (It is only in its structure that the Catholic church remains a formal rather than a semiformal group. If it were structured less severely, it would be a semiformal group like other churches.)

The dichotomy between the formal and the semiformal groups begins *after* the matter of structure. If we have belabored form unduly, it has been to remind ourselves that the differences between these two kinds of groups lie in other areas. Structural form is of vital importance to the group in both its internal interactions and its relationships to other groups in the social environment. Form is a frame of reference for comparison between groups leading to initial choice of membership; unless it is clearly defined and maintained with integrity, a prospective member is lost in a fog. Suffice it to say that, so far as form is concerned, there is no distinguishing between the formal and the semiformal group.

Membership in the semiformal group is purely voluntary. We made a big issue of the fact that any given individual does not have total control over his membership in a formal group. If we disregard the strong influences exerted by his formal group leadership to assume membership in one or more semiformal groups, we can see that his choice of membership in semiformal groups is otherwise uninhibited.

It is interesting, as we noted in an earlier chapter, to trace the migration of some people in their church memberships. Rising through various economic strata, they see that certain sects have greater social status than others. So sometimes they shift their membership if they feel that belonging to a particular church will satisfy social or ego needs in addition to more fundamental spiritual longings. The same thing can be said of lodge membership. In ascending order of status, a man may aspire to and achieve membership in a series of lodges *until membership in these organizations ceases to have meaning for him.* The act of dropping all fraternal memberships can be a milepost in his development.

Membership in any semiformal group—that is, active participation with the expenditure of quantifiable amounts of effort and ego involvement—will be continued only so long as there is a measurable return for the individual concerned.

Consider the case of the man who does not feel the necessity for membership in any semiformal group. This is indicative of either complete satisfaction of all social and ego needs (so rare as to be not worthy of consideration) or a complete lack of introspective activity and, thus, of felt needs. The man lives on a plateau of achievement that is either totally stultifying or is representative of the acme of his desires.

Voluntary group membership assumes a measure of self-determinism, which may or may not be within the grasp of every individual. Involved are community status, financial situation, available time, and amount of ego involvement. When these amount to a strong enough motivation, attempts will be made to associate with a desired group or groups. The struggle for membership itself is part of the developmental activity of every man who attains emotional maturity. He can equate his position in the community with his self-evaluation on a one-to-one basis.

Membership in a chosen group is essential to the peace of mind of any man. He will set aside any other consideration, except the most basic economic ones, until he has been accepted by the group. In other words, his basic objective *is* this membership until he has it in the bag.

The assortment of group memberships finally accumulated by any man is a measure of his stature as an individual. He reflects in his shaving mirror the total security these memberships constitute for him. What he sees may or may not represent a legitimate picture of himself as a man; that is not the question. It does satisfy his own needs, and the resultant peace of mind will make his efforts in his formal group more effective and rewarding. Reinforcement by status and esteem is not to be underrated.

Voluntary membership in the semiformal group can carry over into the formal group. Thus, if enough of our social and ego needs are already satisfied by multigroup memberships in semiformal groups, we may have insufficient motivation to participate fully in the day-to-day activity of the work group. The result may be an undesirable inertia, possibly sparked by the idea that the job is "beneath us." We behave, after all, as we see ourselves in our mind's eye.

In the semiformal group, objectives are rigid. The maintenance of set-in-concrete goals is essential for the perpetuation of the group. Any attempt by members to alter group objectives is looked upon by those in control as insurrection, and the sternest possible means of quelling this activity are brought into use. The semiformal group refuses to recognize progressive change as necessarily desirable. The common approach of semiformal group leadership, to justify this rigidity to its members, is talk about "tradition." Long after the reason for a particular goal has been lost sight of, it remains steadfast for all group activities.

If the goals of a semiformal group never change, it becomes an anachronism in its social environment. It is for this reason that The Establishment is the object of hatred for young, impatient people who see progress being retarded every day thanks to a reactionary ruling clique. The ability of a semiformal group to survive for long periods after it is completely out of touch with the social environment is a tribute to the powerful hold that veneration of tradition can have over its membership. In recent years, we have seen the agonies of readjustment forced upon white citizens of the South who refused to abandon group goals which were obsolete a century ago. The survival of these goals and the attitudes supporting them after a cataclysm such as the War Between the States is a tribute to the power that group goals can exert over both leaders and members of a group. This sort of situation also exaggerates the generation gap so troublesome in these times. Southern youth, exposed as they have been to a more sophisticated and cosmopolitan environment than were their parents, are moving much nearer to acceptance of the change occurring in their midst. Thus a polarization is emerging between the two generations which is next to impossible to resolve.

The inviolability of semiformal group goals produces a narrowed vision in its leadership which reduces its effectiveness. The artificial constriction of the group horizon that results means that significant dangers and significant opportunities for the group both may be missed.

Since many semiformal groups are established with only one major objective, if that one is seriously changed—or deleted completely—the group's reason for being disappears. While a business may undertake diversification to protect itself in a changing world and thereby alter its major objectives with relative ease, the semiformal group cannot do this without risking the loss of its original character and, as a consequence, its appeal for most of its membership. It is interesting to note that some labor unions are semiformal groups. When first organized, their sole objective was to protect the members from a predatory capitalistic management. Now that most managers have changed their viewpoints—and think and speak in terms of the duties and responsibilities of management toward their people—these unions are hard put to maintain their original position of defensiveness against a natural enemy. They reason that their best tactic is to keep their members uninformed of the changes occurring in management and to work on the assumption that all management is still generically bad. This produces an intransigence which is not productive of good results in labor negotiations.

Whatever their reactive behavior may be, the leaders of a semiformal group believe devoutly in the sanctity of the group's goals and will employ any tool they believe effective to insure the continuance of those goals for the protection of the group.

As a result of this attitude and this belief in the necessary rigidity of goals, semiformal groups are self-perpetuating, and group leadership becomes intrenched. This intrenchment is a fallout of the mechanistic design of constitutions and bylaws promulgated at the inception of the group. We are all familiar with the long lines of progression "through the chairs" of lodge officialdom, where it may take as long as ten years for an aspirant to reach the top of the heap as grand mogul. Another common gambit of intrenched leadership is to provide wide latitude in appointive powers for the top leader of the group. In many cases, this means that today's leader has direct control over the choice of his successor without even going through a really democratic election of officials.

If the group leadership is truly venal, an active attempt will be made to discourage the interest of rank-and-file members in election processes. Such a semiformal group will have only a small percentage of its membership present at a business meeting, and those present will all have a vested interest in control of the group. It is in this way that unions are able to perpetuate the same leadership for years on end. This can be the result of only two attitudes on the part of the members—supreme indifference concerning group leadership or respect (even veneration) of the present leaders. The first attitude means they are generally satisfied with conditions in the group. Since the members do not feel a need for change, they could scarcely care less who has control of the group. In fact, their disinterest is so great that they are not even curious enough to learn what the real situation of the group is. The second attitude is a case of "the king can do no wrong." John L. Lewis achieved this position with his miners and was actually able to defy with impunity the direct power of the U.S. government at one time.

There are advantages for a semiformal group that perpetuates a leadership that has shown an ability to protect the group's interests and maintain the status quo against outside attack. There will be less danger of divisive change if the same leadership is allowed to continue without interruption. The greatest danger in this method of operation is obviously the inclusion of large numbers of new members within the group—people who have not had a long period of indoctrination to insure their unreserved acceptance of the group's objectives. A bloc of such new members (if they become insurgent) poses a more real threat to the group than most attacks from without. The older craft unions have been able to survive because of careful screening of prospective members. In some cases, membership may be had only as a legacy from a father to his son. The organization of the industrial unions, embracing without reservation all workers within a given industry, is much more vulnerable to attacks upon its leadership from its own members.

Self-perpetuation and intrenchment may become such an overpowering concern of leaders that no time is left for constructive activity for the general welfare of the group. The result can be either a palace revolution, with the emergence of new leaders, or the demise and disappearance of the entire group. But semiformal groups are not necessarily strongly dependent upon their utility to their membership. It is possible for them to continue many years after their real services to members have become negligible. This they accomplish by such devices as maintenance-of-membership clauses in the union contract. Together with the checkoff method of dues collection, this alone can put the leadership in a nearly invulnerable position.

In a semiformal group, the norms are negotiable. With a rigid structure and rigid leadership required, they offer the only semblance of adaptability that is possible. The leaders can approach norms in two ways. They can subtly or blatantly, depending upon their style, project new norms for achieving the purpose of the moment. This presupposes strong leaders who have no fear of an antagonistic group reaction upsetting the desired end. If the leaders are not so strong, they await proposals from the rank and file as to alterations or changes in mores which seem desirable to the group. Once these changes are laid on the table, the leaders immediately are in a position to negotiate for their own ends. One or more of the new proposals will be accepted in return for concessions from the membership.

Group norms are the day-to-day operating standards by which a group adjusts its effort to the achievement of its goals. Even if the goals do not change, the group's environment and membership will be altered from time to time in such ways as to make adjustments in methods mandatory. The tenor of the group is more directly affected by its operating norms than by any other single factor. Group morale, productivity, and eventually individual identification with the group will be modulated strongly by acceptance or rejection of group norms.

Norms are of more immediate importance in the semiformal group than in a formal one. In the latter case, group objectives are more subject to change and adaptation to the group environment. If the formal group's leaders are alert and competent, they realize that modifying objectives to adjust for outside influences is necessary for survival. Norms are then naturally submerged to a lower level of attention than they receive in a semiformal group.

Perhaps it would be wise to stop and consider the delicate balance which always exists in *any* kind of group among objectives, leaders, norms, and members. The effective group is the one that can find this state of balance quickly and with the least disturbance to individual members. Individual differences will always result in uneven adjustment for particular members of the group; it is the function of the leaders to pull together these valences of varying strength and smooth them out in the total group effort.

The negotiation of group norms within the semiformal group is a major part of its overall activities. Every lodge, every church, every labor union, every P-TA spends an inordinate amount of its procedural time in trying to obtain consensus about its operating methodology. This is why it is relatively simple for a strong leader to take over a semiformal group and intrench himself in the power seat. Most people become bored at the quibbling necessary to negotiate norms; their span of attention is relatively short for this activity. At a point in the proceedings that is easily recognized by the strong leader, he knows that he can step forward and "railroad" through his own slate of norms against only token resistance. Communists spend years indoctrinating their party members in this technique.

Informal Groups

We live among and have memberships in so many informal groups that we lose count of the number. Children are socialized in the groups that they form as soon as they are old enough to be allowed to go out to play. Informal groups accomplish much of our education and imprint most of our cultural values. We acquire our hobbies in informal group activities. An exhaustive listing of informal groups would make this book so ponderous a tome that no one would read it, but there are five kinds of informal groups which are fairly representative and which indicate something of the breadth of the spectrum occupied by informal groups.

Friendship groups. These are the first groups we form in early childhood; we continue throughout life to spend much of our leisure time in the activities of friendship groups. Several common interests speed the formation of a friendship between two people but are not prerequisite to it. The mystique of friendship has eluded exact definition and description for several thousand years. People have many concentric rings of friendship groups. Some persist from childhood; some are formed in our semiformal group interactions in churches or lodges; some grow spontaneously in our work surroundings. Because of the orbital nature of these different groups, it is not common to find much coalescence among them.

Hobby groups. Such groups bring together wildly improbable companions. A chess club may have laborers, managers, reclusive introverts, and the most extroverted of salesmen among its membership. Bridge enthusiasts come from every walk of life, and gross differences of personality and status are ignored in the intricacies of this enthralling game. Bridge comes close to being the international language for its followers.

Informal work groups. Informal groups represent some of the more persistent group memberships. It is common for a friendship to spring up between a new member of the work group and the first person who makes him feel welcome. This friendship leads naturally to the inclusion of the newcomer in the informal work groups frequented by the welcomer. From the standpoint of the formal work group, these can be of extreme importance. A good supervisor is deeply sensitive to the informal groups within his area and will cultivate their goodwill and active cooperation through informal group leadership. They can make or break the enterprise.

Self-protective informal groups. These are found everywhere but especially in the work organization. If a supervisor comes on too strongly, he will find his people grouping against him. The value of the united front against a common threat is one of our first lessons. We are speaking here, not of the semiformal union, but of the small group which arises spontaneously within a segment of a formal organization. This kind of group can spring into being overnight if a threat is perceived; it will dissipate just as quickly as soon as the threat has subsided.

Convenience informal groups. Convenience groups are epitomized by the car pool so common in our industrial life. Five people can reduce their driving responsibility 80 percent by rotating their cars once a week. A subsidiary benefit is that most supervisors hesitate to assign overtime to members of a car pool unless all are included. The proportionate reduction of the stresses of modern driving is often visible in the increased productivity of car-pool members. Many other examples of convenience groupings arise both on and off the job in our everyday living.

One major attribute of the informal group worthy of note is the common practice of rotational leadership. Because of their specialized needs, informal groups are not bound by any set of rules. They are purely functional, with quite fundamental and easily recognized objectives. If one of the members has proved himself to be quick thinking and effective in times of stress, the group will turn to him to guide them when an external danger looms.

Another member of the group, who has demonstrated clear, logical thinking, will be the center of attention in planning activities. He will be influential both in goal setting and in reviews and evaluations.

Every group of any size will assign proper duties to the gregarious and outgoing socializer in its midst. He will plan the party, be responsible for the Christmas program, and know where to go and whom to contact for the summer picnic, whereas the legalist who is good at the bargaining table will have his moments of recognition and know the deference given to a recognized leader as he formulates and guides group strategy.

What the informal group is doing in this process is recognizing pragmatically that only rarely are all these leadership characteristics found to a degree of expertise in one person. The success of the group in different situations is maximized by calling on the one person best qualified for each function. In addition, there will normally be one or two members in the informal group who have achieved *general* status and esteem by the solidity of their achievements in more than one area. These are the "wise old men," who are turned to as a court of last resort in any kind of unresolved difficulty among the group membership.

The informal group judgment of its leadership is quicker, surer, and more coldblooded than that of the management of most formal groups. Only one criterion is recognized: The leader must lead. He must get the job done with a minimum of wasted effort. The average leader of an informal group can make only one mistake before he is deposed, although no penalty is attached to failure except loss of leadership. This characteristic of informal groups reflects its members' knowledge of how vulnerable an informal group is. It has no legal status; all its activities are extracurricular and without the protection of higher authority or formal ordination.

The informal group is a natural source of much of the leadership that will later be officially anointed by the formal group; that is, the management ranks of business and industry. When a man proves himself effective as a leader time after time in the informal group, recognition by the enterprise itself will not be withheld for long. Leadership is too valuable and too rare to be lost. This accounts for the fact that many union stewards, organizers, and officials eventually become powerful and effective members of the management team.

Since it is not bound by formalized policy in every direction, the informal group is an ideal testing ground for new techniques of leadership. The fact that a new gimmick is effective in the informal situation is not a guarantee that it can be transferred without change to the formal situation, where it may conflict with existing policy and procedure controls. But at least it will be worth a try, and the new technique just possibly will become a valuable new tool in formal management. "Management by committee," now enjoying a vogue in some quarters, had its beginning in the informal group, which in most cases is just about committee size.

Norms are of great importance to the informal group. What protection they lack in official status must be made up in other ways to insure perpetuation of the group. For the informal group operating within the formal work group, norms are used many times as a protection against the formal group. If management has prescribed production norms which the group considers to be unfair, the group's recourse is to adopt less demanding norms and bend its ingenuity to discover ways in which it can sabotage management's imposed standards.

Internally, the integrity of the informal group makes norms significant. They become the bench marks by which the behavior patterns of individual members are measured. The informal group is much more fearful of deviance than is a more solidly based formal or informal group. Since informal groups are usually small, the deviance of one or two members can have a much greater effect than would be true in a larger and more heterogeneous group.

Informal group norms may be either proposed by leadership and accepted by the group or originated as a group effort. In either case, once formulated and adopted, they are rigidly enforced until changed. Since normative action is of such importance, the norms will change frequently; the informal group is always attuned to its environment and is responsive to changes in it for self-protective reasons. The tightening or easing of certain group norms is one of the easier and quicker responses to a perceived change in surroundings.

Depending upon the kind of informal group involved, norms of personal behavior (not directly associated with group activity) have varying effects. *Noblesse oblige* has real meaning for members of certain kinds of informal groups, and informal groups exercise a great moral censorship in society at large. For some individuals, this influence may be stronger than that of their church. In fact, a man's informal group membership can color his entire life.

One result of this, however—and a frequent problem in our multigroup living—is appearance of conflict between the norms of one group and those of another. Role conflict is present to some degree in everyone's life today; for some people, it becomes a major disturbance, leading to neurotic and irrational behavior. For, if the informal group's norms are its day-to-day operating procedures and, as such, must be continuously monitored and updated, they assume great importance in the life of the group.

Both the psychologist and the sociologist are intensely interested in group mores, but from opposite ends of the spectrum. The psychologist is concerned with the effect on the individual; the sociologist observes the effect of group norms on larger societal formations. The amount of research by the behavioral scientists in this area is not yet sufficient, but it is increasing rapidly.

Sensitivity to our surroundings is of prime necessity to successful living. That we know *why* we do certain things is more important than the fact that we *do* them. Rational behavior is fundamental to anyone's mental health. It is for this reason that blind conformity can be dangerous to us. Some norms which make eminent sense to groups may be harmful to individuals, *especially to those who do not stop to question their rationale.*

The informal group can only enforce norms through the application of sanctions. As with other groups, these can vary all the way from the withholding of minor privileges to isolation from the group. Informal group membership becomes proficient in devising sanctions which fit exactly the magnitude of the offense. Member sensitivity in the small informal group is often such that direct communication concerning nonobservance of a norm is not necessary. The mere appearance of the appropriate sanction directed against a group member is often enough to bring the offender back into conformity. Although interpersonal relationships in the informal group are ordinarily cordial, they are not necessarily so, since situational developments may have been the reason for the group's formation. For example, if an informal group is formed for self-protective reasons within the work group, it may be grossly heterogeneous, including members who in everyday life are enemies. Even in this extreme case, the group will be successful in applying sanctions so long as the need for the group exists.

The informal group can also apply sanctions outwardly, against its environment. A necessary service can be withheld until a situation inimical to the group has been satisfactorily resolved. This is the basis for a strike action by members of the formal group. Outward sanctions are effective only when those not in the group value its services to an extent greater than they value the situation unfavorable to the group. For this reason, application of outward sanctions is the most dangerous weapon at the command of the informal group, since, if the sanctions are not successful, the life of the group will be in danger.

The decision to apply sanctions, either internally or outwardly, is in many cases divisive to the group. This sort of punitive action brings to the forefront the value judgments of the group membership. Individual friendships may be stronger than involvement with the entire group. When such a choice is forced upon group members, there is always the danger that the group itself may suffer.

The necessity for sanctions results from negative forces within the group, and goal achievement or other types of creative activity will, of necessity, be subordinated until the situation is resolved. Also, for the sake of appearances, it may be necessary to keep the internal application of sanctions a secret from the general public. For example, professional groups such as those of doctors, lawyers, or engineers may put members into the professional doghouse while keeping that fact a closely guarded secret from the layman. This is done for the protection of the group rather than of the individual involved. However, an alert public will soon discover when a physician has lost his staff privileges at one of the important local hospitals, and his practice will suffer—as is actually the intent of his professional colleagues.

There is little a member under sanctions can do except conform or else sever his group membership. The smaller the group, the more critical is the situation when sanctions become necessary. At the same time, smaller deviations from norms are picked up and responded to by the group membership. Group solidarity is of vital importance to the small informal group, where both membership and group objective itself may be tenuous. Another complicating factor is the rotational leadership of the informal group; different leaders will almost certainly attach different values to the same norm. A high crime in the eyes of one leader may be condoned by another.

The informal group is also highly volatile. Volatility in the group may be caused by achievement of a definitive goal, so that the group no longer has a reason for existence. Time-limited objectives, such as elections, will provide an automatic termination date for political informal groups, whether they achieve their goal or not. Another reason for informal group volatility is a change in membership caused by transfers in the formal work group which make impossible the personal interaction necessary for the maintenance of the group. Then, too, intense rivalry between two candidates for leadership of the informal group can cause it to divide or even to disintegrate completely.

The very size of the informal group contributes to this characteristic. Composed as it ordinarily is of three or four or not more than a dozen members, the informal group is highly susceptible to disruptions which larger and more stable groups could take in stride. Especially on the work scene, informal groups are sometimes almost invisible; at least, they operate sub rosa to such an extent as to be inconspicuous in the environment. And this very invisibility contributes to their volatility.

It must not be inferred that all informal groups are short-lived. Some go on for years in formal organizations which have relatively high stability. There are many examples of informal groups which maintain their integrity even though the membership is widely scattered and communication difficult.

* * *

In this chapter the group has been classified into three major categories—formal, semiformal, and informal. These are differentiated by structure and by certain attributes peculiar to each kind of group. The groundwork has been laid for future discussions of how personal group memberships have contact with and membership in many groups of each kind. A conceptual base has been established on which to build a discussion of the broad characteristics of groups and their effects on the group members.

Chapter 4

Properties of Groups

GROUPS of all kinds have several common properties which must be thoroughly understood before one can gain a perspective on interaction between the individual and the group.

Group Cohesiveness

Cohesiveness is that force tending to hold a group together. Cohesiveness varies as a result of many factors. Group cohesiveness increases strongly whenever the membership perceives a threat from the outside. The ranks are closed, and a united front is presented to the enemy. The increase in cohesiveness is a function of the magnitude of the perceived threat and will continue until the problem is resolved.

Group cohesiveness will vary widely according to the type and strength of the leadership. The leader capable of communicating and reinforcing group objectives will have a more cohesive group. The direct relationship between cohesiveness and effectivity in the formal work group is one of the main concerns of its leaders. Because the formal group is more heterogeneous than an informal one, cohesiveness is more difficult to achieve. This is why some supervisors play games by overemphasizing the threat of competition, or the state of the general economy or the particular industry.

Group cohesiveness is positively affected by dissension within the group. Significant deviance on the part of one or more members will strengthen the tendency of the rest of the membership to stick together just as they would face an external threat.

Cohesiveness is directly proportional to the group's identification with its major objectives. If the central objective of the group seems to its membership to be worthy of a considerable sacrifice in order to attain it, group solidarity will be high. Interpersonal relationships prevalent within the group are important conditioners of cohesiveness. It is not necessary that strong friendships exist, so long as esteem and admiration are present. The cohesiveness of the Yankees (baseball) and the Packers (football) during their championship regimes are good cases in point.

Seldom will a group be introspective enough about their own processes to verbalize about the matter of cohesiveness. Attention, if the group is effective, will be centered on goal achievement. If the group is troubled and its effectiveness low, members will be thinking about external problems rather than lack of cohesiveness, which they would call a symptom.

It is possible for a group's leaders to choose their actions with the express purpose of directly raising its cohesiveness. Group tasks can be assigned to teams made up of members who have interacted less frequently or less effectively than others. As these teams succeed in their tasks, new and stronger interpersonal relationships will be formed and cohesiveness will therefore increase. Also, it is possible to choose objectives deliberately for their heightening effect on group cohesiveness. For example, if the leaders maneuver their people into undertaking a task which is unpopular with the general public and brings it off successfully, group cohesiveness will be enhanced.

In general, the most dangerous time for group cohesiveness is when things are going well. If objectives are being met and no serious threats are perceived, either internal or external, cohesiveness will suffer: In this respect, the group is like the individual—and a well man never thinks of his health.

In order to increase cohesiveness, some leaders deliberately devise situations which will put one group into competition with another. So long as this gambit is carefully controlled, group solidarity will increase. The concomitant danger is that the competition will get out of control or, worse yet, will appear among members of the group, thus weakening group ties. The strength of any group is the product of many different factors, most of them not under the direct control of either the leader or the group as a whole. The monitoring of group processes, as already mentioned, is not a common practice unless the group members are highly sophisticated. However, it should be undertaken by any leader who is anxious to improve the performance of his group. Just as the individual wanting to get ahead will train himself to stop periodically and ask, "How am I doing?" so will a well-trained group adopt this practice to measure its growth, progress, and effectiveness. And one of the better barometers of the group's performance will be its cohesiveness. It should be understood that we have no absolute measures of cohesiveness, nor is its quantification possible, yet we can and should make comparative intuitive judgments as to the cohesiveness of a particular group. This will eventually come to be looked upon as a natural and necessary part of group living.

Normative Activities

Group norms are the standards of behavior. They may be set in any context, may cover any aspect of a member's group or personal life, and may be established in several ways.

One method of norm derivation is as old as mankind itself: A norm grows, and is established, by tradition. No conscious creative effort is applied by any member of the group. Suddenly it is realized that this way of doing something is the way most pleasing to the group. Every culture has hundreds of mores which have originated in this manner; cultural differences are most sharply delineated by the variance in group norms. Norms reveal the value sets of a group; this is perhaps truest in the case of those norms which have grown traditionally—without conscious cerebration by any group member.

A second method of norm derivation is imposition upon a group by highest authority. The best example of this is company policy. From the standpoint of the organization, it has the advantage of being generated in an area so remote and aloof from the membership that it is almost impossible to attack. Also, it becomes successively easier for each lower level of management to disclaim any connection with authorship; the first-line supervisor will be held blameless in the eyes of his people for unpopular policy. In fact, it is not uncommon to find conspiracies between employees and one or more levels of management to evade compliance with a certain policy. No matter what its intent, any policy is bad which has the unanimous disapproval of the workmen on the floor. Lowered productivity, sabotaged goals, demotivated employees, and poor morale are too heavy a price to pay for any policy.

A third method of norm deviation is directive imposition by the immediate supervisor of the work group. Here the authorship is recognized, and the norm may be met head on with open opposition. However, because of the closer connection of the author with the group itself, there is a better chance that the norm will have meaning for the group. The members may not like it, but they will be able to recognize its essential reasonableness.

The fourth kind of norm derivation is evolved cooperatively between leader and group at the instigation of the leader. Entailed here is an active selling campaign on the part of the supervisor. Recognizing the value of having the norm accepted by the group, he decides that the effort demanded of him will pay off in lack of opposition from the group to a change in its behavior pattern.

The fifth genus of norms includes those developed by and installed by group action. Numerically, this category is by far the largest. When we think of the myriad of informal groups in existence and the complete autonomy they have over the structuring of their norms, it is easily seen how many we are faced with. The distinguishing characteristic of the group norm established by the membership is its effort to control behavior of the group closely. It is judged by the members to be effective in furthering the achievement of a major group objective. If a group decides that its public image is of significant importance to it, rigid norms will be set in such matters as dress and public deportment. If, on the other hand, a group places high value on good relationships with outsiders, normative action will call for the friendly approach. Similarly, if the objective is the appearance of a carefully selected membership, personal reticence and unapproachability will be the order of the day. A close examination of observable group norms, in other words, will give the clearest single signal as to fundamental group objectives.

Definition of norms therefore is useful to groups in that it assists them in clarifying their thinking about major objectives and codifying them for all the membership. This is why we often see bald confrontations of different segments of the group in the setting of norms. To be effective, especially in the small group, norms must have close to a consensus of the membership. No 51 percent plurality will suffice for the establishment of a detail of behavior. It is a matter of closed ranks and united front.

The ability to influence the group's establishment of norms is a critical element of group leadership. The person who can effectively sway the group toward the adoption of a norm has passed the first test of his leadership abilities, especially if the norm he is advocating embodies a major change from the previous modus operandi. It should be noted that pure logic is the least effective approach to achieving this end; too much emotionalism is involved in normative behavior for serious attention to be given the dictates of reason. Again, groups are similar to the average individual—they believe what they want to rather than what might be good for them.

Normative activity is the change agent for any group's operation. If basic change is to be effected, obviously a change in behavior also is involved. Yet a booby trap is hidden in the assumption that the major objective always precedes the imposition of the norm. As already noted, tradition has its own place in the evolution of group behavior and may change major objectives of the group.

The development and establishment of norms is the highest form of cooperative activity among the group membership. It is the true test of group solidarity.

Group Sanctions

No body of law is worth the paper it is written on unless the power of a police force stands behind it. The norms of the group correspond to its laws; group sanctions are the police power for enforcement of these norms.

Sanctions run the gamut from the lightest of censure to the ultimate punishment of expulsion from the group. The nature and severity of sanctions depend on the critical nature of the norm itself, the person in the group who fails to conform, and the membership–leadership interaction over the situation. The norms of the group are venerated by each member in his own way, but every good member of a group is aware that the system of norms is the framework about which group integrity and continuity are built. Just as a masonry wall has a keystone which is critical to the entire structure, so every group has a few extremely sensitive norms which carry the greater burden of group continuity. If these (and thereby the entire group itself) are threatened by lack of observance on the part of one or more of the group members, the reaction of the rest of the group will be immediate and sharply corrective. The most severe sanctions will be reserved for this sort of abrogation. The group considers expulsion as extreme and dangerous as an individual does major surgery—to be undertaken only when life itself is threatened.

Groups have a real proclivity for "fitting the punishment

to the crime." Sanctions are capable of infinite gradation. Some sanctions are so slight as to be scarcely noticeable by the offender; some will give him a degree of trauma he has seldom experienced before. The amount of the reaction experienced by the deviant will depend on his identification with the group. The more ego involvement he has in group membership, the more effective the application of sanctions will be in curing his deviance.

Reverse effects are noticeable in a group that is contemplating the application of sanctions if the deviant is powerful in the group or ranks high in its esteem. If his position is of sufficient eminence, there can be a reevaluation of the norm itself. It is not uncommon to see a single member of a group make significant changes in its behavior pattern through the expedient of ignoring one or more of the important group norms. Again, if the offender is high in group esteem, there may be a palliation of the sanction finally exercised by the group. This is a tacit recognition that the particular member in question is more powerful in the group than the average member. The choice for the group in this situation is relatively simple: Discard the norm (in which case the stigma is removed from the offender) or, if the norm is kept and punishment is therefore necessary, lighten the punishment noticeably in deference to the position of the deviant.

Unfortunately, the reverse situation also occurs. If the deviant is held in low esteem—perhaps even disliked by a majority of the membership—the sanction applied may be disproportionately severe for the nature of the offense. Then—to consider only the group dynamics involved—the application of sanctions becomes a device for securing both closer conformity and a fundamental change in the behavior of one of the members. If it fails in the latter half of this assignment, the final result is usually severance of that member from the group, either voluntarily or by expulsion. In either event, the overriding objective of the group will have been achieved: greater homogeneity and strengthening of the norm.

The interaction between group members and the leader over the situation in question also affects the sanction. It is quite possible that the leader will take a view of a particular deviant behavior quite different from that of the general membership. The leader may actually find himself in the equivocal position of having to defend an action which poses an apparent threat to the safety of the group. If he wins his case for the deviant, he just may lose his own position as a leader. If he loses the case and bows to the consensus of the group, he has lost face to a degree difficult to repair. On the other hand, it is possible for a group to rise en masse against a leader who strongly demands sanctions for an observed deviance. In the minds of the members, there may be factors which totally outweigh the magnitude of the crime against the group. Their empathy for the deviant makes it possible for each of them to see themselves in the same situation, and they will be willing to grant amnesty because they would hope for the same treatment were they the culprit.

The strongest sanctions are applied when there is complete agreement between leadership and members about the deviance. If this basic consensus is arrived at, the application of sanctions will be swift and definitive. In such a case, the deviant is most likely to see his completely lonely situation and either conform quickly or sever his group membership. One danger to group continuity, of course, is overconcern with these magistral activities—to the point where pursuit of the group's basic objectives suffers. Fortunately, healthy groups have members whose sense of balance forces the group back toward its most fundamental activities.

Determination of Objectives

A group requires, first of all, a stated objective or objectives. The group will coalesce from those people who have identified with these objectives. There is no group which can maintain continuity indefinitely with the same set of goals; the formal group must change its objectives to remain in consonance with its surroundings, to meet the moves of its competition, and to adjust to internal changes within the group itself. The majority of formal groups have their objectives developed and handed to them by their leadership—usually from the top of the heap. In some of our forward-looking business enterprises, an effort is being made to involve the general group membership in the process of goal setting. Such involvement should result in heightened identification and greater motivation to achieve the targets. However, long and intensive training of a group is necessary before the members become sophisticated enough to make worthwhile contributions to the goal-setting process.

The semiformal group faces a special danger when setting long-range goals. The group may fall out of step with its surroundings and eventually become an anachronism. The original membership may be intact, but it will be difficult to attract new members to a group which is obviously out of communication with the rest of the world. The one significant exception to this situation is the honor society (such as Phi Beta Kappa or Sigma Xi), which remains as attractive to potential new members today as it did a hundred years ago. If the semiformal group does enter into a goal-setting situation, it will probably be through an intrenched leadership; rank-and-file members will be presented with the new goals as a *fait accompli*. Moreover, any changes in the goals of a semiformal group are likely to be minor.

In the rough-and-ready world of the informal group, the situation is quite different. Goals must be modified quickly and easily to adjust to both external and internal pressures. Involvement of both leaders and members is nearly equal. The bell is rung by whoever first perceives a change which will necessitate altering the goals. The informal group will use a give-and-take methodology in hammering out new objectives; group continuity is too closely tied to goals and their appropriateness to be stiff-necked about their determination. The one overweening concern of informal group membership is that their goals be *functional*, for the continued existence of the group depends upon them.

Any kind of group is concerned over whether its goals are realistic. A fundamental cleavage occurs at all levels of leadership about whether error in goal setting should be on the high or the low side. There are many leaders who deliberately set goals they know the group will never achieve. This they do under the working hypothesis that, even though the goals are impossible, the group's achievement will be greater than it would have been if the goals were lower. Their philosophical opponents will argue that it gives a group's members a lift to meet their objectives. For this reason, they believe in goals set low enough that they will always be achieved. What these theorists are discounting is the motivation, both personal and group, in the challenge of tough goals. By making people (and groups) stretch, growth and personal development will result. The ideal situation prevails when goals are difficult but are clearly achievable if the group works hard.

The need for clean-cut communication must be repeated over and over again in goal setting. It is mandatory that uniform understanding of the goals be achieved before turning the group loose to start work on them. If two or more interpretations of the stated objectives are prevalent among the group, total chaos is the inevitable result.

The process of goal setting is simple in concept. If the difficulty of the goal has been determined, the rest of the process is concerned with methodology and the setting of controls. It is in the latter area that most groups make their mistakes and fail to reach their targets. This is especially true when working with time-limited goals. The earlier in the time increment that controls become functional, the better chance the group will have of accomplishing its objectives. That is why many businesses establish semiannual rather than annual goals. It is easy for the average man to relax after setting an annual goal until he suddenly realizes that he has a zero chance of reaching the target. A six-month period, on the other hand, retains much more urgency; with this short a time, the average worker will never have far from his conscious mind the imminence of the deadline. Thus the time period itself can be one of the better controls. The trick is to establish controls which are effective without being burdened with unnecessary detail. (Ask any manager about the paperwork demanded by "the system.") These controls must have built-in validation devices in order to be effective. They must measure results achieved, not effort expended. It is in this latter area that many enterprises and managers get lost in the "numbers game"—and are then horror stricken to find that they have missed their objectives by a country mile.

Response to Leadership

The response of a group to its leaders is similar to that of an individual. The determinants are the kind of group, the leadership style of the man or men in charge, and the environmental situation. A group is more than the sum of its individual members; it develops a personality and will react to its leadership according to the elements of that personality. Some groups are more difficult to lead than others because of their strong-willed determination to be self-sufficient. This kind of group will demand *reasons* for the actions designated by its leaders. It will have strong informal leadership within its ranks, either acting as a deterrent to the formal leadership or strongly reinforcing it.

Other groups are nearly helpless without directive leadership. This helplessness emerges when the exact nature of the group objectives has been poorly communicated; ordinarily, it is found in the formal work group. It can be exhibited by a group composed of strong individuals; it is the lack of goal definition which inhibits self-reliance.

The esteem in which the members hold a leader is a modulator of general response. The leader who is liked as well as respected is in an enviable position. Personal regard makes all the difference when that little bit of extra effort is needed to meet a deadline. Concern over letting down its leadership is felt only by the group which likes and respects its leader.

Because of their different structures, it is predictable that there will be some differences in response to leadership in formal, semiformal, and informal groups. In the first case, response is more often prompted by a sense of duty or under duress, either overt or implied. The semiformal group responds to its leadership traditionally, according to well established group norms of behavior which have tradition behind them. In the informal group, response is free wheeling and will be unique to every situation the group faces. In addition, the informal group faces the problem of responding to multiple leadership, which acts as a complicating factor.

Chapter 1, on personal motivation, showed how the

attitude of the leader affects his approach to the group members and how the response of the group is conditioned by, and similar to, the leader's approach. Robert Blake and Jane Mouton, explaining their concept of the managerial grid, describe five typical styles of leadership which elicit widely different responses from group memberships. It becomes the job of the leader to be sensitive to his group, the situation, and his own personality before he can choose a leadership style which will have a reasonable chance of being effective.

One fact, lost sight of at times, remains fundamental. No leadership, whether imposed from above or chosen by the group members, is effective unless it is accepted by the group. The mere designation of a leader does not make him effective until the group members give him the go-ahead. It is this fact which produces the curious anomaly of a leadership void in some formal groups. The designated leader, not having been accepted by his people, is powerless to achieve the group's objectives. Informal leadership frequently takes over in this vacuum and carries on with, at least, the routine chores of leadership. The importance of leadership style in the attainment of goals is just now achieving some of the recognition and attention it deserves. The behavioral scientists are doing some of their most important work in this area.

Neither the group nor its leadership has much control over the general environment outside the group. Yet the outside environment remains the strongest determinant of the group's response to its leadership. If the environment is totally hostile, the leader is reinforced as a father figure; the group turns to him more frequently and with greater urgency for relief from their fears. At the same time, they become more critical of his decisions and watch more closely the results of his actions. In a benign climate, speed of response to leadership will be reduced at just those times when reactive speed is mandatory. For example, the meeting of deadlines does not weigh so heavily on a group whose surroundings pose no immediate threat to membership as on one for which the reverse is true. (We leave unanswered for the moment the natural question of the effect of environment on leadership. This will be treated separately in Chapter 7.)

In general, the response of a group to its leadership is a complex variable, conditioned by the three vectors mentioned. Each vector is subject to variation on a time continuum. Their summation at any particular moment determines the effectiveness of the group in its progress toward goal achievement. The more enlightened the group is about its objectives, the true state of the immediate environment, and the strengths of its leadership, the better the chances are for a response to leadership which will be viable. Latitude must be left for a free choice of response by the members if the best results are to be achieved. Throughout human history, man's response to leadership has always been greater than his response to "drivership."

Blockage

The expression for group blockage in labor relations is "concerted action." This means that the hourly employees are banding together to resist a management action. There are many degrees of blockage this side of the ultimate one—the strike. A favorite form is the slowdown, where the workforce refuses to produce up to standards. Each man advances his own reasons for failure to reach his quota; ingenuity worthy of a better cause is exhibited in the array of rationalizations put forth. Many union contracts are structured in such a way that pseudo safety complaints can be used as red herrings when the real intent is a slowdown, or blockage. Safety considerations must be put above production needs, at least until all possible hazards have been thoroughly examined.

Another method of blockage which can prove effective at times is "misunderstanding" company directives or policy. The time necessary to recommunicate and interpret the orders in question will accomplish the desired interruption of normal activity. A good supervisor will know what is happening to him but, thanks to his own precepts, will be powerless to fight back, at least the first time around. He has preached the absolute necessity of clear understanding of orders for too long to refuse another go at clarification, even though he *knows* that the misunderstanding actually does not exist.

Of course, blockage does not occur only in the formal group. In the semiformal group, a favorite method of blocking a change in the constitution or bylaws is to stay away from the business meeting in such numbers that it is impossible to achieve a quorum. Blockage is also effective when the entire group, with the exception of its leaders, ignores a new rule as if it were not there. The classic example of this ploy was the failure of national prohibition in America when a large part of the citizenry acted as if the Volstead Act had never been passed.

Blockage is a group reaction elicited by the appearance of a threat, real or imaginary, from within or without the group. It is a basic illustration of the reason for group formation—the strength of banding together. It should be noted that blockage implies a passive type of resistance; the use of force is deliberately avoided by the group, either because it has a good relationship with the leadership or because it fears its leaders to excess.

Another use of blockage appears in the power struggle between the incumbent leadership and those who want to supplant it. Followers of the insurgent leadership may not be willing to go so far as to countenance open rebellion, but they are not averse to aiding it through the process of blockage. Once it has been established that blockage is occurring internally, the group must be prepared for some sharp, determined response from the incumbent leaders. What amounts to a complete negation of established leadership calls for action. This type of confrontation is seen with some frequency in all types of groups but is found most frequently in the semiformal group.

Insurgency (using blockage) is a test of established leadership that separates the men from the boys. The *kind* of leadership response to blockage is more often less important than the *timing* of the response. It is urgently important that leadership regain control by a considered offensive of some sort, for the blocking action by the group has changed the momentum in its favor.

When the group reacts to an external threat by blocking, it of course has the active cooperation of its leaders. On the national scene, the Post Office Department has effectively used the threat of blockage several times in recent history. Many upward budgetary revisions have been gained for the postal service after the announcements that service would be curtailed unless more money were forthcoming. And this is not the only service group that has used the same kind of polite blackmail effectively. In most instances, this bold type of threat is a bluff. If the bluff is then called, probability dictates the retreat of the blocking group. Any group employing blockage as a weapon must be prepared to backtrack, either gracefully or otherwise.

The psychological reaction of the group to the continued use of blockage is ordinarily negative. It is a negative type of action; its results are dependent on risking significant amounts of the group's safety and well-being; the adversary at any time may pull the rug from under the group—to its considerable discomfiture. In any event, if blocking is adopted as a tactic, it is imperative that perfect communication be maintained within the group so long as blockage is in effect. The slightest breakdown or clogging of the channels of communication will result in pure chaos. The moment there is any indication of a lack of consensus, the battle is lost.

Notwithstanding its inherent dangers to group effectiveness and even integrity, blockage will continue to be used frequently as a response to a threat, since it has proved to be useful countless times. It is absolutely necessary that the group make a sharp decision about the magnitude and imminence of the threat before this dangerous weapon is employed.

Aggression

Blockage is a pacifistic approach to a perceived threat; aggression is a positive approach to the threat, with accompanying hostility. Aggressive action is taken by a group when it is convinced that it has an even or better chance of overcoming the threat by means of force. Overt truculence may or may not be exhibited. The inherent danger of aggression to the group is that it can appear spontaneously, without direction from the leadership, and spread like any other hysteric action. Anyone who has seen mob violence (a typical example of group aggression) evolve from a static crowd knows how terrifying group action can be. Mob "leadership" shows few attributes of true leadership. More often, it is a focusing or verbalization of the temper already present within the group; it acts only as a triggering mechanism. Suppression of all reasoning activity by brute emotionalism is a requisite. The violence of mob action subsides only with the appearance of a clearly superior opposing force. It is common for individuals who have taken part in mob activity to have no memory of what took place—or even of what they themselves did. The purgative effect of mob action, moreover, is so severe that members often collapse immediately afterward.

More commonly, of course, aggressive action by a group is on a relatively low plateau of violence. In the formal group, the strike—if accompanied by any measure of violence—is a typical part of aggression. The difference between mob action and the average strike is that the latter is the result of calculated and continuing group leadership, although some measure of the mental set present in the mob scene also is found in the strike. That is, many striking workers are not in real sympathy with the group action but are forced to conform by group pressures that are far greater than any they are normally subjected to.

Because it is less explosively violent than mob action, the strike goes through a recognizable life cycle. Typically, the work group first "hits the bricks" calmly and becomes engrossed in the mechanics of organizing the picket line. For the first several hours or even a day or so, light banter may be exchanged between pickets and members of management as they come and go across the lines. The weather has much to do with the extent of this period of mutual forbearance. The midpoint of the strike is of varying duration and is characterized by increasing sullenness in both parties. Communication between the two camps virtually ceases, and the anxiety level of workers and managers rises quickly. The penultimate period of the strike contains whatever violence may occur on either side and whatever countering tactics may be invoked to neutralize the violence. The death of the strike comes when a majority of the group has expressed either formally or informally its unwillingness to continue this form of aggression, although the actual signing of a contract officially ending the hostilities may take place months later.

The first signs of weakening will evoke severe repressive measures by the rest of the membership. Those who cause the first cracks in group solidarity may become the victims of violence from the rest of the group. More strikes are ended by counterpressures exerted by the families of the strikers than by any negotiations. Wives and mothers have notoriously little patience with extended strikes.

Once the strike is over, observers are amazed at how quickly breaches between the working group and management can be healed in many cases. Bitterness will run high during the actual strike but can dissipate quickly after a settlement is reached. Again, note the cathartic effect of the strike on many employees. Past irritants and bitternesses which have accumulated over long periods can be burned out. The major casualties of a strike are commonly some of the leaders of the working group or certain members of management, depending on the outcome of the struggle. Any residual bitterness finds a target in one or more of these people.

According to the behavioral scientists, definition of the word "aggression" indicates that it can also be exhibited in a strenuous effort to *avoid* a perceived threat, rather than in an attempt to meet and overcome it. Just as much convulsive effort is put into avoidance reactions as is put into those aggressions which meet the threat head on. An aggressive reaction occurs when the preponderant evidence tells the group it has only a poor chance of overcoming the threat—the odds are stacked against them. Evasive action can develop a backwash just as violent as any which occurs with positive aggression—the kind of violence shown by a fleeing animal when it is cornered.

A group leader should be alert for the many nonverbal cues any group sends up before actual aggression begins. Communications of all sorts are strained; nonverbal cues show beyond a doubt the anxiety of both individuals and group. Quick diagnostic action, sharp and incisive communication, and the advancement of a reasonable plan for amelioration of the threat can avert aggression before too much damage is done—provided that the leadership itself has not succumbed to fear of the threat. The instigation of aggression is naturally the happy hunting ground of the demagogue. His best chance to usurp leadership comes during the upheaval suffered by the group during aggressive action. From the management point of view, the best way to either forestall or suppress incipient aggression is peaceful but direct confrontation. Running away from the situation is the surest way to precipitate a worse one.

Other Responses to Threat

The group has other ways of responding to threat besides blockage and aggression. One way is to retreat into a protective shell and make no response to the perceived danger. Some of the members will fail to recognize the threat in this regressive position, for there is a sense of false security here which is dangerous to the integrity of the group. As children, we were tempted not to look at an unpleasant situation but just hope that it will go away. Behaving this way as an adult is just as childish as it was in our first three or four years of life. The retreat from reality will only sever communication with the outside world and make it more difficult to appraise the imminence of the danger and determine whether it is increasing or decreasing. The "turtle" reaction is common in semiformal groups as they start to realize they are losing touch with modern times; thus churches and lodges perpetuate liturgies and rituals long after they have lost any real meaning for the membership. Then, when an attempt at modernization is made—belatedly—the group is thrown into turmoil at the damage done to venerable norms. In some cases, this situation can cause a group to split and a new group to emerge around the proponents of the heresy.

Another reaction to threat is the appearance of a sudden desire to learn everything possible about the enemy. If properly handled, this can be a more effective form of protection than withdrawal. The better we know our foes, the better will be our chances of defeating them. Our own nation, both officially (through responsible government officials) and privately (as individuals or members of family and social groups), has a long-established custom of ignoring its enemies. In World War I (and to a lesser degree in World War II), the formal study of the German language was frowned upon to the point where it practically disappeared from American school curricula. We would have been in a much stronger position, both psychologically and tactically, had we redoubled our efforts to learn everything possible about the Germans.

In some groups, not only cohesiveness but acuteness of perception is heightened under threat. Sensitivity to smaller degrees of change in the environment appears, and reactive time is shortened. The same family of protective reactions can be displayed by a group as are manifested in an individual when his adrenal glands are stimulated by either fear or anger.

Under threat, group leadership must lead, or it will be

replaced. No tolerance will be shown for vacillation or indecision. This is why governments of small, weak, and quarrelsome nations are so unstable. Each successive perceived threat, imaginary or real, can topple the current leadership. It is interesting to observe the reactions of the French under the strong leadership of de Gaulle as compared to their instability under weaker leadership. (This observation has nothing to do with any value judgments as to the *direction* in which de Gaulle led them.) Other nations have drastically changed their public image as they turned to strong leadership after deposing a weak one.

The group can also benefit from the mere presence of a threat. Its most innovative and creative actions can be the result of its reaction to danger. Finding the way around the roadblock to the objective can be exciting and rewarding when successful. Cooperative action is at a premium under these circumstances and will be rewarded more visibly than under less urgent stimulus. The common example of this in modern times is the way in which businesses make use of research and development or diversification when their industry is attenuating. Many of our most valued products on the market today are the result of a threat to an established industry.

As the group is strengthened and matured by this kind of process, so does the membership grow and progress individually. Much of our personal advancement is the result of threat to the groups in which we live. Henry Ford, with his production line and $5 minimum daily wage, so threatened established American industry that tremendous growth and development occurred throughout the country to meet what appeared to be a complete impasse.

The trick is to perceive a threat *as it develops*. A true test of any group's vitality is the sensitivity of its awareness of the environment. Group norms are ordinarily the first to be affected. A change in the surroundings will automatically outdate the fundamental mores of the group. Evaluation of the relative importance of the threat and the established norms is the immediate order of judgment for the group. The threat can easily be neutralized in many cases by altering group behavior. If both leadership and members approve, the pathway is easy and clear. However, if the norms are deemed to be sacred, the group must be prepared to fight for its life. The difference between neutralization and destruction of a threat is obvious, so far as the involvement of the group is concerned. Its fundamental character is involved from the moment of perception of the threat; the reaction of the group and its leaders will be indicative of its will to survive. This must be accepted as a way of life in our immensely complex and involved social structure. Survival is automatically the basic goal of any group.

Methods of Self-perpetuation

The group has a human desire to survive and perpetuate itself. Much of its planning and daily activity is concerned with this fundamental goal, which always remains foremost in the consciousness of group leadership. It is because of this desire for group continuity that leadership is of premier importance in the eyes of the members, because, whether they verbalize it or not, they know that leadership decisions are the key to group health and survival. Evaluation of leadership goes on without interruption over a time continuum; a leader is on permanent probation with his members. Yet strength of leadership does not correlate perfectly with its success or lack of it. There are situations in which less strong leadership can actually be more effective than the "take charge and bull a way through" type.

Conversely, there are other situations which demand a strong leader who is not subject to self-doubts or pressures from others.

Perpetuation of the group is closely connected with the maintenance of a virile and active membership. Any group spends much time and effort in searching for fitting replacements for lost membership. A college fraternity or sorority is engrossed with its pledging program throughout the summer and early fall. Competition is keen; the hunting is aggressive; pressure tactics to secure the prize catches are used continuously. In fact, solicitation of membership is common to all kinds of groups. Determinants of its intensity are the size of turnover within the group and the desirability of the group's growing in size or remaining relatively static in number. Whether the group dies, merely survives, or grows and prospers is a measure of the acuteness of the group and its leaders in evaluating prospective members and attracting strong candidates.

Group perpetuation must be correlated with the kind of competitive spirit engendered internally. There are no groups which do not face active competition for the services and activities of membership. As groups proliferate on today's scene, this competition becomes more rigorous with the passing of time. The ability of the group to rise to the challenge and beat its competition for the available members will largely determine the length of its survival. Governing factors include member identification with attractive objectives, thoughtful distribution of the workload by the leaders, and a congenial internal climate for the group.

Corollary to the right sort of members is the development of viable interpersonal relationships in the group. Formal and semiformal groups will often find some members abrasive, especially in contact with certain other members; even informal groups may be faced with this problem.

Group suicide will result unless these personality clashes are satisfactorily resolved. While it would be foolish to expect perfect harmony to prevail all of the time within any group, the target is workable relationships and lack of open, direct conflict among the members.

Group maintenance will be associated with the working habits developed internally. Efficiency and smoothness of operating procedures help greatly in attaining group objectives; both leaders and members must be prepared to give much thought to this aspect of their group living if they expect to be successful in perpetuating the group. It is in this connection that a premium is placed on subordination of individual wishes to the welfare of the group. The amount of personal sacrifice the member is willing to make to keep his group membership is a direct measure of his evaluation of the group.

Continuity and intrenchment of leadership also can be effective in the perpetuation of a group. The image of the "wise old head" is usually sought by a group leader whatever his chronological age. A parallel necessity is the high esteem of the membership, with its concomitant trust in his actions. *His coefficient of reliability is that perceived by the group members, not his achievements, no matter how real or valuable they are.* Of course, if weak leadership becomes intrenched, it will hasten the death of the group.

One of the more critical factors associated with group perpetuation is the vision of both members and leaders. A high degree of conceptual skill is demanded to evaluate changes in the environment and the effect of those changes on the group. In formal groups, this ability to "see the big picture" must extend for years into the future; in informal groups the lead time is shorter but just as important.

Certainly not the least important factor in group survival

is its work output—its success in meeting group objectives and then resetting them with imagination and sensitivity. The effective productivity of the group is ongoing and unremitting in its demands. All other considerations are, in reality, not germane if they interfere with the group's attainment of its goals. Both leaders and members need a proper sense of balance—the ability to juggle the factors which control group survival. Adaptability to change will always remain high in importance, as will judgmental ability to evaluate the relative importance of the changes appearing in the group's surroundings. This is not to imply that it is impossible for any group to survive, but only to suggest that it is necessary to be aware of the many factors militating against any given group in our society.

* * *

All groups have common properties. First of all, to continue to exist, a group must have cohesiveness, in greater or lesser degree.

Every group will develop its own norms by some means. These standards are held most important by the group membership, and their observance is policed by the sanctions which the group exercises against those who fail to conform. Sanctions are graded in severity, according to the importance of the norm being violated and the status and esteem in which the deviant is held by the group.

The group will be occupied from time to time with an evaluation of its objectives; new ones will be set as old ones are met or are found to be no longer viable. The kind of response given by a group membership to its leader will be conditioned by the style of leadership exhibited, the membership mix, and the environment of the group.

What has been said up to now is really preparatory to

getting at the heart of group dynamics—the effect of the group on the individual and the effect of the individual on the group. Because of our own selfish interests, these are the areas in which we have a vital concern. If a knowledge of group dynamics is to have a positive effect on our life, it will be here. Let us therefore consider these topics next.

Chapter 5

Effects of the Group on the Individual

*W*E ARE the product of our group memberships. From our earliest infancy until we lose any sort of perceptual contact with the world, our character, our personality, our general behavior pattern, our dress, speech, and mannerisms are shaped by the forces exerted upon us in the groups in which we have membership. Just as there are general properties of groups, so are there general effects of the group on the individual member irrespective of the kind of group examined.

Conformity

Man is by nature and training such a conformist that much of the time he fails to realize he is conforming. If you ask the average man why he wears a shirt and necktie to work every day, it is difficult at first for him to give you a reasonable response. When he asks you rather blankly,

"Doesn't everyone?" he is genuinely disturbed when you point out that a large part of our working populace never wears a tie at work. His confusion grows as he tries to give a convincing explanation of why he would feel uncomfortable if he were not to wear a tie.

Any person with teenage daughters will affirm the impossibility of getting near the phone from 7:00 to 7:30 A.M., the period when the girls are rigorously checking what is to be the uniform of the day at school. And teenage boys are subject to just as much social pressure to conform to the norms of the moment as are the girls; if anything, their norms are even stricter, if perhaps more whimsical.

Conformity is a fetish of any group, since it is the backbone of group perpetuation. Every civilization is built on a basis of conformity to those mores which, in summation, will most likely lead to achievement of group goals.

We must recognize the distribution curve of conformity in any normal population. At the one extreme are a small proportion of those who conform blindly and without discrimination to any dictate of the groups to which they belong. It may be wild or far out; this small percentage of the group is entirely uncritical. The middle of the curve is composed of the large majority of people who are more conformant than they are deviant. They will, in general, conform rather closely to most of the norms of most of their groups, but occasionally they will deliberately fail to conform to one or more norms in one or more groups. This exercise of their value judgments reinforces their self-image of individuality and is necessary, in most cases, to their mental health. At the far end of the spectrum is another small group of people who are zealously (one might almost say pathologically) nonconformist. The delineation of a group norm for them is the ringing of the tocsin which calls them to arms. These are the loners, the "characters" who arouse ambivalence in the rest of the group membership. Irritation at their flouting of tradition and group norms is mixed with a healthy amount of unexpressed admiration for their ability to withstand severe social pressure with no apparent discomfiture.

There is no question that our culture would cease to evolve if everyone were a total conformist. Progress is made only by those who have the courage to flout tradition and strike out for themselves. However, it must be noted that if this nonconformist instinct is misdirected, the result will be regression rather than advancement. Certain noncomformists have done their best to reduce the entire world to a state of chaos.

The question remaining for each of us to answer personally is: "How far am I going down the road of conformity?" As noted, every person has his own particular tolerance level for conformity. It is true that advancement in our formal work groups will be significantly affected by our ability to conform without becoming rebellious. The higher the position of the individual in the hierarchy, the greater will be the pressure upon him to conform to more and more esoteric norms. The origins of some norms, such as the traditional rising of the audience when the "Hallelujah Chorus" from *The Messiah* is sung, are lost in antiquity. Neither are they understood by the group member, nor is he expected to understand them. Like the mountain, they are there. Beyond them, it becomes a matter of individual decision how far one is willing to conform in order to progress, either in his work group or in any other with which he is involved. The rather dubious argument is advanced that conformity (up to a point) will be rewarded when the individual has achieved a certain eminence in a group by being allowed to set the norms to which others must conform. This, at best, is only partly true. The pressures for conformity are stronger at the apex of the pyramid than anywhere else, and any satisfaction found in dictating norms for those below is submerged in the realization of the severe constraints of the position. Whatever personality elements drive a man toward the top of any group, they must be sufficient to meet and overcome these constraints. His satisfaction and rewards will be in other areas, and he must be able to endure the necessity for conformity in order to achieve them. Perhaps it is this one fact which makes the chief executive or president of a company a truly rare individual. Few of us are willing to pay the price for that position. Most of us treasure a personal life so highly that we are more than willing to stop our ascent somewhere short of the top. This is fortunate, for if all of us were totally dedicated to arrival in the presidential suite, what a donnybrook would result! The happiest man in the world is the one who recognizes his appropriate level when he has found it.

Influence on Behavior Patterns

The groups to which we belong exert a significant influence on our total behavior. The spectrum extends from the fads and hobbies we pick up to the deepest traits of character and personality. We reflect in our own actions the norms of the groups in which we have membership. We shall for the moment ignore the role conflict which will inevitably occur from our multigroup membership, since that topic will be treated separately.

The game patterns of children's friendship groups are quite distinctive as we go from one cultural level to another. (An offsetting influence is now at work which tends to make the behavior of children more uniform—universal television exposure.) Our intellectual growth, too, is noticeably affected by the company we keep. In our school years, the norms of friendship groups determine the depth of penetration and breadth of scope achieved by our mental interests.

Ethical and moral values we acquire from three major influences: the family, the church, and the school. Because it provides our *first* influence, the family remains the *major* source of our ethics and morals. Even though association with new groups may modify our mores as we approach and enter our teens, it is rare for fundamental character to be grossly altered during that decade. The worries of parents about the behavioral vagaries of children during their high school years should be tempered by this knowledge. There is only one factor on the modern scene which might alter the foregoing statement—the undeniably increasing use of drugs by our young people now, a habit which was not prevalent among preceding generations. Obviously, fundamental changes in both personality and character will occur if a young person becomes addicted to some of the stronger drugs.

It is fascinating to observe how the adoption of one new item of dress or the affectation of one current fad can massively change a young person's total behavior pattern. These things usually lead to an "egg and chicken" argument. Does the youth grow a beard as a sign of rebellion against The Establishment, or is it the other way around? Are love beads a symptom, or does their conscious wearing trigger a chain of other responses to stimuli which hitherto were not a cause of reaction?

The contradictory norms of different groups produce some interesting results. The youth is subjected to repeated stimuli of a certain kind during his years in the Boy Scouts —all of them on a high moral and ethical plane. Then immediately, after he normally is through with Scouting, his high school and college associations expose him to agnostic or amoral ideas in direct contravention of his earlier training. We adults have a tendency to forget the trauma arising from this kind of mental and emotional reversal of field. The result is a period of "dead centering" of value judgments. The young person oscillates and is unable to decide what his own values really will be. To repeat once more, as adult values gradually emerge, they will ordinarily resemble those of youth very strongly, even if somewhat modified.

Superficial behavior associated with "culture" is quite likely to be derived from our admiration for a particular small group of friends. This friendship group will first determine whether we are interested in art or are vocally disdainful of it. If we are propelled in this direction, the same friendship group will then determine our likes and dislikes in the area of art. Even our political leanings are determined by our group memberships. Traditionally, the managements of most of our bigger businesses have had Republican sympathies. A young man who identifies with his work group and is attracted toward management as a career will be, in effect, brainwashed in favor of Republican political ideas. For the past 30 years, the complete opposite has been apparent among a majority of our blue collar workers; the influence of both the trade union and the industrial union has steered them into the Democratic camp. There are indications that this latter influence is losing some of its strength (look at the last two or three elections); certainly, some atypical patterns have emerged in the voting of the working class. These might logically be attributed to the rising educational level of our present working force, with a concomitant influence leading to independence of political judgment. Similarly, a difference of reaction can be observed on the management side of our formal groups. Greater numbers of supervisors and managers now openly avow Democratic leanings than did a decade ago.

The increasingly rebellious attitudes and activities of our college students over the past few years can also be attributed to these forces. Independence of political and intellectual judgment is a pearl beyond price, but it is difficult to achieve this without an emotional side effect that vitiates the gains. And we must remember that balance in both judgment and behavior is a product of intellectual *and* emotional maturity. We are being a little harsh if we punish our college students too severely for excesses brought about by their lack of maturity.

Our group memberships, in the long run, will for most of us outweigh any individual in their influence in our behavior patterns. The remarkable thing is that we escape as well as we do from the schizoid tendencies that result from opposite valences. It is a tribute to the fundamental good sense of the average citizen that his entire behavior remains sane and goal-oriented.

Change in Personal Goals

Our group memberships are the biggest single factor which causes us to modify our personal goals. The exposure we get in the group to new value sets, plus the forces generated by our identification with that group, is a powerful mover. Often a normally self-centered person, after joining a service group or a church, is led for the first time to understand the value of giving rather than receiving.

In the formal work group, provided the leadership is blessed with vision and a good perspective, the setting of group goals can act as a catalyst in enlarging the individual objectives of the members as persons. In other words, participation in the group's activity and in the achievement of solid, challenging goals is a fine impetus for better personal performance. Learning is the result of doing something. When the "doing" of the group brings significant accomplishments, individual members will benefit personally from this learning process.

We should not gather from what has been said here that change in personal goals as a result of group membership is necessarily swift. More often, it is an evolutionary process marked by plateaus of growth in objectives. These plateaus are usually associated with the joining of a new group which provides more complex and difficult goals.

Unfortunately, the changes produced by the group in personal goals are not always for the better. It is entirely possible for group associations to have a detrimental effect on objectives. If this occurs, it is likely to be an outcome of social group memberships in young adulthood, either during or immediately after terminal education. During this time of life, a person is especially receptive to change. Total erosion of moral or ethical values, if it happens, will be the product of a relatively long exposure to malefic influences. Normal individuals boggle at a sudden 180° phase change in ethical norms. The first slight adjustment will occur in relatively minor norms. The slope of the change curve may increase later, but the first differences will be small.

Changing personal goals sets off a cyclical effect. Group associations are likely to cause the first change in goals; different goals may then stimulate a person to seek new groups in consonance with these changed goals. This volitional part of the cycle, in turn, gives impetus to the change in norms. It is not uncommon to see major personality changes emerging after personal goals have changed. A common and notable example is that of the introvert who becomes an extrovert. Such dramatic differences are especially apparent to the relatives and close friends of the person involved.

A side effect of radically altered personal goals is the impact on the family of the individual in question. Other members may not understand the changes occurring and may resort to blockage or aggression. In extreme cases, there can be total schism, with a finally divisive result. For example, if one member of the family joins an extreme religious sect and persists in proselyting others, the resultant valences may be too strong for the family ties. It is interesting that final disruption of the family group is often the decision of the deviant member. Second only to the trauma due to religious influence is the upset which comes from a sudden change in the political beliefs of a parent. If the family's political thinking has been in harmony before, this change can be deep and disturbing. It is human to want to rationalize and verbalize a change in basic objectives. This rationalization is perceived by other family members as a threat, and they react variously according to their particular ways of meeting threats. Physical growth is disturbing enough; intellectual or emotional change can be shattering both to the individual and to his close associates.

We should not fail to note the situation arising when a change in personal goals is either an overt or hidden agenda of the *group* rather than of the individual. Special groups with special causes abound in our society. Stated objectives may be far removed from the hidden goal, which would be unacceptable to prospective members. Cryptocommunists are fiendishly expert at this sort of tactic; hundreds of citizens of the highest probity have allowed their names to be associated with groups whose real objectives were subversive. The tragedy, of course, is the stigma which is attached to the innocent upon exposure of the group.

But it does not matter, from the standpoint of group dynamics, whether the changes in personal goals are instigated by the individual or by the group. The outcome will be the same, for better or worse.

If an individual desires to retain a modicum of control over the situation, he must maintain continual vigilance over his personal goals. Here again, we are faced with the necessity for periodic introspective activity to police our progress. The habit of reviewing one's position on a strict time continuum should be established early—and it should be a deliberately inculcated and carefully tended habit. Just as the man wise in finance will survey his assets and liabilities regularly, so the average person should take stock of his personal objectives on a periodic basis. This will evoke some fundamental value judgments as to the appropriateness of his various group memberships. No group is viable if its effect on personal goals is negative or even questionable. Repetitive examination of personal goals can remove from self-control any aura of triteness or cliché.

Interpersonal Relationships

Our own personal characteristics are the most influential determinants of our manner of interacting with others. Our group memberships rank second in importance. Every group has its unique character in this respect. There are those which make a fetish of good relationships above every other consideration. At the other extreme, groups are so pragmatically oriented that interpersonal reactions are not considered at all—the only reason for a group to exist at all is to get the job done. Most groups fall somewhere between these two positions.

The nature of interpersonal relationships is a function of their depth. It is relatively easy for us to maintain courteous and correct relationships with acquaintances. It is more difficult, however, where our emotions are involved. If friendship or love is present, our feelings become much more sensitive. In any event, our group memberships condition our behavior with others. Norms demanded of membership in a particular group habituate our reaction to personal contact. If the group norm is one of open, friendly approach, we find ourselves using this approach outside the group in other contacts. But, if one of our major groups has a norm of reserve and taciturnity, we will likely present this kind of front even when away from the group.

Luckily, multimembership develops ambivalence in our reactions, because it is obvious that one cannot react identically in every human contact. Our group living provides us with a number of ways in which to react to the varying approaches of others.

A changing environment heightens most people's sensitivity in interpersonal relationships. They are aware of the need to watch for hidden motives, gestures, facial expressions, and words in communicating with those about them; after all, they make use of the same devices in their own communications. The extent to which an individual can develop the necessary sensitivity in interpersonal relationships will have far-reaching effects on his life. The person who has everything *except* the ability to get along with others is a familiar tragedy. If this inability is due to a lack of sensitivity, he probably will be insensitive to that fact as well. His whole lifetime will be spent in frustration, trying to determine what is wrong in the world about him. There would undoubtedly be more people like him if a complex society did not give us much training which can be put to our advantage in developing sensitivity.

A byproduct of our sensitivity is empathy. Our ability to understand the thinking and attitudes of others gives us a special position from which to deal with others. Most of our trouble in getting along with people has its basis in a belief that their reactions are unreasonable or irrational. If their fundamental beliefs and feelings are unknown to us, we have little chance of understanding what they say. But a word of caution here: There are those who use empathy as a rationalization for their own lack of principle, yet the fact that we understand the attitudes of others does not mean that we will always accept these attitudes. True empathy on the part of both parties is normally the beginning of a viable compromise. The average citizen will consider himself successful if life is a series of such compromises. No one should expect to win all his battles, and no one could tolerate losing them all. Compromise is the only alternative.

Our group living gives us daily practice in reacting with others, and this provides the beginnings of tolerance. We must learn to overlook the vagaries of others, just as we expect them to overlook ours.

Our approach to getting along with others should proceed from a solid base of self-knowledge. Unless we can predict our reaction to a given stimulus, we have little hope of being able to control it. The pressures of social life demand the development of both self-knowledge and self-control. One of the more frequently questioned facets of modern living is the apparent disappearance of the self-control practiced by our Puritan ancestry. We hear it said, time and time again, that discipline is gone from our younger generation. It is true that pushbutton living, mass communication media, and greater mobility make disciplining our youth much harder than it used to be. We have lost some of the controls our parents had over us. In recognition of this, we see anxious parents turning to the schools or the military service, which they hope will discipline their children for them. They forget that the habit of discipline must be one of the first acquired by any individual if it is to be effective in his life. Parents have no right to try to delegate this most fundamental of obligations to any other agency. Indeed, although it is not always completely articulated, one of the chief complaints young people make against their parents is to deplore the absence of home discipline. They want it, even if they cannot always verbalize their desire for it.

We depend heavily on our group interpersonal relationships to make life a going thing. Normal contacts with other members exert a salutary influence that helps to counterbalance the heaviness of our mental load. The wise employer will encourage, rather than fight, the formation of lunchtime bridge foursomes or other informal social groups. He will recognize how much of the day's pressure can be dissipated by innocuous pastimes. In the same way, we as individuals must find and maintain our own personal balance in terms of the numbers and kinds of interpersonal relationships which are most workable for us. It comes back again to introspective self-knowledge. Most important of all, we must be sensitive to those times when we are not good company and avoid contacts with others at these times.

Socioeconomic Outlook and Beliefs

Our social and economic beliefs will be those of our most important group. Usually, several groups in which a person has membership will have similar outlooks. For generations, a man's political beliefs could be forecast with total accuracy if one knew his street address and the college from which he was graduated. This is no longer the case, but there are still cultural patterns which can be predicted from place of residence and alma mater.

Any group which has partial or complete control of a segment of the local society as a major objective will operate through the medium of social beliefs and economic tenets. The nineteenth-century Irish in New York City and Boston exercised close control over their compatriots through political activity. As ward bosses, they governed patronage and, in many cases, the local elections. A bright young Irishman gravitated toward local politics as the best way to achieve that upward mobility that was so desirable in both social and economic status.

It would be difficult to prove today that colleges and universities have much influence over either the social or the economic beliefs of their students. It is, however, relatively easy to demonstrate that the students' beliefs in these areas are molded during the time they are attending college. What we are saying is that some of the more important groups that mold the opinions of the young are not directly associated with the universities but are peripheral to them and located in the same geographic area. Many of the more activist groups are composed wholly of students, with little influence exerted upon them by faculty members. On the present scene, however, the students more often shape the thinking of the faculty than vice versa.

It is easy enough to understand why one's present social and economic position will have strong impact on one's beliefs. The "have nots" will be attracted to the political parties which profess to have the interest of the little man at heart and display a platform of social reform aimed at uplifting his status. The "haves" can be excused for demonstrating ultraconservative beliefs. Their social beliefs will tend toward maintaining the status quo and an economy which gives special privilege to the rich. Actually, our nation became, shortly after its birth, a country of the middle class, and the middle class is only slightly less conservative than those who are more affluent. It is the belief of middle-class citizens that any major change would probably harm them more than help them. Thus they form a large group that reinforces the beliefs of the grossly rich. Between them, these two economic groups have maintained solid control of our national politics throughout American history.

It is quite possible for the sociopolitical beliefs of an individual to undergo a 180° phase change (perhaps more than one) during his lifetime as his personal economic status waxes or wanes. We sometimes lose sight of the fact that the liberal or radical leftists are more vocal than the conservatives. The latter are greatly outnumbered, but we hear more from them than we do from the more complacent conservatives, and this vocal minority has had a far greater influence on our economy than their numbers would indicate. Having captured the imagination of some of our more intelligent youth during the Depression, they exerted a tremendous impact on our social structure through a sympathetic and powerful president. The increasingly socialistic aspect of our national government is a complete paradox in a nation which was founded on and achieved greatness through individual initiative. Yet this influence has had one totally salutary effect on our society—the appearance of a social conscience in some of our extremely rich families and giant business firms. Public philanthropy and research in the social sciences have progressed much further than anyone could have predicted two generations ago.

Our demographic variables today puzzle the experts

because of certain trends that go against the grain of theory. It is hard to say what the configuration of our nation will be even a few years from now. Such anomalies as labor unions which have become enormously wealthy throw obstacles in the way of the forecaster. For example, a wealthy union will behave atypically; that is, it will suddenly discover that it too has a vested interest in seeing that certain trends are not reversed. This in turn weakens the functioning of the union in the area of its primary objective: continual fighting to advance its members.

The norms of any group will closely reflect the present status of that group. If most of its membership are upwardly mobile, norms will quickly become protective and reactionary. If the members are economically stable or slightly regressive, their norms and socioeconomic beliefs will be militant and activist. This close association between the economic position of the group and its norms makes it hard to tell which is the independent variable and which the dependent. Since we have so little power of self-determinism, we cannot always be positive which is cause and which is effect. Do our beliefs change according to our situation, or do they determine our position? The probability is about 0.5 either way. Nevertheless, we can say positively that our group memberships will have a fundamental effect on our social and economic beliefs. We never get far from the subtle influence of the group on our thinking. And we have it on good authority that "as a man thinketh in his heart, so is he."

Adaptation

Man learns to live in society by adapting to the groups in which he has membership. This process begins in the home if there are siblings or outside if one is an only child. It is disturbing to learn that we are not the center of the universe and that we cannot control our environment unilaterally. We must adapt, and adaptation signifies change. We modify our behavior to fit group norms and make it possible for us to work toward the accomplishment of group goals. Since change in behavior is involved, adaptation is clearly a form of learning. Adaptative change brings about somatic, mental, and spiritual alterations in a human being.

The adaptive process may be initiated by either the individual or the group. If the group discovers one of its members to be a deviant, it will apply its various sanctions to force him back into conformity. This is education in its simplest and most effective form. Public school teachers soon learn that if they can make use of social pressure on a recalcitrant student, they can save themselves much upset and hard labor. Possibly, forced adaptation of this sort will not be as permanent as that which is voluntarily undertaken by the individual. A residuum of rancor remains after a person is forced to accede to the will of the group, and, if the opportunity arises, the same deviance may recur later.

As implied, adaptation undertaken voluntarily by the individual is longer-lasting and is positively reinforced by the subject. Most change of this kind results from a high degree of identification with the group and its objectives, with the resultant desire to be a member in good standing of that group. We should be aware of the process of habit formation if we wish to adapt easily in group living. The first volitional changes are difficult to achieve, since they represent gross differences in behavior. However, as the acts in question are repeated frequently, volitional involvement becomes less and less until synaptic resistance all but disappears, and the stimulus triggers a habituated response.

The difficulty of adapting within the group is minor compared to that of adapting to the differences among the groups in which one may hold simultaneous membership. This is especially true when two of the groups have norms directly contradictory to each other. The confusion this causes in the individual can be reduced only by assiduous attention and concentration. In addition, he must form a workable rationale for having identified with two groups which *are* so different. He must convince himself that the value he receives from each group is sufficient to make this difficult adaptation worthwhile.

Another kind of adaptation is present in our life most of the time—that associated with our own growth and advancement in the business or social world. Each new stratum we occupy on our upward climb is different from the one we are just leaving, whether the differences are slight or profound.

Speed of adaptation is the best weapon any person can have in a complex society. The quicker we accept change and adjust to it, the less we are disturbed by it. It is the same as in any other race: The winner will be the swiftest. It is comforting to know that the ability to adjust smoothly and quickly can be learned and developed just like any other skill. The more often we are successful in our adaptive efforts, the more easily the next change will be taken in stride.

Each member of an effective group will recognize his responsibility to help other members in their attempts to adapt. The strength of the group will be measured in part by the adaptability of its membership. There is a personal reward in our efforts to help others adapt. Each time we give aid and comfort to someone else in this area, we are helping ourselves solve our own problems. There is no better way to learn a subject than to teach it.

Adaptive ability is closely related to the amount of cooperation which a person can extend to his fellow members. In the final analysis, adaptation is not a unitary action; two or more people are always affected by the adaptive efforts of an individual. A large part of adaptation, if successful, is associated with the subject's skill in interpersonal relationships. He finds it much simpler to adapt to change if his contacts with fellow members are smooth and gracious. By this time, it should be evident that the various factors involved in group dynamics are interwoven into a matrix. Almost never does one of these elements function alone. The highest skill in group living is that of handling these intermeshings effectively.

Adaptation is called into play whenever there is a change in group objectives. From the intellectual examination of the new objectives for acceptability through their implementation into the group's activities, adaptation is the name of the game. No living society is static. There will be change, whether it represents progress or regression, and it then becomes the clear duty of the group member to change himself in whatever way is necessary to maintain his effectiveness. How far this can go is illustrated by the tentative flares being sent up to apprise freedom- and privacy-loving American citizens that they must be prepared to live with a "Big Brother" computer which will be able to store and retrieve every detail of a person's life, down to the minute and the ridiculous. This ultimate demand for adaptability is one which may find an insurmountable obstacle. There may yet be rebellion against this degree of regimentation.

The Power of Subcultures

One outcome of the growth of our society in both size and complexity is the emergence of subcultures. Every generation has known a few; our times recognize the largest numbers yet. Take, for example, the group of the "hippies."

This group, although numerically quite large, represents only a fraction of a percent of our total population. If we examine its characteristics, we find certain exaggerations of normal group attributes. The first hyperbole is the intense dedication of the membership to the central objective—protest. Different hippies protest different things, but there can be no doubt that they are all protesting. Certainly in the beginning, a subsidiary to this protest was the conviction that it should be nonviolent protest—an attitude evocative of Mahatma Gandhi and his followers in the early days. The element lacking in the hippies was the religiosity of the followers of Gandhi.

The second exaggeration in this and other subcultures is the absolute conformity demanded of followers, no matter how weird and far out the norms may be. (As a sidelight on the power of subcultures, the expression "far out" comes directly from the hippie vocabulary.) If love beads are decreed, love beads will be worn. If communal living is the norm of the day, the pad will increase its population to the bursting point. This total and rigid conformity to norms goes much further than in the more "normal" group. As a result, only one sanction can be invoked by the group: isolation.

A subculture, because of the intense dedication of its members, does more proselytizing than other groups. The members feel an obligation to "give the word" to their benighted brethren. They will be quite inventive in discovering new media for communicating their beliefs. In most cases, the adoption of unusual norms will assist in getting them before the public. There is a large gap, however, between being known by the public and achieving numbers of converts. Most of us are more vulnerable to ridicule than to any other nonviolent weapon. Not so with the members of a subculture: They are impervious to ridicule and proceed blandly with their efforts at indoctrination and the courting of new members.

The greatest single effect of a subculture on the rest of the population is a forced reexamination of fundamental values by society. Starting with their original protest against the Vietnam war, the hippies made the American public crystallize its thinking about this war, the validity of the universal draft, the position of the home in our society, marriage as an institution, and the ethical and moral values in the use of psychedelic drugs. When traditional beliefs in any such areas are questioned, we are forced to make some basic reappraisals. Thus, if they have accomplished nothing else, the hippies have made the American public take a good, long look at the underlying ethics of our society.

Reversing the telescope, let us consider the various kinds of individual motivation typical of the hippies. The first impulse is to oversimplify and ascribe cowardice or laziness to the total membership. Both of these traits are negated as universal motivators when we see the physical bravery displayed by hippies in their confrontations with the police as well as the hard work they go to in order to mount their demonstrations. The more we look, the more we are forced to conclude that hippies can be motivated normally. In short, the members of a subculture may use unusual methods to achieve ends which, in themselves, are perfectly normal.

There are two possible end effects that a subculture may have on the rest of society. The first is evident in American politics. In the early thirties, a tiny group of activists generated a subculture whose objective was the complete reversal of the country's political and economic ideology. Little more than a generation has elapsed since it sprang into being, but that subculture has disappeared into normal American society. The ideas of Norman Thomas when he first became the Socialist candidate for president were considered dangerously radical, but Mr. Thomas lived to see those ideas become conservative, if not reactionary. The second possibility is that the subculture may arise, make its effort, and disappear after having failed in achieving its goals. That is not to say that there cannot be a residual effect on the rest of the citizenry; but, if the main objective fails, the subculture will be reabsorbed into the population. Obviously, a subculture can be one of the more effective change agents in society when its objectives are reasonable and timely.

A psychological reason for the appearance of a subculture (as in the case of the hippies) is a general revolt against the complexity of what we have come to call "normal" living. Any person over 30 can look back at a childhood significantly simpler than our present environment provides. Complexity is the product of an affluent society which has to work less to support itself and a technology which spews forth innovations, both attractive and expensive, at a staggering rate. The balancing of these two factors (both tending in opposite directions) is not an easy job, and the task raises the anxiety level of the average citizen to a barely endurable level. The result, in many cases, is the coalescing of a new group based on protests, with the objective of major "reform." Such attempts at simplification rarely succeed; they are going against an immensely powerful stream. Their true value lies in making us reexamine our basic principles.

The Individual as the Sum of His Group Memberships

When we say that a person is the sum of his group memberships, we are speaking the truth but not the whole truth. Actually, this statement is intended as an attention-getter and an incitement to controversy. It is true to the extent that man's social interactions of course do take place within the group. Our contacts with one or more other persons will add to our cognitive perception of the world about us.

One of the more important effects of group memberships is the formation of those habits by which we control the greater part of our life. As complex as it has become, living would be insupportable without the help and lubrication given us by our habits. A major part of our day's activities requires no conscious attention on our part, simply because we are accustomed to its routine. What if we had to stop and consider judgmentally the dozens of actions we go through in arising and starting the day? How frustrated we would be were not the mechanics of driving a car submerged below the surface of our consciousness! Even a large part of our group activities has become habitual. The rituals of greeting, certain kinds of one-to-one interaction, the small tasks of the individual within the group, and many other familiar acts are by now ingrained. Good or neutral habits are supportive and strength-saving many times a day.

We have already mentioned that much of our cultural life is strongly influenced by our most important group memberships. We should now amplify this statement to the point of generalization by noting that almost all of our attitudes are the product of one or more of the groups to which we give allegiance. This is no denigration of our own individual freedom of thought or action. For the most part, we have the right to maintain membership in a group or sever it. If we maintain it, there can be little doubt that the group will rank high among the determinants of our attitudes and beliefs.

Some of us, true, give little thought to how great an

influence our group memberships have on our public image and reputation. It is quite possible to be drawn into a group through strong ties with one or more of its members, only to discover sometime later that the status of that group is far from desirable. Our position in this case is complicated by the knowledge that withdrawal from the group will probably cost us the friendships which were the original attractive force.

With no intent to belabor the point, we should still reinforce how much of our personal motivation is conditioned by our group memberships. Strong identification with any group carries with it an automatic involvement with the achievement of group goals. Personal motivation and group motivation have a synergistic effect upon each other. In the final analysis, there is little that is conducive to strong personal motivation which is not connected with some group or another. No man is more terribly bored than the one who attempts to live unto himself alone.

Since, as we have reiterated, life today is a cooperative affair, our individual progress will be directly correlated to the advancements made by our various groups: formal, semiformal, or informal. Along the same line, almost all innovation and progress in these times are triggered by group interaction. Only the true genius is capable of solo flights of creativity; the rest of us will make progress by striking sparks from each other. The best illustration of this is the fact that 99 percent of the American technology is the work of teams. Membership in such teams imposes a restraint in the form of self-control which might otherwise be lacking in our existence. The work can flourish only when each member of the team is prepared both to make an individual contribution and to give respect and a hearing to any other member.

Our personal rewards reflect our effectiveness in group

membership. Society repays us on a comparative basis for our contribution to the achievement of group objectives. The essential unfairness of this system is ignored by all mankind. It takes no cognizance of individual differences and gives no weight to greater or lesser ability as they appear in individual endowment. Those who have are rewarded; those who have not are doomed to a lifetime of relative struggle and frustration. To be sure, the theory of the survival of the fittest cannot be applied to our present society, which is so loaded with buffers and life-preservers that the unfit are unfairly favored. The difference between survival and triumph, however, is still considerable. What has happened is that our modern society has succeeded in simultaneously protecting the weak and rewarding the strong.

We should reflect for a moment on the differing (some of them opposing) valences to which we are subjected in our multigroup memberships. Inevitably, some of these will be in opposition, and it is this factor which sharpens our evaluative powers. Daily we are called upon to make differential judgments in our actions according to our various group memberships. This honing of our discriminative powers is all to the good. It keeps us alert, and each iteration of forced judgments reinforces our basic principles and beliefs.

We could continue this inspection of the way in which we are individually molded by our group memberships to the point of diminishing returns. Its significance lies in the integrative effect of such memberships. We grow, mature, and—we hope—progress, as a result of our choice of groups.

* * *

In this chapter we have centered our attention on how the group affects the individual. In every society, the group acts as the policeman to enforce conformity to the norms which it has established. Conformity to norms of its own making is, in fact, the only real way a group has to perpetuate itself. Individuals find safety and reassurance in conforming to groups which they think can protect them. Nevertheless, all of us must exhibit a slight flare of nonconformity on occasion to reassure ourselves as to our own identity. Consciously or otherwise, we will carefully choose one of the lesser group norms to flout, so that the resultant sanctions will be light.

In addition to demanding conformity, the group will mold the general behavior of its membership. There will be close similarity in behavior patterns, and related to it will be the influence the group has on the personal goals of its members. Any group that ranks high in a member's value system will in large measure determine his personal objectives.

Multigroup memberships force us as individuals to become highly adaptable in order to survive. Our adaptation must extend even to membership in groups which have totally antithetical objectives. We must be schizoid enough to tolerate this sort of situation if we are to live in modern America.

The individual—to repeat—is the sum of his group memberships. His basic behavior, personality, reputation, and character are products of the groups he chooses.

Chapter 6

Effects of the Individual on the Group

$\mathcal{W}$E WOULD be seriously in error if we assumed that, by simply reversing the outlook of the last chapter, we could intuitively understand how an individual affects a group. His influence is *not* the mirror image of the effect of the group on the individual. A group is more than a collection of individuals; it has a personality and a spirit which are entirely its own and are only in part determined by its composition. This matter of group individuality and character is about as fascinating a facet of group dynamics as can be found. It takes a close student and a trained observer in the field of social psychology to make predictions about the behavior of a specific group with any accuracy.

Leadership Qualities and Changes in the Group

The quickest and surest way to change a group is either to cause the leader to change one or more of his characteristics or to replace him with another person. For example, a frequently seen change in a group, and one that is directly associated with its leadership, is its work tempo. The leader, with his personal involvement in reaching the group goals, is more often than not the change agent for speeding up production. If his leadership is good, he will maintain controls so that feedback will keep him posted on mileposts toward goal achievement. The matter of controlling the working speed of the group will account for a considerable amount of the time he spends with the group.

We carry into adult life one attribute developed as young children—an unconscious imitation of the mannerisms of our heroes. The more we admire and respect a group leader, the more we will imitate him so far as we can. Therefore, the personality of a group's leader will have a strong influence on the personality of the group. Certain of his personal mannerisms will often be noted in the group at large. Likes and dislikes can be traced through group behavior back to their origin in his attitudes.

Such character traits as a leader's way of responding to a threat and his views on quality of work are quickly picked up and copied by devoted followers. The influence and example of the leaders are especially critical in relation to quality performance—not only in the formal work group but in other groups as well. Pride in accomplishment and workmanship is not indigenous to the human being; it must be acquired, like a taste for olives. American businessmen would do well to reflect more deeply on the value of this highly intangible attribute. The customer chooses quality over many other characteristics in his purchases; repeat sales of a product are traceable to high quality more than to anything else. And the leader has more control over quality of workmanship than does any other individual. If his efforts are consciously bent in this direction, big strides can be made in the improvement of quality.

The leader's formative influence on change in the group goes far beyond any volition on his part. Much of this change will come as a result of the nonverbal cues he gives constantly. The responsiveness of the other group members to these cues is, of course, a measure of his leadership effectiveness. One of the responsibilities of a leader is to be aware of these subtle aspects of his leadership; he must be alert to effects on the group he had no intention of initiating. Inertial momentum is controlled by a group leader in much the same manner that a symphony conductor shades the nuances of his orchestra—by looks, small or grand gestures, vigor of attack, and an indefinable rapport which goes beyond any and all of these. Every means of human communication is used by a good leader to change the behavior of his group.

While still in the area of the imponderable, let's look at the matter of esprit de corps. The term "group morale" does not completely cover the phenomenon of group spirit. Actually, it is entirely possible for the morale of the group to be at an all-time low without having any significant effect on its esprit de corps. A Marine platoon on the battlefield, cut off from the rest of its company, will find its morale too low to measure, but the spirit of the Marines will make them rise to the occasion and give a good account of themselves even in a hopeless situation. Group spirit is an asset analogous to the goodwill which the owner of a company finds has a cash value when he puts the business up for sale. It is the balance wheel which makes it possible for a group to operate efficiently in bad times as well as good. When the leader is effective, the commonest expression of group spirit is a conscious unwillingness to let him (and thereby the group) down. People will go to lengths for the group which they might not be willing to undertake solely for their own purposes.

The leader's charisma is important in the generation and maintenance of good group spirit. It is one of the intangible and unquantifiable components of the group which makes the study of group dynamics both fascinating and frustrating. It sounds trite to reiterate so many times how the impact of leadership affects group performance, but nonetheless the effect is there, and it must be reckoned with whenever we appraise the performance and effectiveness of the group. Like any other powerful motor, the group must have an ignition system and a distributor. This is the function of its leadership.

The Impact of Splinter Groups

Important as he is, the leader is far from being the only individual with an effect on the rest of the group. Every member has his impact on every other. Individual influence in the group may be either positive or negative. A person may be so constituted that his personality attracts new friendships quickly and easily; his entry into a group will be felt as soon as these friendships emerge. If this new member identifies completely with the goals of the group, his entry can help in their achievement by strong reinforcement they receive through his personal contacts. All of us have seen a group rejuvenated and revitalized by the addition of one or two new members with strong personalities. If the group has a wise leader, no friction will be generated by this sort of development. The leader will be glad to accept the contributions of the new members and will actively encourage them to form friendships and increase the positive valences within the group.

The reverse of this situation is just as possible. New members, if their personalities are abrasive, can stir up trouble where none existed before. It is not necessary that these persons be men of ill will; if their demeanor is an irritant to their fellows, their total effect on the group will be negative. The strongest disruptive factor resulting from the appearance of such persons in a group will be the damage to old and smoothly functioning relationships. Morale will suffer first; actual group effectiveness will be lowered if the situation persists.

Truly negative results may be noted if a new member has an outright personality clash with an older member, especially if the latter is a leader or otherwise exerts a strong influence on the members. The course of such a confrontation will follow a fairly predictable path. As the enmity between the two develops, both members will have a human tendency to become more involved in their infighting than in the overall good of the group. A coup on the enemy will be more important than progress toward group goal achievement. The tactics adopted by one or both of the fighters will more than likely be inimical to the welfare of the group. The early detection of such personality clashes is the job of group leadership. Ordinarily, the advantage will lie with the older member; his group history will speak for him, while the new member is an unknown quantity. However, if a contest develops quickly and sharply, some new facets to the personality of the older member will become apparent, and there may put him in an unfavorable light with his comrades. They will soon remark, "John seems to have changed a lot lately, don't you think?"

The final outcome of a fight between two members of a group can easily be the formation of a splinter group. In almost every case, the membership will be polarized about the two contestants. In a short time, what started out as a rivalry between two individuals becomes a schism affecting the entire group. This situation is a familiar one to church congregations. What began as a personality conflict quickly spreads to involve the whole membership, and the real reason for the battle will be engulfed in controversy over form of worship or fundamental dogma. The proliferation of religious sects in our country is ample evidence of how deep and shattering this kind of conflict can be in a church group.

A second area where personality differences may have some serious aftereffects is politics. Every political party at every level, from the strictly local to the national, is replete with examples of discord and damage caused by personality conflicts. It is possible for these to flare up so violently that the leadership is helpless to quell them before severe damage has been done to group solidarity. More than one national candidacy has had its origin in a fight with the regular party machinery. The success of such a tactic is "iffy"; the chances are slightly against it.

It is not impossible for a splinter group to have a positive effect on the entire group's activity. For example, if a new member has a strong interest in public relations, he can pass his enthusiasm to his new friends, producing a splinter group which is working toward a positive new group objective—the betterment of the group's public image. In a manner of speaking, it could be argued that some of our larger groups are run as a collection of splinter groups. Most P-TA's function more effectively as a collection of committees, which are really nearly autonomous splinter groups in their sphere of activity. General membership meetings then come to have two functions: the hearing of committee reports and the establishment of policy for the organization.

It should be obvious by this time that not only is the

individual altered by his various memberships, but he will have a measurable effect on any group in which he is truly active. In fact, the more the individual is changed by his group associations, the greater will be his chances of controlling the groups with which he works. The summation of these individual effects will amount to the overall "yeastiness" of any group. The only group to which individual activity poses a threat is the one which is fiercely dedicated to the maintenance of the status quo. In this kind of group, the greatest heresy is the introduction of innovation to the group's agenda.

Modification of Group Goals

Changes in group goals are more often triggered by one member than by cooperative action among the total group membership. A change is first perceived as a felt need by one individual; his efforts to have this change accepted by the group membership take on the aspect of a crusade. This deep ego involvement is the impetus needed to change the inertia of a group.

It is quite natural that proposed changes will be personally advantageous to their sponsor. Even when this is understood by the other members, it can be forgiven if the sponsor can demonstrate an advantage for the whole group. Most ordinary adults will agree that the sponsor *should find some personal gain in the new goal.* They will demand only that his proposal be well thought out and smoothly presented. This much is necessary to bolster their own egos to the point where they can finally accept the change. There is no general formula for effecting change in objectives. However, logical presentation and demonstration of results useful to the group are always vital to any change action.

The one element that is ordinarily necessary if an individual is to make a change in one or more of the group's goals is *time*. At best, behavioral change is a slow procedure, with all its attendant trauma and its raising of the anxiety level. The sponsor of the change is asking that new habits be substituted for old. This requires first the extinction of the old habits and then the formation of the new ones—both long processes when working with adults.

It is logical to assume that more proposed changes in group goals will be originated by the leadership than by any single individual. This will be true, that is, if the leadership is alert and active. A man is a leader partly because he *is* able to conceptualize desirable change and then sell it to the membership. In fact, the general health of a formal or a semiformal group has a positive correlation with the rate at which it changes major objectives. To be functional, any such changes must correspond to the changes occurring in the group's environment. It is a truism to note that a group's effectiveness is dependent upon the validity of its major objectives, but we should remind ourselves frequently of this basic fact.

A natural parallel to effecting change in objectives within the group is the construction of new norms to support and control the achievement of the new objectives. It is the norms, rather than the objectives, which will cause the visible change appearing within the group. To most of us, basic disquiet is associated with a change in our behavior because change represents the new and the unknown. We are unable to predict exactly how we will react to this new requirement, which is fundamentally disturbing to us. We demand predictability in our own behavior just as we do in that of our leadership. A little analysis of a typical group will usually show the persistence of one or more norms which actually impede progress toward the existent goals.

This naturally results in lowered group efficiency and all the upset which accompanies it.

The innovator who would see his proposed goal change realized should spend much of his planning and selling efforts in the area of new group norms rather than merely specifying the goal change desired each time. In some cases, the decision will be made to keep the new objective as a hidden agenda and to work toward it purely by way of superimposing new norms. If this gambit is successful, the installation of the new goal may appear as a most logical and inevitable event. Many astute operators prefer to use this approach rather than enter into an extended philosophical discussion of the desirability of changing the goal. It is, in any terminology, manipulation of the group membership.

Remember that it is just as possible for a proposed goal change to be engendered by altruistic motives as by base ones. The individual who truly is totally identified with the group and its welfare is the one who literally burns with desire to implement a new goal which he sees to be intrinsically valuable to the group. He becomes a true zealot and will be invincible against all the group's resistance to change.

In the final analysis, however, there will be no change in goals without the acceptance of the entire group. The process by which this is accomplished is traceable in broad terms of time, changed thinking, and different behavior, but the roadmap for such a procedure is unique to each instance, even within the same group. The variables involved are too many and too complex to predict a generic outcome accurately. Finally involved will be cooperative action between leadership and group membership, with a resultant learning curve for the installation of the new behavior. Implicit here, also, is the ongoing evaluation of the new goal after its adoption for a variable period of time. A change in goals is always an emergent situation in the life of a group; calm will return only after the membership at large has been convinced of the advantages of the change.

Effects on Cohesiveness

There are two ways in which an individual may have an effect on the cohesiveness of one of his groups. The first is to be deviant. Any group will react reflexively to a member's deviant behavior with a swift rise in cohesiveness. It is a purely defensive reaction to a perceived threat. Since norms are established by the group for the dual purpose of self-perpetuation and achievement of a group goal, it *is* threatening to see one of them flouted. At the outset, this is a reaction, not against the deviant as a person, but against the act of deviance. If the villain does not respond immediately with a return to conformity, the group quickly personalizes its reaction against the deviant. This maintenance activity of the group is so important to its safety and general well-being that there is seldom much discussion about the proposed course of remedial action. The person refusing to conform ordinarily is aware of the consequences of his act. Only a grossly insensitive individual could expect to go directly against the considered judgment of the rest of the membership without incurring some sort of punishment.

The increase in cohesiveness resulting from the appearance of anormative activity will continue, and continue to intensify, so long as the activity is present. Group pressure is usually slow to build up, but it is capable of increasing nearly to infinity. At some place along the line, good leadership will begin to probe for the reason for the deviance. If it is discovered that the person concerned (especially if he is new to the group) is apparently or admittedly just trying to gain attention, the punishment will probably be light if the deviant mends his ways at once. Should an investigation show that the deviance was the result of pure ignorance of established norms, there may be no punitive action at all. Possibly the act of deviance may be an effort to assume leadership; naturally, then, it will constitute an open challenge to the established leadership, and again group cohesiveness will rise significantly. The decision to "take on" the rest of the group is seldom undertaken lightly. There must be extremely high motivation behind such an act. Of course, it is not unknown for a person gifted in leadership to unseat the "ins" and take over power. But, even should this occur, there will still be a sharp increase in group cohesiveness during the course of the battle. Whichever way it goes, the group members will be aware of the threat to their security and continued existence as a group. It may be that the deviant will be the only relaxed member during the incident.

The second major way in which an individual can have an effect on group cohesiveness is by his personal influence on the rest of the membership. If his commitment, identification, and influence with the group are high, the resultant change in group cohesiveness will be on the positive side. We have all seen how contagious enthusiasm and dedication can be when continually displayed by an individual. The crusaders for any group do make their contribution by reaffirming the group objectives and their accomplishment for the rest of the membership. Perhaps this is the only real contribution the zealot makes to the good of the order. The unfortunate truth is that the opposite of the situation can also exist. A vocal, dissatisfied member can, if he is highly respected, become a change agent for lowering group cohesiveness to the danger point. The alert leader will quickly observe that a destructive climate exists, and he will move in ruthlessly. Morale will be the first casualty; cohesiveness will suffer a little further down the line.

Group cohesiveness can also be affected, either positively or negatively, by a personal attack from the outside on one member of the group. Whether cohesiveness will increase or decrease under such a circumstance inevitably will be dependent upon the victim's esteem and status within the group. Again, we look to politics for many familiar examples of this situation. Personal attacks upon presidential candidate Al Smith because of his religion sharply increased cohesiveness within the Democratic ranks during the 1928 campaign. In this case, morale was high, even in a losing cause. On the other hand, attempts to establish anti-Semitic overtones to Goldwater's candidacy had little effect one way or the other; the Republicans were so demoralized during this campaign that nothing could have had a strong effect upon their group cohesiveness. The fatal rift within their own ranks had occurred long before this tactic was employed by the opposition.

It may be too obvious to point out that the ability of an individual to affect the cohesiveness of his group will be a function of his personal stature among the membership. Every group has its quota of faceless members who receive little consideration from their fellows. There has to be some distinctive quality of distinction about a member for him to exert a personal influence. The normal bell curve of distribution will immediately show that only about 16 percent of the membership can affect group cohesiveness on either the plus or the minus side. Yet it will happen often enough to be of significance in the life cycle of any group. If we could pinpoint such a thing as a "normal" group, we would observe a sinusoidal curve chronologically in group cohesiveness.

Changes in Action Levels

As a reflection of their leadership, the membership mix, or both, groups evolve a method of initiating action. If the leadership is strong and dominant, action will begin at the top level by its direction; members will acquire the habit of waiting for direction before doing anything. If, however, the leadership is permissive or encourages participation, the members may be accustomed to initiating action at the grassroots level. In more complex organizations, such as our present large corporations, top-level management will make and disseminate policy, leaving the implementation to the various layers of middle management. It is possible for the entry of one strong new member into the group to have a visible effect on the point at which action is initiated.

Take, for example, an old, established corporation which operated strictly by the book. Unless there was an operating procedure which documented exactly the action to be taken, nothing happened. Procedures were beautifully explicit, and operation was smooth within the prescribed limits. Under the unusual situation which arose during the early part of World War II, a new supervisor was hired from the outside for the control lab in the factory. This man was strong, alert, and full of determination to do a job. Actually, his first few months were full of trauma for everyone around him. Because he was totally unaware of the sacred processes by which the company was run, he ignored them completely and cut across all sorts of taboos and forbidden areas. Before his actions could be reviewed by middle management, it was discovered that his unit (a new one) was setting records daily in both production and quality of work. The reaction of the responsible management was fascinating to observe. A considered decision was made to let him proceed according to his own methods *in his own area*, but he was completely walled off from any attempts to extend his heretical methods to other areas with which he had liaison. More than this, a total conspiracy of silence was built up about the whole situation. The job was recognized as part of the wartime emergency, with no expectation of being built into the permanent organization. It is interesting to note that no plans were made for retaining the deviant, either.

The effect of an individual on the action level of the group will, of course, be directly associated with his own level of entry. One of the more upsetting events in the life of any group is to have a new leader installed whose philosophy diverges widely from that of the leader he replaces. Changes under the new leadership can happen in either direction. If the group has been running free and easy under a Theory Y leader, it will suffer greatly if the new boss is disclosed to be a Theory X man. The shock is no less if the reverse is true, but the eventual outcome for the group will be much happier.

We should not overlook the possibility that a change in action level can also be instituted by the present leader as a calculated gambit. The leader may discover that the environment of his group has changed to the point where a different posture is demanded of it. Perhaps he determines that his group *must* be more flexible if it is to remain competitive. He will then shift responsibility for emergency action to the individual concerned, with the proviso that this individual communicate with him immediately upon making a decision and starting the action. The reverse is possible too. If the leader feels that a free-wheeling organization has been too impetuous, with a concomitant waste of effort and money, he may decide to draw in the reins and return some of the latitude for decision making to himself.

Yet another situation must not be overlooked. Thus far, we have perhaps intimated that all changes in action level will be started by group leadership. This is not so. A member, either new or old, may be motivated to make a move which will precipitate action. If his influence in the group is significant, the change in action level will be well under way before it is even discovered by the group leadership. Naturally, a confrontation of the first order will result if action initiation has previously been controlled tightly by the leaders of the group.

We should reinforce heavily the fact that the origination of action is more often than not a function of the climate and surroundings within which the group operates. No group has any major autonomy of action per se. All of us, both as individuals and as group members, must compromise between subservience and self-determinism. This kinetic equilibrium becomes a way of life. Our adaptability must be great enough for us to retain peace of mind and continue to function efficiently under these constraints. If the action level of a group is responsive to its leadership, its group mix, and its surroundings, the individual who will have the most effect in introducing a change in action level is the one most sensitive to a different climate. The effective group will respond to the intuition of this observant member and follow his lead toward a better adjustment to change. It has been the happy faculty of the American public to do this repetitively. Only in this way can we survive the tremendous pressures of our exploding technology and the resultant strain upon both individuals and group members.

Status—Individual and Group

The entry of one person into a group can change the status of the rest of the membership. If the president of a corporation takes up golf, his choice of country club can elevate its status significantly. Any social group keeps an alert eye open for certain people in the community because of the prestige their membership can give. Of course, the sought-after member will have a human tendency to join the group which he considers is already the most prestigious —unless, that is, his own position is so unassailable that he literally cares nothing about the status of his groups. And this type of person is extremely rare.

The entire matter of status is so ephemeral as almost to defy close definition. A group (like a person) may achieve status for many different reasons; likewise, its status in different segments of society may vary from the highest to the lowest. It may gain this status through accomplishment, individual high-status members, expert knowledge, money and power, and a multitude of other attributes. Also, status may be time-limited. Whoever heard of the Burning Tree Country Club until President Eisenhower began to play golf there? For that matter, how much has been heard of it by the general public since Mr. Eisenhower left office?

There is always the possibility that group membership will have a reciprocal effect on the status of both the new member and the group at large. If the prospective member has already arrived at a position in the community only a trifle this side of preeminence, he may make the calculated decision that this new membership will be just the touch needed to solidify his position. At the same time, the group will be happy to gain this solid citizen, who is already generally recognized as such.

The American scene is unique in the modern world because of the complete mobility possible to any citizen who contributes creatively, earns great wealth, or simply becomes notorious for some reason. The rags-to-riches plot is too hackneyed to revive here. We all have friends or acquaintances who have carved a respectable place for themselves in their community and have noticeably raised their position during their lifetime. This kind of person will generate several satellite groups in which he will be the leader. These groups will have high community status simply because they are associated with him. Membership in his poker club, his golfing foursome, his duck-hunting associations will be much desired within his circles. At the same time, it should not be forgotten that there are the unique achievers, such as Howard Hughes, who maintain a fierce hands-off policy toward the rest of the world. These figures of mystery gain even greater status in the eyes of the public because of their inscrutability. The elder Henry Ford built an aura about himself which was the exact antithesis of the nature he displayed in his business activities. Perhaps the most famous and fascinating recent example of mutual enhancement of status occurred with the marriage between Jacqueline Kennedy and Aristotle Onassis.

It is unfortunate that, in order to complete the picture, we must examine the reverse situation for a moment. It is just as possible for an individual to reduce the status of his group as it is for him to raise it. The industrialist indicted by the government for tax fraud or illegal price fixing brings quick and certain disgrace to every group in which he has membership. The greater the previous status has been, the mightier the crash when the idol falls. A drug firm that was more than a century old and had an impeccable reputation was nearly ruined when high corporate officers systematically looted the company by means of false inventories and fictitious sales. It took the enterprise nearly a generation to regain its reputation after this event. The real tragedy was that, had the acumen and intellectual power of the two offenders been bent toward legitimate ends, the company would probably have become a colossus.

We have already taken a cursory look at the dangers of placing too great emphasis on the matter of status, but it might be well at this point to reassess just how much importance the status of a group should assume in the minds of the members. The determinant *should* be whether the status involved is earned or artificial. Recruiting new members on the basis of how much they can enhance the status of the group is a dangerous ploy. These members just may be completely satisfied to consider their presence as their total contribution to the group effort and may exhibit supreme indifference to the achievement of the group's basic goals. This kind of "nonmember" will soon become a drag on the group rather than a contributor.

There is a constant give and take between the individual member and the group with respect to status. The internal status of the member is indissolubly linked with his contribution to overall group effectiveness. It is in this area that he will be judged by his peers and his group leadership. He may have been chosen purely on the basis of the status his presence will give the group, but this motive will have spent itself at the moment of his arrival. From there on out, he will be judged on the basis of his solid efforts in behalf of the group. In the last analysis, status (either individual or group) is nice to have but is not one of the fundamental necessities for the group life.

The Group as a Collection of Individuals

A major part, but not all, of a group's personality is made up of the individual characters and personalities of the membership. Although the group acts most of the time from consensus, time is spent in reconciling differences in opinions among the membership before actions can be taken which are neither routine nor covered by established norms.

Much of the ego satisfaction which accrues to group membership arises from the knowledge that the individual member does influence the group decisions. This is recognition from peers in its purest form. Inputs to group decision making constitute a large part of the practice we get as adults in both reasoning and persuasive activities. At least, we had better have done our reasoning before we attempt to persuade others, or we will be shot down without mercy.

Both the momentary mood and the general morale of the group will be the summation of the individual contributions of the membership. Here we see the position and status of the single member assuming major importance. It is not rare to have the even tenor of a working group badly upset when one member comes in nursing a grudge or expressing ill will. The reverse of this is a little harder to accomplish, but it can be done. One unflappable member can set about to raise the low spirits of a group and show some definite gains by dint of persistence.

Thus the group does vary its mood and temperament just as does the individual. Groups can be lethargic, calm, even-tempered, ebullient—even manic-depressive, depending upon the mix of the membership.

The effect of the individual member will be felt in the goal-setting process. Ordinarily, as we have seen, it is an individual who first conceptualizes a change in an old objective or proposes a new one. Group introspection is accomplished by the efforts of single members; the pooling of their impressions and beliefs will result in a reading of the group.

It is easier to trace personal contributions in the day-to-day work toward goal accomplishment than in any other area of group life. True though it may be that the group will show a nearly normal distribution of effort on the job by its members, the measurement of what each person contributes toward achieving the target is relatively simple. The group *is* more than a collection of individuals, but the total amount of work done cannot be more than the sum of the individual contributions.

The leader of the group will be quite conscious of individual differences whenever he considers the interpersonal relationships as they ebb and flow in both quantity and quality within the membership. A single member, by showing exceptionally good or exceptionally bad relationships within the group, may leave a mark on its life. Approximately 95 percent of our interpersonal relationships are within a group context, rather than on a one-to-one basis. They are, for this reason, complicated by changing valences within the group. A deterioration in our contacts with one person will have repercussions on several others. Similarly, improved relations will be a help to several others. Remembering this at all times will make our social living smoother and more pleasant.

We have neglected so far to correct one misconception which may have arisen from our having emphasized repeatedly how the individual melts into his group associations. Although it is becoming more difficult day by day, it *is* still possible for a person to maintain his own identity and individuality by knowingly nurturing those characteristics which tend to set us apart from those about us. It is the one area of self-determinism open to everybody. No one can do this for another person; any attempt at maintenance of identity is a purely personal one.

There is little to gain from an exhaustive iteration of all other characteristics, major or minor, which are to be found in the makeup of a group. The essential thing to remember is that groups are composed of human beings, with all their many strengths and weaknesses. Interactions among them will set the group's tone, determine its survival, and account for the ease or difficulty with which it meets its objectives. The group is sentient: It makes judgments, is capable of fine discrimination, and will order its life in nearly the same way as do any of its members. The understanding of this strong parallel between the individual and the group is one of our better tools for successful living in our various social units. It can give us the perspective by which to judge the fitness of our own decisions and resultant actions. Without this balance wheel, we are helpless to assess our success or failure as a member of any group. Others will most certainly be making a judgment of this sort about us; our best defense is to beat them to it and be able to rectify our navigational errors before they become fatal.

* * *

If there is any difficulty in understanding the individual's influence on the group, it is due to the difficulty of putting into perspective the infinite variety of human characteristics found in any normal population. Not only is there wide variety among individuals, but each person himself will change from day to day in his interests and emphasis. Yesterday's passion may have been replaced overnight by a new interest even more consuming. As group members, we will do well to achieve an understanding of how one person can affect a group and guide our own actions accordingly. If we see an unusual situation developing and have a knowledge of some of the valences being engendered, we may be able to predict the outcome and choose our own course to avoid disaster or perhaps even to benefit ourselves. Predictability of human behavior can most certainly never be exact. One must allow for a margin of error whose magnitude will be governed by the number of independent variables operating within the group. For example, management in predicting the outcome of union negotiations, will be concerned with such variables as the general economy, the strength or weakness of the international union being dealt with, local union politics, and even the state of mind of the union members' wives. These same variables will have their effect on the management people concerned. Even with a working understanding of the principles of group dynamics, there is no formula into which we can grind raw data and come up with a sure thing for an answer. The best we can hope for (and this is no inconsiderable thing) is the greatly enhanced probability of making a correct prediction about human behavior.

Groups will evolve, grow, prosper, or fail and die as a result of the effect on them of their individual members. We can be sure of having a better chance of personal success if we understand how groups operate.

Chapter 7

Leadership

So much has been written, both generally and technically, on the subject of leadership that we could inquire whether this chapter is really needed. Our excuse is that, for all of the writing done, disappointingly few definitive conclusions have been reached by the behavioral scientist in the area of leadership. It then becomes essential that we agree on, or at least state, the ground rules of leadership in this book.

"Qualities" of Leadership?

At this particular moment, the heavy preponderance of opinion holds that there is no list of traits or characteristics which can really describe what it takes for a person to be a leader. On the other hand, in order to be able to define the term, we must discuss certain behavioral aspects by which we recognize those people whom we are willing to follow. For the fact that people are willing to follow a person is the absolute minimum for leadership to exist; no man is a leader until he is acknowledged as such by others. This matter of acceptance is sometimes lost sight of, especially in the work group, where leadership—or managership—is imposed on the group from above. What we are actually saying is that in a number of cases the group will be managed by a nonleader, simply because the members refuse the necessary recognition. (Incidentally, the void left by the absence of true leadership will be filled de facto by another member who acts as the group's informal leader. This person will assume many of the functions normally handled by the official leader of the group.)

One of the most discussed attributes of the leader is *intelligence*. Most people find it necessary to respect the person they follow, and it is human for us to admire high intelligence. Therefore, if a leader has better-than-average intelligence, he will be in a good position to get the respect of his people. However, if his intellect is so great that the disparity between him and his people in this matter is evident, big trouble will ensue. Communication will be too difficult for smooth operation. Directives which the leader feels to be perfectly self-evident will fail to register on his followers. As this becomes clear, the leader will be irritated, he will begin to speak sharply, and there will be the first chipping away at the good relations of the group. As the moderates would say, the good leader should be smart but not too brilliant.

Another requisite for leadership is greater-than-average *motivation*. The leader must be at least as strongly desirous of attaining the group's goals as any other member, and more so than most. This fundamental drive will give him the needed energy to carry on when others are ready to call it quits. Note that we have not specified what his motivation will be. There are many who assert strongly that the commonest motivators among leaders are power, position, and prestige. Strong as these are, however, there are many other motivators to be found in ascendency among recognized leaders. The basic trait is strong motivation, no matter what the kind.

A leader must be willing to make *decisions*. We have a tendency to lose sight of the fact that many, many people have a reluctance to make decisions which amounts almost to fear. The absence of the word "correct" in this statement is intentional. There are major leaders in world history who rarely made a correct decision but, were never wanting when the situation demanded that *some* kind of decision be made.

At the risk of total confusion, let us observe here that better-than-average ability in *interpersonal relationships* is not always found in a leader. A little retrospection will recall leaders who were pretty cold fish even though their ability to judge others' capabilities and weaknesses was above average. But all of us have at some time probably been willing to follow a person we did not like. We had trust and confidence in his drive, intelligence, motivation, and perhaps his talent for survival and allowed these traits to mitigate the fact that he had no friends. Napoleon, Alexander the Great, and Hitler were good examples of this sort of great leader.

On the other hand, there have been many other world-famous leaders whose warmth and personal charm attracted followers in hordes, even when people knew that this great ability to relate covered massive gaps in the other aspects of leadership. In the same vein, it is unfortunate that many famed leaders have not been noted for their *personal integrity*. It is a sad commentary on human nature that we are willing in certain cases to trust our own future to people to whom we would not give our purses. This type of leader will abound in personal charm and overpowering verbal prowess.

Few leaders of note have been lacking in *stamina*. The

ability to go on that extra step beyond the capability of any follower is rewarded by acceptance as a leader. Sheer staying ability will overcome in some cases where other desirable characteristics are lacking. Some call it "determination," others "stubbornness." It all depends on whether you are for him or against him.

Conceptual abilities cannot be omitted from our list. The ability to grasp the implications of the entire scene must be greater in the leader than in the follower. *Creativity* is not so important in the leader as is his ability to recognize and make use of it among his followers. In fact, a truly creative leader presents a traumatic picture to his followers because of his unpredictability. Far better that he be the catalyst for others' creative skills. As to *fairness*, it is more urgently needed by the members than is mercy or sympathy. Inequities in disciplinary action or in rewards for excellence will move group members to open revolt quicker than any other single fault in the leader.

And so we are about to do what we said at the beginning of this chapter could not be done—create a "laundry list" of traits and attributes which can make any person automatically functional as a leader. It is no simple task, no matter how long we romance about the problem and how minute we make the distinctions between the traits propounded. However, let us consider some of the factors in leadership beyond the characteristics we have mentioned so briefly.

Charisma

Charisma is an aura possessed by some leaders which is well-nigh indefinable, totally unquantifiable, and invisible. It separates the great leaders from the run of the mill.

Franklin Roosevelt had it; Wendell Willkie had it; so did John Kennedy, and so does Billy Graham. Who could imagine a more dissimilar group than those men just enumerated? Yet it is universally agreed that all are charismatic.

Charisma is of the spirit, if not spiritual. Some fortunate human beings *do* have a special gift that helps them in relating with others. When this gift can be multiplied indefinitely to include almost everyone within sight and hearing, we have a leader with charisma. There are many who flatly deny the existence of it. They argue that such a leader's many followers are attracted by his physical presence (Mahatma Gandhi?), his oratory (Charles A. Lindbergh?), his instantaneous decisions (Abraham Lincoln?). But the absurdity of such an argument is self-evident. The examples named were some of the most charismatic people who ever lived.

Some tremendously charismatic people may give the appearance of personal coldness to those immediately surrounding them. Their magnetism is much more strongly felt from a distance than in direct contact. One of the best known examples of this was Winston Churchill. Absorption with personal interaction will in fact dilute the effectiveness of a leader with the many. Intuitively or otherwise, leaders know they must impartially dole out their strength to the entire group, rather than vitiate it by means of deep relationships with a few.

The reaction of the group to a leader with charisma is dramatic. Results will be quicker and of much greater magnitude than would have been expected from similar groups under lesser leadership. The Nazis went from ignominious defeat at the "beer hall putsch" to mastery of a nation under Hitler in an incredibly short time. Followers multiplied in geometric progression as the man's hold over his public came to be felt.

We have already stated that charisma is of the spirit. If there is any one element of leadership which can neither be grafted onto a man nor consciously developed by him, it is this. Simply and finally, he has it or he doesn't. Followers seldom verbalize about this quality. They talk about everything else in their leader's makeup except his charisma. They eulogize his accomplishments, his understanding of the situation at hand, his fighting instinct, his ability to diagnose the position of the enemy—anything but the one quality which really attracts them as followers.

The people who should make effective use of a leader's charisma are those followers who have the most influence over him. The leader himself would not truly understand if they were to tell him of his particular power. His cabinet, formal or informal, must develop a fine sensitivity for those situations which will demand full exercise of their leader's mystique. Obviously, these will be crisis situations. Franklin Roosevelt's entire administration was one of continuing or abutting crises; there was never a moment during his presidency that charisma was not called upon for its fullest influence. Perhaps a future historian with better perspective will be able to tally the situations in which F.D.R. demanded that the country follow him on blind faith. It is impossible to predict whether a truly charismatic leader will be piping his followers to triumph or disaster, and the leader himself will be the last to know.

The possessor of this characteristic has it for life, no matter what his situation may be. He can win, lose, or draw the various battles, but the war is won because of his gift. It is a fruitless argument, but grave doubts remain that any true Nazi was ever reconstructed. Their blind devotion to Der Fuehrer was completely impervious to attack from any source. He could do no wrong, and his downfall was a nightmare from which they will someday awake to a belated triumph.

To recapitulate, the charismatic leader has an advantage over his competitors which should be exploited to the fullest degree. This must be done by his first lieutenants rather than by the man himself. The accomplishments of the group will be superior, both in amount and in speed of achievement. Followers will undergo few doubts about their leadership and will be free to devote their entire energy to attainment of the group objectives. The whole climate is ideal for smooth, competent, and rewarding performance.

Mass Rapport

The leadership quality of any person is measured in part by his ability to generate and maintain rapport with the members of his group. He must know what is going on in their minds as well as what their activities of the moment are. Leaders have many different methods for taking the pulse of their group at a given time. Some use a communications network composed of confidants whom they can trust implicitly and who are charged individually with the job of reporting happenings and trends among the membership.

A second method of maintaining contact is for the leader to make personal tours and communicate directly with as many members as possible. The danger inherent in this procedure is the possibility that members may tell the leader only those things they think he wants to hear. These bits of information may well be the truth, but they are seldom the whole truth. If the group is of any size, the presence of the leader in the area constitutes an element of artificiality which militates against good communication. This artificial atmosphere can be alleviated only after the leader's visits have become habitual and thereby commonplace.

A third method of reading the group is the use of carefully selected random samplings of the membership at varying time intervals. This method is useful principally in gathering data on no more than two specific questions. It will never do a complete job of keeping the leader in touch with his people.

Whether he uses these methods or others, the leader knows that the maintenance of open lines of communication with his group is of vital importance. He must know what is going on, just as he must tell his people what is expected of them. One of the more significant fallouts of group rapport is in the confidence that the leader engenders among the members, who will not accept him totally until they are reasonably certain that they understand him. They are particularly anxious to learn his personal motivation; his reason for assuming leadership is individually important to all group members. Leader-follower rapport will be born when the leader's sincerity is obvious and unquestioned. He will be forgiven many mistakes in judgment and tactics; the day his integrity is suspect, his effective leadership is dead.

With the establishment of good rapport, the effectiveness of the group starts to increase geometrically. The necessity for detailed orders and work instructions is sharply reduced. Members feel more certain of their responsibility and can move with more comfort in their own area because they know that their actions will be approved. Two-way communication makes changes in group goals much easier to achieve and then implement. The physical symbol of strong rapport is high cohesiveness within the group. The members' reaction to threat is much swifter and more powerful when they know the leader's thinking and have his full support in their projected action. Essentially, good rapport with the leader will provide much more freedom of action for all concerned.

The values of good rapport for the leader are similar, but not necessarily identical, to those for the group. Normally, the first benefit to the leader is heightened self-confidence. He can now entertain the thought of change in objectives, controls, or methods with the knowledge that communicating them to the group will be relatively simple. At least, he will not have to face a major battle whenever he proposes a change. At the same time, his general effectiveness will also be increased. The time spent in communication will be repaid over and over in the release of energy formerly spent on frustrating details. There will be more time for planning and a careful review of progress toward long-range goals.

It is only right to mention here rapport between leader and group is achievable under many kinds of leadership styles. The most directive of leaders can still inform his followers of his intent and give them a picture of his operating philosophy. At the other extreme, a permissive leader will communicate the necessity for members to assume a larger share of personal responsibility than they may have been used to. It all comes back to the fact that every person demands to know the rules of the game he is playing. Only then can he put a semblance of order into his own responses according to whatever may be the style of the leader.

The matter of rapport is one area where the leader never dares allow himself the luxury of being mistaken. He must really know the truth about the level of understanding between him and the group. Nothing but resounding failure for the whole enterprise can result when the leader tries to fool either himself or his people. This is one of the more critical booby traps for the young or inexperienced leader. The carrying of hidden agendas is possible only under the most expert leadership—and even then, it is a tremendously dangerous tactic.

Once rapport has been achieved, the other danger is for the leader to assume it will continue with no effort on his part. Not so. Rapport demands, and is worthy of, continuing attention and care on his part, as well as goodwill and open response from the group. It is a cooperative activity of the highest order, but the results in better operation and quicker realization of group goals will make the effort eminently worthwhile.

The Father Image

No matter what his chronological age, one of the principal tasks of the leader is to stand in place of a father for the rest of the group. The fundamental reason for banding together as a group is protection. Our childhood memories are of our father as the ultimate protector against any perceived threat; his invincibility gave us the measure of security necessary for our mental health and normal development.

To assume this attitude is not equally easy for all people. Responsibility for the basic security of others is the heaviest burden anyone can undertake. The knowledge that his decisions and actions will directly affect the safety of his people accentuates the vulnerability of the leader's position in his own perception. There are some "leaders" who never do face up to this fact, with the result that the group disintegrates at the first challenge to the leader's protective ability.

The father figure not only must protect but must be

the all-wise sage, to whom members can go for information on almost any subject. This role must be played especially carefully by the leader. It is imperative that he remind himself constantly of his own human frailty and of the fact that his position of leadership does *not* automatically make him a universal authority. Doctors can easily succumb to this temptation; surrounded as they are by patients, druggists, and nurses, all of whom adopt a sycophantic posture toward them. It takes an extremely strong personality to resist the assumption of omniscience. The step from a position of authority in medical matters to the assumption of authority in politics, economics, education, or what have you, is a short one. And perhaps we should not single out doctors as the prime examples of this sort of omniscience—we see many in all the professions who fall into the same trap. To reiterate, the leader must exercise especial care not to make this error as his people continue to defer to what they think of as his superior knowledge in all areas.

The father figure must frequently act as judge–arbiter in disputes among the membership. Just as dad used to be the final court of appeal in family jangles, so the leader will naturally be turned to when there are disagreements in the group. This is a legitimate part of his responsibility, and it will evoke every ounce of objectivity at his command—though man is by nature anything but objective. We are putting him into a highly artificial situation when we demand that he ignore his own emotional involvements in situations and make his judgments purely on a factual basis. The trouble is, no leader ever feels that he has enough facts on which to base a fair decision, and this added trauma may have an effect on his decision-making ability. Yet his group members will be disturbed if they see him hesitate and postpone a decision. In fact, this can be the beginning of their loss of faith in his leadership.

Unfortunately for his peace of mind, the leader, in his

role as a father, must go one step beyond the role of judge and be an executioner as well. That is, he must dole out punishment when he sees nonconformity anywhere in the group. Whenever nonconformity arises as a result of interpersonal conflict, the greatest fear of the leader is that he will misjudge the facts of the case and punish the wrong parties. Actually, this fear is not too well founded. One has only to examine one's own position as a group member to realize that almost all people are basically fair in their judgment of a leader's action. More than that, they are willing to give the leader the benefit of any doubt as to his objectivity—at least until he has repeatedly demonstrated a subjective approach to group problems.

The other side of the coin is that good old dad not only punished, he also dished out rewards to the "good" members of the family. If an objective overview of the problem situation is demanded of the leader, the same objectivity is at least as essential in his recognition of meritorious service. Commendations, raises, and promotions are subject to the intense scrutiny of every member of the group, and every member will make his personal judgment as to the fairness of these awards.

In spite of the extra pressure upon the leader, it is psychologically sound that he assume the father-figure role. With few exceptions, human beings do require at least the illusion of security if they are to function as members of their various groups. Our security blankets change in form as we mature and age, but the need for one never disappears. The fact that mature people joke about this need does not mean that it is not there, or that they fail to recognize it. The leader of any group must therefore resign himself to this part of his job and find the extra strength demanded from whatever source he can. Of course, he in his turn will recognize a father figure in some other leader and can thus shuck off part of his load onto that person. All of us are seen as leaders by some; all of us consider others our leaders. It is this reciprocal and cyclical arrangement which makes it possible for a man to act as a leader without cracking under the pressure. By shifting part of the weight of responsibility to another, he is able to retain his mental health and general well-being.

Goal Identification

The leader, to be effective, must be closely identified with the group's goals. He must place his personal stamp on them, either as author or as signatory. This statement does not imply an authoritarian attitude by which goals will be imposed upon the membership. It signifies only that he as the leader must approve of them and that the membership must be aware of this approval.

Depending upon the leadership style of the man in charge, goal identification may vary from pure ukase to a complete draft by a participating membership. The role of the leader in this process will likewise vary all the way from sole authorship, with no contributions from any of the membership, to mere service as a catalyst while the group conceptualizes and evolves its own objectives. In any event, the group will naturally (and rightly) expect to draw on the wisdom, experience, and guidance of its leader.

The leader of goodwill can be expected to see his part in the process as that of a facilitator in arriving at viable and useful goals. His job is largely one of communication. He will constantly remind the membership of the general perimeters of their activity and will call up for frequent review the most pressing of the group's current problems. A thread of evaluation should run constantly through the job of goal determination. The leader can make a strong contribution by comparing the probable condition of the group after it has achieved the tentative new goals to its present status.

A principal responsibility of the leader is motivation of the group in its continued thinking about goals. It is all too easy to put off goal determination under the pressure of day-to-day work and crises until a state of emergency exists. To prevent this is a recognized part of the leader's job. The inciting spark and the perpetual drive must come from him. Group morale is often at low ebb during the process of goal identification; many people perceive this period of uncertainty as a threat to their security, and they react predictably. Thus they turn to the leader in full expectation of drawing upon his strength as a buttress to their own uncertainties.

Normally, the leader will have access to sources not open to the group membership in determining the probable reliability of the proposed goals. He must compare the experiences of similar groups in similar circumstances and be guided by the results they achieved or failed to achieve. This is only one of the many situations in which his status as a leader allows him to make contact with others and receive confidential material for his own use. Sometimes he can even get such material from competing groups; it is common knowledge that the top managements of rival companies often share information for the good of both.

The leader must determine the timetable attendant upon goal identification. He must first recognize the necessity for a change in major objectives and then plot a carefully calculated course toward effecting that change. This does not mean that goal identification is necessarily a one-man show. Under Theory Y, the leader will stay largely in the background and be more concerned with inspiring and guiding the participation of the group. His contribution will be the identification of those group members whose qualities make them especially fitted to undertake particular parts of the goal-setting job. First of all he will put to work those members who are best at determining the broad outlines of goals. Next will come the activity of the organizers and detail men and, finally, the synthesis of work from the rest of the group preparatory to implementation of the goals. It is during this synthesis that the leader's overview and knowledge of his membership will be most severely tested. To a greater extent than in other group activities, the success of the project will be dependent upon the correct use of the available people.

At this point, it is imperative that the leader reassure himself that his members correctly understand their new goals and their full implications. This understanding is more critical to their final achievement of the goals than the actual work which lies ahead. If the group is individually working toward an assortment of goals, nothing but chaos can ensue. The period immediately after the goals have been determined and before the everyday work toward their achievement begins, is the time when the importance of the leader will be paramount. The vital spark which will set the group into motion must come from him. It will be his job to blow the whistle. His assessment of the group's reaction to the completed process of goal identification, with his reading of their mental and emotional state, will make or break the job. He must decide whether another attempt is in order before putting the machine into high gear. He must satisfy himself that all systems are operational and that the mood of the group is both receptive to the necessary action and restive.

It is here that the leader will truly lead. His sensitivity

to the necessity for change and his finesse in handling his people are urgently needed for the success of the project. He can depend little on guidance from within the group; he will stand or fall upon the extent of his own inner resources.

Power Drive

A desire for power is one of the more common motivators of leaders. Power in this case is derived partly from the status and partly from the ability of the leader himself to escalate his position. As human beings, we have a tendency to ignore the benign use of power; it is only when power is abused that we become conscious of the strength of a leader. There is no office in the world inherently as powerful as the presidency of the United States, yet evil leaders (such as Hitler) are thought by many to be the only powerful ones.

Each leader will seek to increase the power of his position in a different way according to his leadership style and his basic philosophy. The anatomy of power is rather simple. It can come only from position itself or from the personal influence of its holder. The benign use of power is more far-reaching than is its evil use, because the beneficiaries will continue to live and prosper rather than be confined or die. In any event, by its definition, power implies the application of force against an object. Some observable change must take place in the followers before a leader can have power.

Most leaders seek to gain, increase, and hold power by building a personal organization within (and perhaps outside) their own group. Continuity of power depends on individual contribution and submission to the power drive of the leader. Control over the actions of others is one of the strongest and most insidious temptations to which man can be exposed. It far exceeds our desire for belonging or for material wealth. To be able to give an order and see it executed satisfies one of our deepest needs.

Not all leaders have in anything like equal amounts the ability to maintain their equilibrium in the use of power. This is a key measure of the stability of any man. It takes great self-control to exercise power and be able to judge one's own actions with any degree of objectivity. The behavioral sciences have made one of their better contributions in this area by continuing to insist that any person nominated for leadership must be emotionally mature. The lack of this trait will be fatal to the career of a leader in many aspects of his job, but nowhere more so than in his abuse of power. Civilization has established a norm demanding that leaders publicly deny any aspirations for power and continuously maintain a facade of humility and self-denial. This is patently ridiculous. No person will actively seek a position of leadership without assessing the power concomitant with the title. The only person in history who truly sought leadership without power was divine.

Power acts as a narcotic in two ways: The dosage must be increased regularly, and it is addictive. There is no more pitiable figure than the deposed leader shorn of his power.

The group itself is the only agency which can exert any measure of control over the power drive of its leadership. It will be the first to note the change in the behavior pattern of the leader and must be quick in its response to the symptoms. If he is curbed early, the leader will have a good chance of regaining his perspective and putting reasonable limits on his acquisition of power. Conversely, a group which follows its leader blindly will be doing him no favor. There must be both bench marks by which to measure power and controls to prevent its increasing too rapidly in the hands of the leader. That is to say, any leader will have a modicum of power as an integral part of his job, but it is the responsibility of both the leader and the group to keep a running check on the growth of his power drive.

This is another of those areas in which continuing cooperation is the only way of life if the group is to be effective and the leader successful. Power is measured by the impact it has on the people it affects. So long as the even tenor of their living is not seriously disturbed, and so long as they still have all reasonable powers of self-determinism, we cannot really say that the leader is abusing his power. The detection of the point at which power becomes malignant is extremely delicate—it is always an intuitive process and will be conditioned by the previous status of the group with respect to power. Obviously, the reference point of a prisoner in a state penitentiary and that of a small businessman are not identical. All of us see power in relationship to our own degree of independence; what is oppressive to one is perfectly tolerable to another.

The wise leader will recognize that power is a part of his job. So will his followers. The problem then becomes one of achieving a state of dynamic balance between just enough and not too much of an aura of power openly perceived by the group membership. The knowledge that enough power is there will satisfy their security needs; too much of it will directly threaten their safety and cause them to react immediately and defensively. Nor should we forget that external variables will affect the amount of power the leader will find it necessary to exert, either externally or internally.

Manipulation or Self-realization?

The ultimate effect of leadership on the group may range from pure manipulation to the highest form of self-realization. If the leader is venal or self-seeking, the members of the group can expect to be pawns in his game, and any personal gains they get will be totally coincidental. On the other hand, the leader who considers his followers to be people, with normal human expectations and aspirations, will believe that his and the group's best interests will be served by leading his followers toward the best possible goals.

Much of human history is the chronicle of "drivership" rather than leadership. Operating under a Theory X concept, leaders have always been suspicious of the motives of their followers and have not trusted either their desire to help achieve the objectives of the group or their personal attitude toward their leadership. As we have already observed, if a leader has this sort of distrust, he will probably find his people responding in a way that confirms his beliefs. The emergence of the Theory Y type of leadership, in contrast, has been relatively recent. Only in the past few years have enough leaders adopted this posture for it to be a significant factor in group dynamics.

The most vicious type of leadership imaginable is that in which the leader gives lip service to a permissive, humane philosophy while, under a hidden agenda, he manipulates his followers to his own advantage. This is the most shattering situation in which a group can find itself involved. The resulting destruction of faith will of course completely vitiate the effectiveness of the group and permanently damage the spirits of many of its members. Betrayal by the leader is the one unforgivable sin in the lexicon of the group. Happily, this sort of leader is relatively rare and, once discovered, naturally will not last.

The majority of leaders fall somewhere between the two extremes we have delineated. A man is as human as any of his followers. He will discover early in his career the methodology most comfortable to him in working with his group and will adjust his operation accordingly. But the discovery that is most valuable to any leader is that growth and development among his followers will work toward *his* advantage as well as theirs. On the modern scene, a leader is judged as much by the quality and achievements of his followers as by anything he accomplishes as an individual. To be honored for having aided in the development of other leaders is the finest tribute he can receive.

We would be less than realistic if we denied that all of us are manipulated at some time in our lives. No leader can continue his career for long without finding himself in a crisis which demands fast, definitive action involving his entire group with no chance to consult with them or consider their personal desires. Once action is taken however, the leader with any consideration for his people will communicate with them as soon as possible—certainly, before they discover for themselves what has happened. Even if it is after the fact, the word should come from the leader first. Then there will be less group reaction at having been used; rather, most people will recognize that the leader had no choice.

The leader who is committed to the involvement of his people in goal determination and participation in the resulting activities for the good of the group has the most difficult leadership job of the entire spectrum. It is also the most rewarding. Involvement with the group, not to mention participation in the identification of the group's objectives and their achievement, cannot be accomplished without growth on the part of everyone concerned. The natural fallout of this sequence is that the objectives will become cyclically more difficult and challenging. As this happens, the maturation of the group (and the individuals comprising it) will become visible to all concerned. The leader will find that his own development is at least as great as that of any of his followers in this environment.

There are those who believe that the analogy between the life of a group and that of an individual is almost perfect. They say that just as a human baby must be completely directed and controlled during its infancy, so must a group—that is, until it has attained a little maturity. These theorists claim that the job of the leader is exactly that of the parent: He must guide the new group through a period of helplessness, teaching as he goes, and make his own decision as to the time when the group is ready for more permissive and advanced guidance. It is true that many leaders new to a group will feel misgivings about operating under a 9.9 style * at first, simply because "the group isn't ready for it." There will be a period of indoctrination, of getting acquainted, before he is ready to let the group go full speed ahead on their own.

Whatever may be the leader's position on the continuum at a particular point in time, he should be committed to bringing his group along as soon as possible toward a more advanced type of operation. This is his responsibility. Nothing is more stultifying than to drift along for a period of years in a group which shows no sign of growth. Members become bored, lazy, and apathetic. Group productivity suffers; group goals are missed; quality deteriorates—the entire operation decays, in short, and the death of the group

---

* A 9.9 style is participative and permissive as opposed to a dictatorial and directive 9.1 style.

can only be a matter of time. Unless the leader takes his responsibility for development seriously, the group is doomed.

The attitude of the leader toward his people is the most critical factor in his success or failure. It is never possible for him to hide his true opinion of his followers for long. And, once they know what it is, they will respond in kind.

Inverted Leadership

When part or all of a leader's authority has been usurped by group members, the group has inverted leadership. In a clean case of documented delegation, the leader loses none of his authority or prestige: Everyone understands that the work must be divided into manageable pieces. But, when the position and status of the leader are chipped away by power drives from below, everyone suffers. The first symptom is ordinarily loss of group effectiveness. More wheel spinning occurs, objectives are dimmed and lost sight of, and the work output is diminished. The second sign is a lessening of the prestige of the leader within the group. His ability to control weakens progressively, with a shifting of the power base toward the challenger. Group morale suffers, even if the leader has been unpopular as well as weak. Most people are made uncomfortable by any attack on recognized authority. The fact that the raider or commando group responsible for the move takes away part of the power does not always mean that it will assume that power. A power vacuum can result, with no one in the driver's seat, that will intensify ineffectiveness and lower morale. The ensuing struggle for the leader's spot can be the death of the group.

Inverted leadership does not always signify weak leadership, especially in large groups. A communications block at a critical point can produce a situation favorable toward a power takeover. The ambitious underling may seize this opportunity and become well entrenched in his new function before the real leader knows what is going on. This is not an excuse; it is simply an explanation.

Leadership may be inverted as the result of a conspiracy among a few key members of the group. This conspiracy can remain hidden until the inversion is accomplished. The choice of the leader here is simple: He can either abdicate or carry on an open and direct conflict with the raiders. If he abdicates, it may be possible for him to hold his nominal position indefinitely, but his days as a leader are over. If he chooses to fight, there are three possibilities. The raiders may win and become titular as well as de facto leaders; the leader may win and restore the original configuration of the group; or the group may die.

In those cases where inversion of leadership is the result of perceived weakness in the leader, the situation is much stickier. This is revolution in its clearest sense, and risk to the conspirators is at its highest. Involvement in the takeover will reduce productive work to the point where group goals will certainly not be realized. Interpersonal relationships will be severely strained, if not irrevocably ruined. The coup, even if successful, will find the group disorganized. Achieving a semblance of order out of this chaos will be a Herculean task.

The lesson for the leader is plain. He who maintains clean and open channels for the gathering of information will be much harder to surprise by an attempted takeover. Also, delegation of authority must be completely understood by every member of the group, both as to the amount and as to the recipient. And, finally, good organization within the group is immunization against inversion.

Inverted leadership is found in both formal and semi-formal groups. It is rare in informal groups, since leadership is usually rotated. Where specialists are to be found in each of the various phases of leadership, there is little chance for its inversion.

Inverted leadership will have a negative effect outside as well as inside the group. Relationships with other groups, either formal or informal, will be strained or completely broken because, as a result of the intense concentration on internal difficulties, it becomes impossible to maintain normal outside activities.

Leadership inversion is a *symptom* rather than a disease. It will be attempted when there is little faith in the titular leader, when one person or a small group feels it has a better than even chance of taking over, or when major aspects of the job are not being properly handled by the present leader. And this job of leadership will continue to become more intricate and demanding every day. Increasing social complexity is reflected directly in the life of every group, even our informal friendship groups. Maintaining friendships is getting harder and harder logistically. A group of friends spread over one of our modern cities finds it extremely difficult just to get together; deteriorating surface transportation and the terrors of freeway driving militate against free and easy social access. We are fast reverting to the days of our grandparents, who had to plan for weeks before "making a trip to town."

Many factors, in fact, are adding to the difficulties of our group living, and all of these can contribute to the inversion of leadership in a group. Actual inversion is not too commonly found; what is significant is that its frequency is on the upswing. The capable leader will keep this in mind and practice those preventive therapies which will lower the chances for a successful raid on his position.

Responsibilities of Leadership

Each year, thousands of men and women refuse proffered positions of leadership because "they don't want to accept the extra responsibility." Just what is meant by this statement? Is it true that the leader has a heavier burden than any of his members? The generic answer to these questions is that the leader has really only one responsibility: to get *the best for the most.*

This definition naturally covers hundreds of splinter responsibilities. The one thing the successful leader *must* do is condition himself to weigh the effect of any projected action on the entire group. This is why a leader's decision and action may appear to be (or actually may be) harmful to one or more individuals. For example, in the business world reduction of the workforce is always painful to the group. In making his choice as to who stays and who goes, the leader must be able to show that those who remain have greater potential for the good of the group than those who are released. This is not to belittle the often tragic effects on those separated. Also, we should note the use of the word "potential." The leader must make a considered value judgment upon the *future worth* of every member of the group in a surplus situation. It is for this reason that we so often see the compounded tragedy in which the older members of a group are released, many times at an age when it will be terribly difficult for them to find a place elsewhere. The good leader, irrespective of his emotional involvement, owes it to the group to make these judgments about the value of individuals in a completely objective manner. Anything less is an abdication of his responsibility to get the best for the most.

This same mental set must be carried by the leader into his evaluation of every leadership situation. The great labor leader, for example, is the one who can resist the temptation to accede to a tempting offer from management which, in his considered judgment, is not in the best interests of his union's members. He may even run the risk of losing popularity among his followers by pursuing what justly he feels to be the best course of action. In this case, he has the further duty to communicate to his membership fully the reasons for his actions and to convince them that he does truly have their best interests at heart. This he must do, not for his personal protection, but to prevent a loss of cohesiveness and morale within the group.

In the informal group, this sort of decision may be quite blurred, since the members probably have little interest in looking downstream for more than a few days or a few weeks ahead. Their primary concern is with the here and now. It is predictable that they will even resist leadership which attempts to provide for their future welfare as against the advantage of the immediate moment. This neo-hedonism, which has become a characteristic of a large part of our group living, is directly traceable to the gradual inculcation of a socialistic philosophy upon the American public. If the underachiever is, in effect, to be rewarded almost as well as the average member of the group, what value lies in planning for the future or in self-denial on the present scene? It remains the evident responsibility of the leader to fight this tendency. The best-for-the-most theory demands it of him.

There is one aspect of leadership responsibility which is overlooked by many dedicated leaders—the duty they owe to themselves. No leader who sacrifices his own health or well-being is discharging his duty to his people. If he has any value as a leader, it will be enhanced as he gains in experience and wisdom. He will not be available to the group if he disregards his own health. This is the hardest lesson the leader has to learn. After all, it is fun to play the martyr just a bit.

Simply because the leader's overriding duty is to the group as a whole, it does not follow that he is not responsible for the individual member. On the contrary, anything which he can do to maximize the growth and development of a member of his group is clearly a continuing part of his job. It is only when the individual and his interests come into conflict with the group that the former must be sacrificed.

These cases are often complex and difficult. The leader, because he is as human as any of his followers, will in the long run be making his decision without all the facts; and he will have only his own intuition to guide him in weighting the facts he does have. His greatest temptation will be to succumb to the fallacy of overrating the importance of this particular person to the group. If this happens, his decision will inevitably be muddy and questionable.

All this has been intended to imply that the critical element in leadership responsibility is focused in the decision-making aspect of his job. This is the plain truth. The forging of decisions makes the job of the leader different from that of the follower. Decision making generates the instability and risk of the leader's position and contributes the greater part of his uncertainties and anxiety. Thus we have come back full circle to the reason why many people not only do not seek but will refuse a position of leadership if one is offered to them. Here is another example of the delicate balance of nature. If everyone were equally willing to accept the onus of leadership, life would then be filled with even more hatred, conflict, and tragedy than exists today. We have trouble enough in this life without adding to the contents of Pandora's box.

* * *

This chapter has been conceived as a stimulant and catalyst to thought, rather than an exhaustive survey of the subject of leadership. The literature on leadership is voluminous, and the interested reader can explore it at his leisure.

Principally, the difference between the leader and the rest of the membership, with one exception, is a matter of degree rather than character. The exception is the quality of charisma. We say that a leader is charismatic when he is possessed of an aura which will activate large numbers of people to follow him without any conscious analysis of the reason for doing so. It is unfortunate that evil leaders as well as good have possessed charisma.

There is no definitive list of traits which must be possessed by a person aspiring to leadership. The whole of a leader's duty can be expressed in the concept of "the best for the most." In looking for the best for the most, the leader is involved in the kinds of decision making that his followers never meet. This responsibility and all the possible danger and unpopularity that go with it make the majority of people unwilling to accept leadership.

The position of the leader has never been more difficult and will not get any easier in the future, thanks to a technology which becomes more complex by the day and a group of followers which is better educated, better trained, and more sophisticated. Groups are more demanding and more critical of their leadership than ever before, and rightly so.

Chapter 8

Followership

*T*HERE are many more followers than leaders in man's social structure—which is as it should be. Moreover, every leader is a follower in other groups. There are certain characteristics and behavior patterns which will help us to be better followers and to have more successful group memberships. The single trait that is most important to our living with others is a high degree of sensitivity concerning our impact on them. Each person has his own method for getting feedback from his peers, and sensitivity, as such, is an indication of our degree of maturity. There are additional, less fully understood attributes of followership, and it is to these that we shall devote our attention in this chapter.

Security Drive

Our never-ending search for security is one of our stronger motivators; it begins with our first breath and ends with our last. Several of our major decisions are modulated by security considerations; we use the safety factor of a given situation as a determinant of whether to get involved or remain aloof.

Common security drives are the cause for more group formations than almost any other. We seek security from hunger, pain, outside threat, air pollution—the list could go on indefinitely. Many of our reflex actions are geared to increase our security, and our survival often depends upon their proper functioning.

Our security drive also makes us content in most situations to be a follower rather than to seek leadership. With a few notable exceptions, we are more comfortable when we can look to another, stronger person as a bulwark against disaster. As has already been pointed out, we like to see the leader as a father image, with all the protective might with which that concept is endowed.

Lest there be any misunderstanding, a strong security drive in no way indicates that its possessor is necessarily a coward. Some of the fiercest fighting in the world is done by those who are seeking security from an enemy in the only way they think is possible. Of course, devout cowards may also fight fiercely if they find their security threatened.

Some behavioral group reactions have their origin in the security drive of the group's membership. Isolation of a deviant is a good example. The miscreant is either sealed off or amputated, depending upon the severity of the danger he represents to group security. Trusted leadership is maintained over long periods of time because the group feels secure under its aegis. Group norms, rules, and regulations are established to increase safety.

Security drive is often a stimulant to creativity. We become inventive under the pressure of threats; we discover and implement new ways of avoiding them. The new policy or procedure may be the group's lightning rod against an approaching storm low on the horizon.

Security drive is the reason for the follower's avoidance of the risks of leadership. He calculates the odds and finds himself unwilling to expose himself for the sake of rewards which he considers not worth the danger to his safety. This is a more "normal" reaction than that of the person who does seek leadership. Many of those judged by their peers to have the qualities of good leadership will refuse to accept the role when it is offered them. Their excuses will cover the whole spectrum; essentially, all boil down to a reaction engendered by their security drive.

Much of the behavior triggered by our security drive is subconscious. We are not aware of the motivation underlying the gyrations we go through to avoid a perceived threat. The threat itself may not be consciously verbalized as such. Man has become quite adept at fooling himself, even if his actions are transparent to the observer. Our self-esteem demands that we not acknowledge all our actions as security-motivated. The suppression of motivation can occur in persons generally adjudged as quite mature. This is simply another method of securing mental security—peace of mind!

On the overt side, our planning exercises are strongly flavored by security considerations. We attempt repeatedly to build safety factors into the projected actions of all kinds of groups. The weightiest debates of boards of directors concern the amount of "risk capital" to be allocated to new ventures. The great fortunes and the most profitable enterprises are the result of good luck in the use of risk capital, but most businessmen and the majority of companies are content to be smaller and less wealthy. Better the certain beans and bacon than the possible filet mignon and caviar.

Conditioned as we are from birth by our security drives, the wonder is that we ever make any progress at all. Progress, however, is the result of another common human trait:

boredom. There comes a time (or several times) in every person's life when he rebels against the oppressive grayness which gathers about a perfectly secure course. Unless he kicks over the traces and takes a chance, he feels degraded and less than a man. There are equal chances of success and failure in these situations; the flip of the coin will determine whether we go on to glory or land in the mud.

During our day-to-day operations, the security drive common to all of us acts as the governor does on a motor: It prevents excesses and conserves our strength for constructive activities. It also prevents the great majority of men from seeking or accepting the position of leadership. It makes us better followers.

"Inner Directed" versus "Outer Directed"

Some psychologists hold that there are two kinds of people so far as the way they receive their direction is concerned: "inner directed" and "outer directed." The inner-directed man holds to standards and bench marks of behavior which originate within himself. Intrinsically, he accepts leadership from others only after making value judgments as to its correctness and after having compared what is asked of him to what he would decide to do in the same situation. Strong leaders, according to this belief, are inner directed.

If we accept this tenet, we must recognize some essential differences between this person and others about him. For one thing, his self-confidence level is high. He does not often feel the necessity of checking his thinking with others. It does not even occur to him to do so. The inner-directed man will have small patience with vacillation or indecision in others. Whenever he sees signs of it, he will attempt to impose his thinking on them, since he abhors the vacuum that results when a decision is needed and none is made. The fact that he often stands alone because of this lack of patience causes him no concern. He satisfies his need for group activity by bending the group toward his way of thinking. Responsibility per se holds no terrors for him; he will more likely look upon it as a challenge to his strength, and he will enjoy the conflict concomitant with the role of the leader.

Because he is strong-willed and rather thick-skinned where he himself is concerned does *not* mean that the inner-directed man cannot be sensitive to his impact on others. In fact, his general alertness will be high, since he is used to being a stormy petrel at the center of a conflict situation. As a result, the inner-directed man may be well aware of how he is affecting others *yet still continue his course of action*. The desired objective is more important to him than the feelings of his peers. His self-assurance is great enough to support him.

Predictably, when inner-directed men come in contact with each other, an abrasive contest of wills may be precipitated as soon as the point of decision making is reached. This clash will probably not be ducked by either person in his attempt to gain leadership. Such a struggle for ascendancy will have a more traumatic effect on the rest of the group's membership than it will on the antagonists. Followers always feel insecure and threatened when they are uncertain as to who is in the driver's seat.

In the total population, the proportion of inner-directed individuals will be small, because, as we have seen, there are always more people who are content to follow than there are people who are desirous of control. To further complicate matters, an individual may be inner directed in some aspects of his life, and be quite content to accept direction in others. What we are saying is that, on the basis of these parameters, there are few pure types. Almost all of us are psychological mixtures—a fact that accounts for the uniqueness of the individual.

Outer-directed people react quite differently from inner-directed people. First of all, they avoid whenever possible the making of an important decision. They are upset at the very thought and much prefer to delegate the responsibility to another person. This is why many will follow a leader whom they fear or dislike rather than strike out for themselves.

It does not inevitably follow that outer-directed persons will be docile. Although they avoid leadership or decision making themselves, they will reserve the right to criticize their leadership harshly. They are unaware of the inconsistency of their position and will be full of hurt surprise when confronted with it by others.

We can infer that, in general, outer-directed people will have less self-confidence than their opposites who are inner-directed. They will find it difficult to derive internal reassurance as to the correctness of their position. This constant feeling of uncertainty reinforces their tendency to rely on others for decisions and direction. It also increases their gregariousness and tendency toward group formation for mutual protection. The power of numbers is vastly intriguing to outer-directed people, and they put unswerving trust into its efficacy.

It is interesting to note that creativity does not seem to have much correlation with inner- or outer-directedness. There are examples of both highly creative leaders and highly creative people who have never sought leadership and would be disturbed if it were thrust upon them. The ability to combine the old in new ways, to see new relationships, or to penetrate the unknown is like mathematical ability—it is where you find it.

Outer-directed persons are less demanding of life in general than are their opposite numbers. They are willing to exchange significant rewards for the basic security that comes from trusting their fate to others.

Interestingly, too, our complex society is now evolving a class which lies outside the leader-follower relationship—that of the individual contributor. He is not burdened with the duties of leadership, because he has no followers. His specialty may be so esoteric that, in effect, there is no one to lead him. As a loner, he is free of the normal constraints of the formal group and will be judged by the effectiveness of his contribution as it relates to the achievement of the group's goals. This judgment must be deferred for long periods of time, until his effectiveness can be put into perspective retroactively and historically.

However, the majority of people still are categorized as either inner-directed or outer-directed, with more of us falling into the latter than into the former group. Followership is essentially the job of the outer directed.

Subleadership: The File Closure

Just as there is a full spectrum of leadership behavior ranging from the "great" leader with charisma all the way to the nominal leader whose leadership has been inverted, so are there various levels of followership. A minute percentage of a group is willing to follow on blind faith, never questioning its leadership. The majority of followers follow, but they do so with some degree of considered judgment. Another small percentage of followers assume a position of quasi-leadership or what, perhaps, might better be called "subleadership." They are willing to accept a small amount of leadership responsibility and execute some of the routine duties of the group leader. They occupy the same position that the platoon sergeant has in the army company. Their principal function is to relay directives and monitor the group's compliance. Every group of any size needs one or more subleaders, since the leader cannot personally check on all the details. He will be too involved with planning the action "downstream" to limit his daily time severely by assuring himself from personal observation that everything is on schedule.

The subleader will have a greater sense of group responsibility than most of his peers. His conceptualization of the group's total job will be more complete than average. And—not the least important—he will be willing to assume a load greater than the usual front-line soldier. Ordinarily, subleadership duties are over and above regular performance as a member of the group. Some industrial organizations recognize this by creating a "lead" job within the structure. The holder of such a job leads and counsels the rest of the workers and is responsible for production and quality, but nowhere in his job description will there be found any mention of authority. His position and his status with the rest of the group depend directly upon his own abilities and the way he relates to his peers. Another important aspect of his assignment is his responsibility for reporting to the group leadership any unusual events, either good or bad. This is functionally management by exception in its purest form.

The subleader's personal position is schizoid. He is clearly somewhat more than a "regular" member of the group, yet he is not recognized as a full-fledged member of the leadership hierarchy. His adjustment to this situation will determine his effectiveness. In most cases, he will be an isolate in his normal group relationships, yet he will not be accepted on a full and equal basis by the group's true leaders. The ability to prevent all this from being traumatic is essential to the subleader. Fortunately, he may find a stabilizing influence in the realization that he is contributing more than his fair share to group goal achievement. He will get his reward in the satisfaction of ego and self-actualization needs.

The subleader will need sharp and incisive judgmental ability as well. Since he operates on the front line, where the action is, he will be involved in decision making of such urgency that there will be no chance to check with absent leaders. With no real authority to do so, he will find it necessary to make the "go" and "no go" judgments of the day's activity. The rest of the members will turn to him here as naturally as they would to their nominal leader; all that is necessary for them is not to have to make an action decision. The subleader will find himself with full responsibility for errors in judgment but with little credit—at least, *public* credit—for his successful decisions. Of course, his position in this respect is no different from that of the regular leader.

With these facts in mind, it is not surprising that the subleader's position is usually considered a training ground for actual leadership. In the formal work group, a manager can test several things about a management candidate by making him "lead man." He can determine whether the candidate is ready for a modicum of responsibility and whether he is able to enlarge his sphere of activity and, at the same time, continue to function in his old job. Many things can be learned about his commitment, dedication, and loyalty. His judgmental ability will be put to frequent and repeated testing. There will be a chance to see how effectively he communicates, both up and down the line.

Any trouble with interpersonal relationships will be magnified and thrown open to inspection.

From the other side, the man will have a chance to get the feel of how a manager operates without committing his entire future. If he decides that leadership is not for him, he can retreat to his old job as a line worker without having prejudiced his future. The subleader's job is an ideal time to form and crystallize a personal philosophy of leadership and try on for size different styles of leadership. A man can increase his personal sensitivity without jeopardizing a formal job and become secure in his knowledge of policy and procedure. The entire position is exploratory, educational, and formative.

It should not be inferred that only the formal group needs the subleader. Semiformal and even informal groups can use one or more subleaders, whose contributions to ease of administration make them valuable in most kinds of group operations. Benefits will accrue to group leadership, to the individuals chosen, and to the group members in general.

The Maintenance Needs

Professor Herzberg, in his two-factor theory, accounted for a direct need of all followers by postulating maintenance needs. The follower is kept busy by—sometimes almost buried under—the pressures of countless details in his daily living. He may or may not find real motivation in the kind of job he has or in the other group activities in which he participates. Therefore, it becomes quite important that some of his surroundings be so structured as to bring him to a zero state, a state in which he is not actively unhappy in his surroundings.

Most followers spend a great part of their conscious lifetime in a frantic, frenetic chase for money. This does not motivate them to do better in their group work. Their total concern is to get enough money to pay essential bills and provide a short list of comforts. The herd instinct naturally takes over among followers in money considerations. Group leaders such as union officials find it an easy job to get their membership solidly behind them in economic bargaining. Followers believe that the only way to make gains in this area is to act in concert. It is difficult to convince them that their formal group leaders will pay attention to individual excellence in performance.

The same thing can be said about working conditions. If work areas are dingy, ill-lighted, or ill-ventilated, it seldom occurs to an individual follower to go directly to his supervisor with suggestions for the alleviation of these discomforts. His reflexive reaction is to huddle with his group and make an issue—usually presented in a hostile way—of the matter. He can become obsessed with working conditions to the point where his performance will suffer badly.

Maintenance needs can cause a schizoid leadership relation in the formal group. Since followers do react as a group to problems with working conditions, and since they expect their formal leaders to resist correcting them because of the expense involved, they instinctively turn to the semiformal leadership of the union to carry the brunt of the contest for them. This is, in fact, the theoretical basis for the use of collective bargaining. It is interesting to observe the reaction of followers when working conditions are bettered by the formal leadership. Their acceptance of the change is gracious but completely bland. They might as well verbalize it by saying, "It's about time!" Formal group leaders should understand that they are caught in a difficult position with respect to working conditions. A fine balance must be maintained between doing what is reasonable and possible and allowing the situation to deteriorate to the point where the group membership rebels. For example, the location of a parking area on grossly expensive land in the center of a large manufacturing complex may be more than justified if the alternative is to relegate employees' cars to its fringes, leaving them with a long, arduous walk in all kinds of weather to get to the work area. The resultant disgruntlement, in this latter case, could have a serious effect on productivity and costs.

Another of the maintenance factors constantly in view in any kind of group is supervision—or leadership. The leader who is unaware of the impact of his leadership style on his followers is unnecessarily handicapping himself. We have mentioned before how a hardheaded adoption of a single style of leadership can militate against success. The group situation is far too fluid, in both surroundings and membership, for a style to be set in concrete. Followers, especially in our modern economy, have more autonomy in the matter of group selection than they did a generation ago. If they don't like it where they are, they can go—and they often do. Voluntary attrition in American industry as a result of unmet maintenance needs costs uncounted millions of dollars annually.

Hand in hand with supervision as a maintenance factor go company policy and procedures. In a sense, company policy is only an extension of the immediate supervisor's attitude, for he will normally reflect a clear image of what *his* management propounds. The extent to which top management can be blind to the feelings of the man on the floor is unbelievable. This is particularly true when management moves in and takes away, or denigrates, privileges enjoyed for a time in the past. This action can only be regarded by followers as punitive, no matter how much it may be backed by cold, irrefutable logic. Followers have found over the years that cold logic is neither palatable nor nourishing, especially when it concerns economics.

It is easy to see how followers can become so involved with maintenance factors that they have little time to become motivated by the work itself or by the prospect of recognition, achievement, or advancement.

We are, however, in danger of overlooking the most important aspect of maintenance factors. That is, *followers become intensely involved with them, whereas leaders have a strong tendency to give them scant consideration.* This is one of the more significant differences between the two kinds of group members. If the leader becomes deeply engrossed in his salary history, it is for quite a different reason than that of the follower. The leader uses his salary history as a criterion of his hierarchical progression, but the follower still equates it directly with the satisfaction of his physiological and safety needs.

All of us have maintenance needs. The extent to which we are involved with them is a function of our leadership or followership potential. The man who is so engrossed in the fascination of his work that he loses track of time on the job will be more likely to succeed as a leader than the one who fidgets for a half-hour before the quitting whistle blows. But, once again, in our society followership may quite properly be a matter of personal choice.

Identification with the Product

The good follower will find it necessary to identify with the product he makes. This is perfectly true in all three kinds of groups but, above all, in the formal work group. Centuries ago, pride in fine craftsmanship led to the establishment of the guilds, which in turn set rigid standards for quality of product. Artisans could ply their trade only after having received the cachet of their guild. Modern industrial methods of mass production have undermined the concept of pride in workmanship until millions of workers have never felt the thrill of accomplishment to be had from a fine piece of work they can claim as *theirs*.

Alert leadership must recognize a particular responsibility in this area. There are ways of getting a workman to identify with the product by taking pride in his contribution to the total effort. If he can be made to realize that dereliction on his part will jeopardize the product, his own pride will rise to the occasion and evoke a better effort from him.

As a case in point, a group in an aluminum rod, bar, and wire plant produced at intervals in its production schedule an alloy which then was used to make a tiny part for jet engines. This part, of course, was never seen by either the crew or the passengers of any plane, yet heat failure from incorrect alloying of the metal could cause failure of the part—and thus failure of the jet engine and possible tragedy for the entire plane. The plant manager, when making a cross-country flight, began to think about this situation. When he returned, he huddled with his communications man. As a result, a series of pictures and displays was set up at the plant gatehouse. Considerable interest was aroused among the employees, especially in the crew concerned with the alloy. Of their own volition, they tightened quality standards to the point where the alloy began to come out significantly better than specifications required. Here was a perfect example of *group* identification with a product which led to observably improved performance.

Naturally, it is not always this easy to improve followership performance through product identification. More often, it is an individual rather than a group problem and must be attacked as such. Results will be slower when leadership must spread its efforts individually over a crew. Improvement, if any, will be sporadic.

Another potent force in modern society militates against pride in workmanship—the planned obsolescence carefully engineered into many products to insure they will not last too long. Industry is maintained and grows through repeat sales. If a product is excellently made and lasts too long, the delicate balance of an expanding economy is in danger. (If all American cars were Bentleys or Rolls Royces, every family would buy only one automobile per generation.) The effect of quality on the worker is immediate and lasting. If he is a party to the manufacture of a product that is less than excellent, this will be reflected in his attitude toward his work. Slipshod products are made by shoddy workmen.

However, it should not be inferred that every follower must be engaged in cutting a diamond or manufacturing an exquisite watch in order to have pride in workmanship and identify with his product. He will recognize the justice and logic of a leader's call to cooperate in the production of a quality product within a vast range of prices and materials. In a furniture factory, for example, a carpenter may work in rotation on pine, fir, cherry, walnut, or teak. He will automatically adjust his concept of product quality according to the nature of his materials. Furniture made to the same patterns in these different materials can be quite satisfying to the workman whose standards are high, even though their intrinsic value will vary widely.

Identification with product makes a better follower because it tends to reinforce and strengthen his own self-image. All of us enjoy being connected in the minds of others with an object worthy of admiration and desirable as a possession. This sort of feeling is analogous to the vicarious pride we take in the comeliness or achievements of our children. Thus the bolstering of the follower's ego is firmest and most enduring when it is associated directly with the objectives of the organization, and these are viable only when they are of high quality.

To take another case in point, a large airplane manufacturer introduced a new, medium-range transport jet which almost immediately captured an entire new market. For a period of two years, its performance record was flawless. Then came the first crash of the model. Conversation among workmen in the plant was wholly concerned with, "What happened to *our* plane?" The fact that it had been sold to a specific airline customer was irrelevant. It was *their* product and would remain so throughout their lives.

Product identification to this degree can only result from pride in workmanship and excellence of followership. We must revert again to the natural conclusion: Good followership will be present in a majority of workmen only where there is good leadership. The greater part of the leader's continuing concern will be to aid and abet the inculcation of this pride of workmanship in every member of the crew. Its presence will also be shown in heightened morale and esprit de corps.

The Front-Line Soldier

Many people remain followers all their lives because they want to be where the action is. Generals die in bed; it is the front-line private who has all the fun. To the front-line soldier personality, the challenge in life lies in coming to grips with the physical part of the job—he could care less who gives the orders, makes the plans, or devises objectives for the group.

This sort of person is invaluable, because he and his fellows carry on the real work of the group, make its product, and ultimately insure the survival of the enterprise. It does not follow necessarily that his endowments are any less than his leader's. He may show much inventiveness in meeting the day-to-day problems on the line which never reach the attention of the leader. His judgment is often superb in choosing the proper work method. He may have interpersonal skills of the highest order, and his ability to predict the actions of others may account for his personal success in getting the job done with a minimum of friction.

The individual who is a front-line soldier by choice is sometimes a trial to his leader in that he is quite insistent on knowing the reasons for the directions he receives. He has his own methods and shortcuts; an impending change is going to need his consent before he will install it without a fight. He has been conditioned to react with suspicion to the communications of a group which he thinks of as "nondoers"—his leaders and any staff people with whom he does business. He has tunnel vision to the extent that he believes the real world is made up of himself and those like him.

We have been describing a person who may not really seem to be a follower. This is not so. He does follow—most of the time, willingly. Company policy in the abstract he could not care less about; but at his level, and that of his immediate leader, he is a pragmatist of the first order. He acknowledges the fact that there must be someone who directs the group. His real concern is, first, to evade being put into that position and, second, to live as peacefully as he can with his leaders so that his joyous battle with the physical can be pursued in relative calm.

Leadership of the front-line soldier is not an easy job.

Because he retains his own values as paramount and is stubborn about being allowed to attack his job largely in his own way, he is often less than an admirable teamworker. Not that he is hostile or antisocial; rather, he is absorbed in his little world and its challenge so deeply he has trouble letting others in on the fun.

The leader's job with the front-line soldier—often a long one—is to convince him that others do have his best interests at heart and are vitally concerned with seeing him do his job in the easiest, quickest way. If this message gets through to him, he is all ears—quite receptive to suggestions. The idea of helping others is novel to him because, all his life, he has concentrated so single-mindedly on his own affairs that it has not occurred to him that others might have time to offer him constructive help.

In most aspects of his job, the front-line soldier is steady and dependable. Just because he gets so much fun from meeting a challenge and beating it down, he is seldom absent from the job, and he is not inclined to be a clockwatcher. In his own odd way, he is doggedly loyal to the leadership and the organization which furnish the continuing opportunity for his working pleasure. He seldom verbalizes this loyalty and would be embarrassed if forced to do so, but it is there. Here is the man who unobtrusively becomes the "old employee." His entire working lifetime is often spent on one job, unless he is displaced by conditions not under his control.

Thoughtful business leaders are at last coming nearer to realizing the value of this kind of group member. The solidity he gives to the organization, the contributions he makes to steady production and manageable costs are not found on every bush.

From the standpoint of motivation, the front-line soldier is operating on the ego and self-actualization levels as much as—or more than—any other person. The fact that he can see the physical results of his efforts quickly and often is strongly reinforcing to his self-image. He thinks of himself, rightly, as a "doer." He is the man who, as he matures, develops rigidly high standards—for himself—and lives by them religiously. He will actively resent any attempt by others to sacrifice quality in the interests of production or cost savings. His is a home-grown attribute that group leadership labors mightily, and often in vain, to develop in others less dedicated.

Strong bonds grow between splinter groups of front-line soldiers in large groups. These informal groups have a steadying effect on the rest of the membership. Their status is usually high among their peers. Even if others do not always emulate their actions, they have respect for good workmanship and for integrity as they find it.

It is obvious that there are many first-line soldiers, as we have described the type here. This country could never have grown in strength and power without the backbone and sinew supplied by these people. They have made American industry preeminent throughout the world on a continuing basis.

It should not be imagined that this breed will disappear with the "old" brand of American industry. The "new" technology has just as much need for them as it ever did. His training will be longer; his expertise will be greater; he will be more sophisticated; but the same characteristics he displayed in a less complicated business venture will have their usefulness—even at premium rates—in our brave new world of the future. His personal rewards will be more substantial, because he must come to grips with the demand for combined hand- and brainwork of a sort he has never dreamed of before. Everyone will benefit from his being there.

The Impersonal Observer

We have mentioned the individual contributor, and seen how he fits with difficulty into the pattern of followership. There is, however, another person who likewise is atypical to the pattern. This is the one who spends his lifetime in fascination with the rest of mankind. He is absorbed in their activities, their motivations, their interactions—so absorbed that he neglects to get himself into the picture to any great depth. This man is the impersonal observer. He records, documents, comments, and generalizes, but he himself is not committed or involved to the point of being either a typical leader or a typical follower.

In fact, the impersonal observer can never be a leader because he refuses to put himself sufficiently into the arena. He is not the best of followers because his commitment and ego involvement are not sufficient to produce beyond the barest of minimal standards. He has been hard put, throughout his life, to maintain his place in the pecking order, since others sense his lack of deep involvement in "their" struggle.

This group historian must maintain detachment and objectivity if he is going to report correctly what is going on about him. He constantly weighs, evaluates, and balances, keeping the record in meticulous detail. He is tolerated by his peers, since they are human enough to like to see their actions recorded and immortalized. His leadership distrusts him, for he is an enigma and doesn't "fit in the pattern." Occasionally, both leaders and peers will turn on him, and he takes his lumps in more than average severity in loss of economic progress and even rejection or expulsion from the group. This is especially true when there is trouble. The man who records the ills of the group is a handy target to blame for those very troubles. If a scapegoat must be found, the impersonal observer is a natural candidate, since he refuses to let the rest of the group ignore what they have done.

The psychology of the observer is interesting. He is not a recluse, for, if he were, he could never uncover the data which are the lifeblood of his activity. He does interact. But his contacts are to an extent sterile, since they do not result in a direct contribution to the group's achievement of its goals. They are purely for the sake of reportage, and all concerned know this. The observer's personal feelings about others' troubles can be even deeper than those of the group members who are totally self- or group-centered. He will recoil from taking directive action, since to do so would be to affect the "natural" outcome. His sensitivity to all sorts of cues, verbal or nonverbal, is higher than average; he has a "nose for news" of radar intensity. His memory is the first of the data banks, and it is still the best. A fact, once stored there, can be recalled at any given moment and fitted into the overall picture. Above everything else, the sense with which he fits the bits and pieces together is impeccable. He constantly searches for the *meaning* of facts and the way that they mesh.

This man makes an invaluable, though seldom recognized, contribution to the life of the group, although he may even be punished for having made his inputs. Whether the rest of the members like it or not, and whether the leader may be disturbed beyond his ability to tolerate it, all know at the base of their consciousness that a historical record of a group's life and activity is a *sine qua non*. To maintain our perspective, we must know where we have been before we plan where we intend to go.

The impersonal observer sometimes does as much good for individuals as the leader. The man who is interested in his own personal growth and development will make constant use of the historian's fund of facts to chart his own path and development. This resource is his for the asking.

The group life of the impersonal observer is hazardous in the extreme. He must be aware that he is constantly expendable, *as an individual*, because his personal contribution to the achievement of group goals is less than average. He cannot be considered a leadership reserve, since his motivation and line of action are neither goal- nor people-oriented.

If we are to be pragmatic, however, we should begin to integrate an impersonal observer into the life of every group. His peculiar contribution will become increasingly more important as our social living continues to become more complex. In a sense, he is staff to the group in the same sense as a physician or a minister. Like those two public servants, he should be tolerated and supported in times of plenty (or good health) and turned to when things get tough for an evaluative comparison.

From the standpoint of group process, the impersonal observer is a control center. His sensitivity, feedback, and evaluation can provide balance when the rest of the membership cannot be trusted to have any degree of objectivity. We know how hard it is to maintain balance when our total effort is required just to get the job done from day to day. If we can turn to a member of the group who keeps himself *just a little* out of the mainstream for the purpose of comparative judgment, we have an added strength for our collaborative efforts. We are exactly like the little boy who sails into a fight with one of his companions, secure in the knowledge that he can go back home and receive solace for his wounds and moral support for the mistakes he has made.

In short, the group position of the impersonal observer is as unique as that of the subleader. Both make a different kind of contribution to the welfare of the group; both have their peculiar punishments and rewards.

The Mosaic Decad

The area of followership has been neglected in the literature, while the subject of leadership has been beaten half to death. We recognize intellectually that there are many more followers than leaders, but we seldom attach any quantification to the relationship. If we were to look for it, we could find documentation in some quite respectable sources of the proper numbers relationship. One of the earliest instances in our cultural heritage was the Mosaic decad. In his leadership, Moses established the group of eleven—the leader and ten followers. We have little evidence as to whether this arrangement was intuitive or the product of pragmatic observation. At any rate, in the paramilitary organization of the Hebrews under his aegis, this was the unit structure.

Some of the reasons for the decad are obvious. Ten people can be kept track of visually by a leader over the average area of their operation. Reportage can be reasonably quick, with no fatal waiting in line until the serious situation has become a crash emergency. Delegation can be fractionated to this extent practicable in almost any situation, yet the leader can have an overview of his sphere of responsibility without unduly stretching his lines. Linkage with peers at the first level of leadership will integrate a viable group of groups with mobility and flexibility. Strategy can be translated into tactics with a minimum of friction and time loss.

Historically, the Mosaic decad has been repeatedly adopted by other cultures and other leaders. The Romans' centurion, or leader of 100 men, actually had ten groups under his command and was recognized as the key military figure in the growth of their empire.

In terms of group dynamics, a group of ten followers is ordinarily comfortable and flexible. Interpersonal relationships are not compounded by sheer numbers, and familiarity and friendship can be developed with little strain. Any one member can communicate with any other quickly; the transmission of directives at either first or second hand is subject to a minimum of attrition. Anyone inclined to a superstitious interpretation of this arrangement could pursue it further to the decimalization of our monetary systems and the oncoming prevalence of the metric system of weights and measures. Assuredly, proliferation of a numerical arrangement does not insure its correctness; retrospectively, however, it has proved to be functional.

After having gone to some trouble to establish the historical predominance of the decad over several millennia, we shall now attempt to establish the fact that it will cease to be effective in the near future. When technology becomes so complex that the leader has no possibility of being expert in all its compartments, he will have to reduce his span of control. There must be a reasonable communication of expertise between membership and leader. If the leader is responsible for decision making, he must have a basis for those decisions founded in technical knowledge of the subject matter. If it were possible to delegate all the decisions to subordinates, there would be little reason for the existence of a leader. The follower must respect his leader, and that respect will be rooted in large measure in his reading of the leader's technical competence. He is convinced of his right to turn to supervision for answers to his work problems at any time.

How far will this skewing of an ancient numbers system

be carried? As we now look at the formal organization, we see many instances where the ratio of leader to followers has been reduced to four or five to one. Controls have become so complicated that one man's time is required to monitor them effectively and prescribe corrective action for as few as four or five others. We have every reason to believe that this trend will continue and even accelerate. The day is most certainly not too far away when it will be common to have work groups composed of one or two workers reporting to a first-level leader—and this prediction is totally unrelated to the increasing sophistication of automation of data recording and data interpretation. Our infinite fragmentation of our increased knowledge has placed it absolutely beyond the power of an individual to master his own discipline, let alone become expert enough in others to maintain directive control without assistance.

At this point, of course, there must be a modification of our intergroup method of communication. Peers will have an increasingly significant impact upon our effectiveness; we will maintain our channels with them, or our own work will be fruitless. The matrix type of organizational structure will become universal, since compartmentalization will have proved to be incapable of doing the job.

If this nearly one-to-one relationship between worker and leader does achieve universality, what will happen to the status of the follower? Superior–subordinate relationships will tend to merge into the never-never land of the "colleague." It is immediately apparent that the color gray will take over! The leader's function will be reduced in status; the follower's responsibility will be hugely increased. Their positions in the hierarchy will be nearly equal; their contributions will be almost indistinguishable. In and of itself, this is a questionable gain. The leader will find it harder to define his responsibilities; the follower will find it harder to get proper support.

Followership, like leadership, will become much more difficult in the future.

* * *

Some of the aspects of followership are nearly the mirror images of their counterparts in the leader. The leader's power drive is balanced by the follower's security drive. The follower is outer-directed; the leader is inner-directed. The leader is not deeply concerned with maintenance needs, whereas they are most important to the follower.

An especially critical segment of followership is that of the subleader. His position is quasi. As a training ground for future leadership, it has the respect of managers at all levels. So do the front-line soldiers, who are lifelong followers. They have no interest in leadership because it would remove them from the field of action and the excitement attendant upon it. At the opposite extreme are the impersonal observers, whose commitment is to historical chronicling rather than the immediate achievement of the group's goals.

Technology and its growing complexity will reduce the span of control in the near future. The Mosaic decad, functional for thousands of years, will be replaced shortly by very nearly a one-to-one relationship between leader and follower.

Chapter 9

Multigroup Membership

*F*ROM the time of our earliest memories, we have lived in more and more groups. This is a function of our own maturation and a society which spins off new groups at an unbelievable rate. Our work group, a generation ago, was on the average small and uncomplicated. Now, enterprises have become huge and correspondingly more complex in their organizational structure. We customarily must be members of many groups just to hold a job in one of these industrial giants.

The Exponential Curve

A man whose recollections extend back half a century can easily recall a childhood in a social organization that was much less complicated than the one now extant. There were the family, the school, the church, and one or two closely knit play groups of children of the same age. Interactions in this small number of groups comprised a boy's life. Moreover, it was an eminently satisfying and rich existence.

Some 30 years later, this man's children had memberships in many times the number of groups which he knew. Their education began much earlier, with nursery school, and was much more regimented and group-oriented than his. It became necessary that they join what seemed like an endless parade of clubs, societies, and groups whose objectives included only a small segment of the school's overall goals. The social life of their schooldays, almost in its entirety, was formally organized into clubs and fraternities.

As adults, these sons and daughters too claim to have had a rich childhood and to remember it with pleasure, but the difference in complexity of organization is clearly evident. And now, as they become parents, the same cycle is being repeated. Their children have memberships in more groups before entering school than their parents did halfway toward graduation. They accept with equanimity and aplomb membership in groups whose names—to an older generation—do not even signify their objectives or organizational purpose. Yet all three of the generations under consideration would be considered "average" or "normal" by anyone's reckoning.

Groups beget groups, either as satellites or as direct competitors. When the functions of two groups are conjoined, simultaneous membership in both is common; if they are rivals, the membership will be discrete. It is in the former case, of course, that multigroup memberships appear in the life of the individual. Man is a highly adaptive animal. He can adjust to a changing environment quickly and efficiently—up to a point. As our exponential curve of group memberships approaches infinity, we can only wonder at what point our memberships in groups will cease to be effective and start to cause us frustration and anxiety. Too great a scatter gun effect in our total effort can only result in lowered efficiency and failure to achieve satisfaction from one or more of our group activities.

The watchword becomes *self-control*. No one else can possibly undertake the responsibility of blowing the whistle on our various joinings. No one else can judge the point at which we cease to have pleasurable results from group interactions. Each man must judge for himself the point at which group demands on his time and energies become onerous rather than pleasurable.

A word here about the meaning of "meaning." Unless membership in a group is truly meaningful for an individual and contributes to his overall welfare and satisfaction, he should refuse to associate himself with the new activity. This is a purely defensive reaction to conserve general energy and efficiency.

What is behind this proliferation of groups? The main factor is the pure mathematics of the permutations and combinations of an increasing population. We all know the old booby trap about shoeing the horse—you pay one cent for the first nail and double the price for each of 32 nails in the four shoes. The total bill, amounting to several million dollars, is incomprehensible unless we have some understanding of the weight of sheer numbers and the effect they can have on our lives. A town of 5,000 inhabitants presents one set of problems in its social organization; another of 10,000 has more than twice the difficulties in interpersonal associations, and with populations of the hundreds of thousands and millions, the resultant troubles become astronomical in number and staggering in effect.

The second independent variable is, of course, the infinite complexity of human nature. A man may present one face to the members of a few simple groups, while his entire personality may be radically altered if he is forced into too many associations with all the attendant problems. Conversely, it is true, some people are bored with a simple structure and bloom only when subjected to the pressures of multiple membership, increased challenge, and concomitantly increased rewards for effective action.

There can be no question that the curve is still rising and that its slope has not leveled off perceptibly. Oncoming generations perhaps will be conditioned in their infancy and youth to accept this as a fact of life and may even accommodate themselves to ever increasing group memberships without trauma. Whether they can do so and still maintain their efficiency as group members is another question. Perhaps they can. We have only to observe the advances made in the past two or three generations to be half-convinced that the process may continue without interruption.

Kinetic Equilibrium

Little in nature remains static for long. Balance is achieved in the universe by an infinite number of forces acting with each other, partly with each other, or against each other. The vectors active within any group *are* forces, whether physical, mental, or emotional; and we learn to live with them, for better or for worse, as we mature. Our only defense against the pushings and pullings of these forces is to be alert, adaptive, and responsive.

The kinetic equilibrium which must be attained among the stimuli of our multigroup living does not come easily. But there is a procedure which, if followed, will minimize our trauma and shorten the period of adjustment.

The first step in this procedure is to be cognizant of the forces to which we are subjected. Awareness must come first. This includes recognition of these forces, source, their strength, and their probable duration. Before any counterforce is exerted, we must be sure that is what we really want to do. Perhaps the force is working to our benefit, and we should take advantage of it rather than neutralize it. Our first cognitive effort stops short, however, of complete evaluation. This part of the job is one of cataloging by source and number.

A value judgment must then be made about each of the vectors. Is it for us or against us? How great will its effect be on us? Will its proper control require a major or a minor effort? How much monitoring will be required? What we are saying is that this process will be the basis for our decision to remain in a particular group or leave it. In most cases, it is better to leave the group (if the evaluation is negative) than make a major effort to meet and destroy the vector. It should be pointed out here that such an action is not an indictment of our courage but a tribute to our good judgment. But remember: The words "in most cases" must be underlined.

At this point, all the vectors must be totemed by their importance (strength) in our lives. Whether their effect is positive or negative, we should be exerting much of our effort on those forces which are most significant in terms of successful group living. Here is where we repeatedly face the dangerous threat to a calm and peaceful life among our various groups. The insidiousness with which a malign influence can gain a hold over us is an ever present hazard. Like the iceberg, some of these forces exhibit only 10 percent of their volume above water; it is that which lies below the surface which is dangerous to our navigation—just as it is not the first cigarette which is a threat to our health, and the tenth carton is not nearly as evil as the five hundredth. Some of the forces in our multigroup living are as deadly to our mental, emotional, and spiritual life as smoking is to our physical well-being.

Once we have finished our comparative evaluation, summing up the forces bearing upon us, we can proceed to the planning stage. How do we meet and handle these influences? What procedure will we use to achieve the balance we know we must have? What tactics should we employ to neutralize opposite forces or attenuate the effect of the dangerous ones? How shall we act to take the greatest possible advantage of those forces which are working for us? This fourth stage is the critical one, and it will determine our eventual success or failure as a member of this or any other society. The most basic requirement of all is to recognize that this planning *must* be done. Successful living is not the result of happy chance or an uncharted course through life.

The final step is obvious—implement our plans and put them into practice. This is often not as difficult as it sounds at first. If our planning has been careful and reasonably thorough, the tactics that should be employed are many times self-evident. Remember, we are talking about a *moving* balance among the forces operant upon us. Our lives are not static; we must move forward—toward our more important goals—or perish. As we become practiced and successful in this lifelong balancing act, we condition ourselves to the cycle of meeting new and strange group forces, evaluating them, toteming them, and applying the prescribed methodology of defeating them or making use of their help.

Actually, the constant change in our environment implicit in multigroup living is what makes it worthwhile. We would all become terribly bored and apathetic were we never to be aware of a new force acting upon us. In learning to meet and adjust to it, we become more or less expert at being change agents—a sort of expertise which is the most valuable tool modern man can acquire. Being a change agent implies control over a situation; we are in the driver's seat when we *cause* change rather than meet it.

It is obvious that failure to fabricate this kinetic equilibrium is a principal source of neuroticism and psychosis. We react negatively to a loss of control over our response to our environment—not control over our *environment*, that is, but control over our *response* to it.

Multigroup membership is obviously a must in today's living. Acceptance of the fact that society is complex is the first step toward adjusting to it successfully. The versatile man is the one who survives and prospers. Besides, he has more fun.

Since multigroup membership has become a way of life— the only successful *modus vivendi*—every effort we can marshal to become successful at it will pay large dividends later. The necessary first effort is to achieve kinetic equilibrium.

Goal Competition

The more groups we belong to, the greater the chance that the goals of one group may come into competition with those of another. It is more likely that this will develop into a severe problem if the goals are only a trifle out of synchronization than if they are directly polarized. The difficulty lies in trying to remember the slight difference in mental set required in each of the two groups. What we do as a member of one group to help in gaining its objectives may be too much, and our come-on too strong, to be effective in the other. (Direct and total opposition between the goals of two groups will be treated in Chapter 10.)

When goals compete, we are the battlefield. An individual will find anxiety inherent in the situation where it becomes difficult to satisfy the goals of both groups. This is especially true if the two groups are of equal importance in our scheme of things. The forced choice which sometimes results is as painful to us as being made to think. Our natural tendency is to try desperately to keep both groups within our sphere of activities.

This forced choice actually is an effective mental catharsis. In casting up the accounts, pro and con, for both groups, we are doing a necessary job—that is, evaluating our total effectivity. The choice will be made on the basis of the depth of our identification with the two groups and on a concurrent judgment as to our contribution to each of them. When we determine that our ego involvement is perceptibly greater in one group than the other while, at the same time, our contribution to this group is significantly greater, the choice is fairly simple. It is when the two independent variables are going in opposite directions that big trouble begins. It is upsetting to have to quantify anything as imponderable as an objective and our contribution toward it.

One of the sneakier maneuvers of an imaginative leader is to deliberately incite goal competition among his membership. In undertaking this gambit, he is assuming a calculated risk that his group may lose some members that he values highly. However, if his group wins, he has solidified and strengthened it by the necessary reevaluation his followers have made of their relationships with it. Almost always, after this sort of assessment, a spurt of sharply increased activity occurs which is of great benefit. The sophisticated follower may well recognize what is being done—the games being played by the leader—and still go along for what is in it for him. The value to the individual member of competing goals lies in the sharpening of his faculties and the increased concentration on the group process attendant upon goal achievement.

Some peripheral forces are set in motion by goal competition. If a man is being forced to reexamine his relationship to one group, it is only a short step to a reexamination of his relationships with other groups. Not uncommonly, a chain reaction is triggered, resulting in a general overhaul of values and group interactions. The hygienic effect of this process will result in a more orderly arrangement of both numbers of members and individual contributions to each group.

Since the goal is the group's keystone, even its reason for being, we are getting at the real basis of our social structure when we find ourselves the victims of goal competition. The "far out" groups are the ones that feel this the most. Their membership is composed of individuals who live defensively. In adopting the mores and norms of a fringe group, they are announcing to the world their own aggression and hostility. The fact that they often cannot verbalize the reasons for these emotions does not deter them from joining the group. By publicizing their deviance, they become the target of the day for the rest of society. Leaving aside those exhibitionists who gravitate toward the weird and the outré, let us acknowledge the sincerity of purpose that is characteristic of the majority of these groups, even if we cannot admire their judgmental process. Up to a point, membership in a protest group is therapeutic and may help an individual troubled by his inability to adjust to today's living. Unfortunately, membership in the deviant group only points up and escalates the goal competition with other groups to which such people belong or with which they have contact.

The posture of protest is hard to drop. If one is a dissenter in one milieu, it is difficult to change mien in other group memberships. The primary demand for membership in a protest group is invariant rigidity. There can be no change in group configuration, no dropping of the guard by individual members. The natural son of this marriage of a dedicated individual to a deviant group is violence. It is completely logical that the universities, with their touted academic freedom, should be the arena for the confrontation of the deviant and the normal group.

Social conflict is a product of goal competition. Our differences are reinforcement of our ego involvement in groups with differing goals. The usual approach to the settling of "differences" is fallacious in its basic concept. We waste thousands of man-hours in exploring "issues" totally irrelevant to the fundamental problem: simple goal competition. Much more productive peacemaking efforts would result from a sincere and determined desire to bring into consonance goals which may, at last analysis, prove to be only slightly divergent.

Invitation to Schizophrenia

Our universal multigroup memberships have caused much of the emotional and mental disturbance in present society. Our mental health is founded upon and conditioned by the amount of equilibrium we can achieve among our various groups.

For most people, the major trauma is associated with the formal work group. The knowledge that we are effectively its prisoner (or trapped by some other group quite similar to it) puts tremendous pressure on our entire being. We have little if any control over our group goals, our leadership, our working conditions, or the members of the peer group at work. It is not so much that adjustment to these is difficult as it is that we are completely helpless and at the mercy of "them."

According to our individual characteristics, we react in a variety of ways to this overpowering knowledge. Some of us become apathetic, withdrawn, and unresponsive; resisting any effort to get to us, we remain in a defensive posture while in the work group. Others react with vigor, showing all the common signs of aggression, in an attempt to escape the perceived prison. Fortunately, a majority of us are still able to adjust successfully enough that our general mental health is at least normal. What is ominous about the picture is the rapidly increasing incidence of recognizable neurosis and psychosis directly traceable to the work situation.

Only in the past few years has business leadership developed an awareness of this trend. Awareness, however, does little for us unless we put forth solid effort to correct the basic situation. It will not be possible to free everyone, suddenly and magically, from the constraints of his working group; with imagination, it will be quite possible to make people more receptive to the way things are and to help them in their adaptation. Herzberg's two-factor theory provides a handy tool (job enrichment) with which to work this problem. Also, many business leaders who set up participating managerial interactions are getting some promising results. Psychologically, the man who is convinced that his leader and his peers are men of goodwill is not subject to as much mental disturbance as the man who feels himself to be entirely alone in a hostile world.

Many workers in less than desirable surroundings are able to leave their work problems behind them and make a pleasant life among their semiformal and informal groups. For these people, there is an actual therapeutic value in membership in many groups; that is, these numerous outside contacts perhaps neutralize the effects of the unpleasant formal work group. In this sense, the goals of the outside groups are in competition with those of the work group—the formal one—and the result of the arrangement may come close to being a standoff.

Simply because most emotional problems arising from group membership are centered in the formal work group, it does not follow that it is impossible for trouble to arise in semiformal or informal groups. If ego involvement is high, goal competition in these groups can be troublesome. A person can become so deeply involved in his lodge work or his union activities that trouble there can cause him a serious mental upset. The trick is to resist excessive involvement in these groups. This may be difficult, since they are often operant in the social- and ego-needs levels, where satisfaction is of great importance to us. Achieving and maintaining emotional maturity becomes harder each year in our civilization as socialistic philosophy and practices continue to proliferate. When not only our parents but our government and society itself refuse to cut the cord, it is small wonder that we find it hard to grow up. There are many things to be said for an older (but currently discredited) theory that a man grows and matures on the basis of his own effort and self-sufficiency.

So far as the informal group is concerned, the one that gives us the most trouble in the area of mental health is the friendship group. Peers here are associated purely through emotional bonds. The friendship itself and its maintenance are the only valid group goals. It is entirely possible for a friendship group to display a complete mélange of mores and personal objectives which may be quite abrasive as they come into direct competition with others tending in the opposite direction. In addition, small help is available from any other single member of the group, since all have their own problems of reconciliation in maintaining an equable membership. Actually, the friendship group runs a close second to the formal work group as a source of possible mental and emotional disturbance.

There is no magic formula by which one can resolve these conflicting pressures. The man who keeps his mental health in multigroup memberships will do so by means of his own strength and his own ability to make the necessary discriminations and value judgments. Of course he may, if sufficiently troubled, seek help from a qualified counselor, but the final decision and concomitant action must be his alone. No other person can hand to us a gift of mental stability; it is ours to earn as one of our more precious attributes. As a personal goal, this must rank well toward the top of the pyramid. Our general effectiveness in all our groups will be of the same order of magnitude. We must keep as a central goal our own personal well-being.

Group Hierarchy

Since goal competition is inevitable under a system of multigroup membership, it also follows that a rational man must organize his memberships into a hierarchy in order to maintain any semblance of order. If he were to give equal importance to every group, nothing but chaos could result, and next to nothing would be accomplished.

Every male in our society has three choices for the No. 1 position in his group hierarchy: the family, the job, or the church. Let there be no misunderstanding. No one can declare them an equilateral trilogy; at some time or another, a definitive choice must be made for at least first place, and it may be necessary to assign second and third places as well. One's life will be significantly different according to which choice is made. It would be difficult to estimate what percentage of American males opt for the job as against the family. The church, by any count, would come in a poor third.

The man who chooses the job as the peak of his group pyramid will have some special problems. Time for his family will be limited to the point where guilt feelings can cause him considerable disquietude. Even when "home," he will either be carrying a burden of paperwork or concentrating on a business problem. He may successfully—for him—rationalize by pointing out that his business success makes it possible for him to "give his family everything." Everything but himself, that is. His wife will be left the unenviable task of being both father and mother to the children. The offspring will feel, either consciously or subconsciously, the deprivation of the half-orphan.

The man who puts his family first on the list will live in the midst of an anomaly. By putting them first, he will probably deprive them of many of the material benefits we have come to expect as a right, because no man can *really* put his family first and *really* be successful in his job. The two are mutually exclusive. The time spent with wife and children will have to be subtracted from that time which other men give to their jobs, and the husband-father will find himself less than competitive in the business world. This can have serious repercussions, with the costs of raising and educating children escalating at a dizzy rate. Because he loves them, the man puts them first; because he does so, he denies them advantages their neighbors will have. What a dilemma!

The person who puts the church first among his groups

may not have as great a problem as either of the other two, because he is "other worldly" in his mental set. In all honesty, he may not care too deeply about either temporal success or how his family fares. His rationale is, of course, that he is doing the best for them by insuring their eternal security.

It would be false to leave the impression that all situations are so clean-cut. A person can put his wife and children first and become a slave to his job in order to support them. Because of his personal goal, he finds it impossible to make the sacrifices necessary for outstanding job success, yet he is caught up in a squirrel-cage existence in order to care for his family as best he can. On the other hand, the man who puts the job first will compensate by showering his family with all sorts of material goodies until they are thoroughly spoiled. He can even be elected "father of the year" by the local P-TA and accept the award without visible embarrassment. And the same thing can be true of the religious zealot as well.

The surface of our society has recently been seriously disturbed by the antics of a subculture which rejects all the choices mentioned. The "great protestors" have apparently put all their money on one group—themselves and their like. Such excessive absorption with self can only be classified as a sickness. Supremely egotistical, they assume that the universe revolves about them and has been created for their particular delectation. Words like "duty" and "social contribution" have no meaning for them. Parasites of this sort can exist only in a rich society; but any parasite, if unchecked, will destroy its host.

As pointed out, one's group hierarchy determines one's general tenor of life to a large extent. This is natural enough when we consider that the determination of the hierarchy involves a toteming of objectives for each of us. We are answering (for our own satisfaction, at least) those fundamental philosophical questions about the meaning of life and the right way to live it. We are announcing the depth to which we will commit ourselves in all areas. The kinds and numbers of our intended interactions will be put on display. All this, of course, takes place purely by indirection. Few people formally put these things into writing or verbalize them except under the most extraordinary of situations. Yet the signal is clearly given to those who have any interest in it.

Significantly, our social organization now permits this ordering of our personal values to be delayed longer and longer, as "preparation for life" is extended in each generation. First, high school graduation was recognized as terminal for most young people. Then came college graduation, and now the trend is for a majority of college graduates to go on to graduate study, generally with the terminal degree as an objective. And this is only the beginning. The emotional immaturity of our "young" (age 30) graduates is shocking to observe in a tragic number of cases. Their preparation has been, not for living, but for a continual putting off of essential decision making about their own lives. The perennial student is a dropout from life.

However, be that as it may, group hierarchies can be determined only when the person concerned is ready to do so. No one can force another to do this against his will, and no one can do it for him.

Making Adjustments

Several times in this chapter we have indicated (rather lightly) that it is necessary for the individual to "adjust" or "adapt" to a given situation. This is true, but the real question is—*how does* a person adjust to a grossly changed environmental factor? For the greater part of his behavior, man is a bundle of habits tied together with protoplasm. Every person knows how hard it is to extinguish a habit, once formed. There are basic electrochemical changes which must take place in the body during habit formation. These must be either reversed or substituted for by new reactions when a habit is discarded.

The steadier and more dependable a person is, the harder is the job of changing him. This kind of person may feel physically upset at just the prospect of a major change in his behavior, and the trauma is increased during the actual change process. We should never underestimate the effect on this man. On the other hand, a person whom we judge to be "flexible" or "easily adaptable" may not form deep habit patterns. For him then, the upset accompanying change will be less than for others. And obviously, if changing his habits is less troublesome to him, he can accomplish that change more easily and more quickly.

One of the higher hurdles to be overcome in making a personal change is the original decision to do so. When the pressures of our multigroup memberships come to be perceived as oppressive, we ordinarily decide it is time to make an adjustment. This part of the decision is simple enough, but what change should be made? In which group? Should it be merely a lessening of involvement, or will it entail severance from the group? In either case, what do we judge will be the effect on our own operation? Are we sure that this decision and the ensuing action will result in a net gain to us? Even harder on us is the fact that, once it is evident that a change in one of our group memberships is desirable, we cannot seem to effect this change quickly enough to suit us. We urgently want to have it over with, but a dangerous situation can result if we rush in too quickly to rearrange our group memberships.

However, once the die has been cast, the procedure is quite stylized. It consists principally of dropping a habit or substituting another for it. What most of us are unwilling to allow for is the time lapse mandatory in this situation. We retain enough of our childish impatience to want this thing done as quickly as it has been conceptualized. For example, unless we change our physical surroundings, many aspects of the environment will remind us of the old situation and make the change more difficult. We often develop guilt feelings over making a change which have no basis in logic but which can still have a deep effect on us. In many cases, these feelings have their foundation in the fact that our interpersonal relationships within the group will undergo a change. If we sever our membership, even for a perfectly valid reason, our friendships in that group are bound to be affected. And friendships are notoriously not under logical control; our action in "deserting" the group will uproot many amicable relationships.

Another major factor to remember is that no change in group relationships is ever unilateral. When one person makes a change, he forces change on many other people, just as he might cause ripples in the pond by tossing in a stone. This kind of disruption in our group interactions, when initiated by others, can be hard on us. We especially resent unforeseen change when we have no relation to its cause. The end result may well be a feeling of basic insecurity and anxiety that is hard to combat.

Nevertheless, continual adjustment in our multigroup memberships is inevitable. It is a product of our own growth and development, just as the purchase of new clothing must follow physical growth in children. To continue this analogy further, the purchases must also be paid for, as already noted, by the upset which normally accompanies change.

We can ameliorate some of the trauma by our mental attitude. A continuing mental set receptive to the concept of change is the greatest asset we can have to help us here. A shibboleth has arisen which holds that people are "by nature" or "instinctively" resistant to change. This is not necessarily so. We can condition ourselves to a positive attitude toward change just as we can toward any other given situation. *This attitude can become as habitual as any other.*

In the long run, adjustment is a personal matter with each of us. I have my particular way of accepting change, and it may be entirely different from yours. The single criterion is that each method must be functional. It is important that we survive continual change in our society with a minimum of mental or emotional disturbance; moreover, each of us has a parallel obligation to see that our peers are as little upset as possible as a result of our own changing environment. The greatest difference between life today and life a century ago is that our personal actions impinge directly upon many more people than did the actions of our grandfathers. The interlock becomes tighter with each half-generation. If the trend continues, it may be significantly greater every quarter-generation.

Adaptability to change is a positive virtue for every one of us—within reason. It must be controlled as each of us sees his own natural endowments.

Withdrawal Symptoms

Present-day man has conditioned himself so thoroughly to multigroup membership that his behavior displays some odd changes if he severs relations with one or more of his groups. A significant lessening of group activity leaves a partial vacuum in his existence, which he tries to fill in a number of ways. The first of these is hyperactivity in the remaining groups. He increases the tempo and the number of his interactions to the point where he often disturbs the other members. This frenetic activity will take its toll in increased tension, greater irritability, and possibly even abrasive interpersonal relationships.

Another withdrawal symptom is sharper criticism of the conduct of a given group. This may be spread fairly evenly between leaders and followers. Things which would not have ruffled the former member's calm before can now excite him wildly and elicit a violent response. This reaction is a defense mechanism to prevent further erosion of multigroup involvement. It can set in even if his leaving a group has been perfectly voluntary and the product of his own reasoned thinking.

Regardless of his reason for having left a group, the ex-member will predictably downgrade the group gradually in both his thoughts and his speech. He is no longer a member; *ergo*, the group is not as good as it was. This reaction is completely understandable and unavoidable. Naturally enough, if the ex-member verbalizes this thinking in the vicinity of the severed group's membership, his old friends and acquaintances will undoubtedly be disturbed.

Another concomitant of departure from a group is a fairly deep examination of personal goals and objectives. Of course, this examination may *precede* the individual's leaving; but, if it does not, it will be a natural result of his departure. If he is sharp and interested in personal growth, a period of rapid development should follow one of these reevaluative sessions. It is entirely possible that, almost immediatley after dropping one group, he will join another. This may not be the same kind of group, and, if the growth-development cycle is normal, it will usually be a little more select than the one just abandoned.

Taken in the aggregate, this process is what accounts for the evolution of a society. Not only individuals but groups themselves maintain a continuously selective process as they grow and mature. A study of the current American concept of democracy yields some ideas which the founding fathers would have found completely incredible, but it must be remembered that they fought bitterly among themselves before achieving anything which even approximated consensus about the meaning of the word "democracy." Some of the original signers defined it in oligarchic, autocratic, and completely totalitarian terms. They sincerely believed themselves to be advanced and liberal thinkers because they were a shade less severe in their concept and oppressive in their actions than were others in power at the time. Conversely, what now passes for democratic thinking and action would have been considered blatantly revolutionary in those days. That our concept of democracy has evolved is undeniable; whether that evolution has assumed a desirable direction is one of the burning questions of our day.

In any case, this process of growth, replacement, growth, and pruning is a healthy one. One is reminded of the unremitting efforts of the nurseryman in the care of his plants. He is kept constantly busy with a cycle reminiscent of the process we have just described.

The withdrawal syndrome is traumatic to any person. We can expect him to react to it just as he does habitually to any other threat: He will avoid, evade, or attack. The fact that he may have originated the withdrawal voluntarily is immaterial; he still perceives a change in his behavior pattern as a potential source of trouble. At this point, there is little that another can do to give aid or comfort. Everyone with this problem, must extricate himself. It is an individual "operation bootstraps."

Anyone will hesitate to place himself in jeopardy again, once he has experienced severance. Thus successive severances from major groups become rarer as a person ages. And, for the elderly, the remaining group memberships take on greater and greater value, with a correspondingly acute aversion to any other severances.

The group dynamics involved are relatively uncomplicated. The departure of any one individual from a group of normal size is a loss quite easily recoverable by the remainder. One person's interactions are so small a part of the total that their subtraction has little effect on the whole. The important consequences are felt by the individual. They are a recognizable part of his "growing pains" as a maturing organism. As the receptor of the stimulus, he is the only one who can respond.

One possibility we have not yet considered is the arresting of personal development at a given level by an especially difficult severance. If the resultant upset is so great that the person simply cannot bear the prospect of a repetition, a developmental plateau could result in his "peaking out" at an early chronological age to his own great detriment. However, our concern in group dynamics is ultimately *for the individual;* groups are only incidental to the welfare of those who make them up. The Judeo-Christian ethic is the cult par excellence of the individual. We have a *personal* God. We are *personally* responsible for our behavior and our impact on others. We *personally* can help or hinder others by the manner in which we interact with them. Thus any withdrawal symptoms we experience should remain our personal problems for our personal solution.

The Integrated Life

Looking back over this chapter, we see that there are several rather negative aspects to multigroup membership. All these, however, will be more than counterbalanced if a person achieves proper integration of his life through a careful balance of his group memberships. The word to keep in mind here is "balance." Ideally, anyone's development should be aimed toward a symmetrical personality. It is proper procedure to take advantage of our innate assets—unless we overwork them in an attempt to compensate for weaker areas of our personal interactions. Our group memberships must be chosen with these facts in mind—there should be one membership for every area of recognized weakness. If this sounds too methodical, remember that in building a fine piece of furniture, both the tools and the woods selected are of equal importance.

The mere building of strength where it did not exist before does not insure that our personality will be properly integrated. The facets of our personality are not discrete particles, but should fit into a unified and pleasing entity. This implies fine discrimination on our part in judging comparative strengths and weaknesses; it also entails careful attention to the amount of activity (in amount and depth) to be allotted to each of the groups we join.

A major factor in the integration of group memberships is the care we exert in gathering, examining, and judging the feedback we get from our peers. In essence, we are talking here about our sensitivity to our impact on others and their reaction to it. It goes without saying that much of this feedback will be nonverbal. All of us perceive the cues our fellows give us; relatively few of us, in contrast, gain full advantage from the cues they send. To do so requires us to develop an extremely objective attitude toward ourselves; there is no place for wounded vanity or stubbed sensibilities.

Proper integration of our group memberships will make life much easier for our closest associates. Chapter 14 will be devoted to group dynamics in the family, but suffice it now to note that proper integration will ease interpersonal relationships.

A well-integrated personality is notable for peace of mind and lack of tension and anxiety. Abrasion produces friction; friction produces heat. When two maladjusted facets of our personality conflict, unease cannot help but result. And peace of mind becomes more and more important as we age in a society which is compounding its complexity. We seek mental peace as addicts turn to drugs. It will not be found if we have failed to adjust our own personality to the various pressures exerted in our multigroup memberships.

A properly integrated life will seek its own level in preferred associations. This accounts for the wide variety of our friendships as we progress toward self-actualization. If our peers make roughly the same progress in their integrative activities, there need be no interruption of our interactions. If they lag behind, we will drift away from them; if we fail to keep up, they will drop us. There is nothing cold-blooded or calculating about this sequence; like will seek like, while dissimilarities will repel. The man who "never loses a friend" is either a completely stagnant pool or a supernally lucky person surrounded by those progressing at exactly his own rate toward personal integration.

We have already mentioned that symmetry is desirable in personality development. The pursuit of this objective is a major activity during the greater part of life. The key to the integration of memberships is a keen awareness of our deficiencies. However, spotting a weakness is only the first step toward its correction. The choice of therapy has to be one of our more important decisions, because this is where we take full advantage of all those whose judgment we respect. The seeking of counsel in integrative efforts is a must. Naturally, the matter of whom we turn to is a measure of our discrimination of our peers' achievements. The balance of nature is nowhere better illustrated than in this area. Each of us seeks help from those whom he considers to be better integrated and generally stronger than himself. One of the aspects of strength is that it can give of itself without being harmed. No one who helps us will be robbed; neither will we feel any loss from having "shown the way" to people who seek our counsel.

Out total achievement as a member of our various groups will be determined by our ability to integrate those memberships into a viable admixture. There remains an important question to be answered: When can we be personally assured that our integration is sufficient and effective? The evidence, over all, will be largely circumstantial. We will notice a significant diminution of our personal fears and anxieties, we will find it easier to plot activities without worrying about their consequences, and we will find that our efforts are more richly rewarded than before. As evidence of all this, there will be less effort involved in attaining a particular group's goal.

The integrated life is the one goal each of us has in common with every other human being. We almost never verbalize it in these terms, but the meaning is there. The parts must fit. Life must gain simplicity in its functional aspects so that we can relate more easily with peers and leaders and assume individual group duties with equanimity and lack of tension. It's the only way to fly!

* * *

The number of groups in which each of us has membership increases exponentially every generation. As the complexity of our social interactions increases, so does the number of memberships necessary for successful living. It is necessary in these times that we develop a condition of kinetic equilibrium in balancing the forces exerted upon us by our various memberships.

There is severe and continuing competition among the goals of our various groups. If we are not adaptable, the situation can become traumatic, even to the point of precipitating neurosis and psychosis. The only viable means of avoiding this is to create our personal group hierarchy. We must prioritize our memberships according to our own standards and expectations.

If it becomes necessary for any reason to withdraw from a group, certain recognizable withdrawal symptoms will be noted. Principal among them is a period of hyperactivity among the other groups, in order to fill the perceived void.

We must integrate all these memberships into our lives, making them fit and complement each other rather than be competitive and abrasive.

Chapter 10

Role Conflict

*I*N Chapter 9 we delineated some of the problems growing out of our multigroup memberships and some of the benefits to be gained if we succeed in integrating our lives properly. There is, however, one particular problem which causes trouble for almost everyone at some time in his life. That is the matter of role conflict. If our memberships in two groups are about equally attractive (that is, if our involvement is about the same in both), and if the objectives of the groups are visibly out of phase, it becomes impossible to reconcile the widely differing roles demanded of us.

The Penalty of Multigroup Membership

Role conflict will occur sometime in every life as a result of the sheer pressure of numbers. Group norms and the conformity demanded by every group will bring us into intrapersonal dissonance as we try in vain to be, both the good church member and the convivial lodgeman. The policeman whose beat is a tough area in a ghetto finds a massive readjustment necessary if he is to function as a Boy Scout leader in his off hours.

The human mind, although theoretically capable of infinite adaptability, in practice can make only a limited number of instantaneous role shifts as one moves from group to group. The mental and emotional shock caused by these sudden transformations is reflected in body chemistry. Discontinuity of self-perception lies at the base of our difficulties. When we cannot receive a consistent picture of our own personality configuration, we are in big trouble.

Of course, interpersonal relationships are strained in both the groups involved. Our uncertainties are visible to our peers, sometimes before we are consciously aware of them ourselves. We become unpredictable, and this is a cardinal sin. The surface serenity of the entire group is disturbed as the members grow restless and unsure of themselves. The role conflict of a single individual can infect and destroy the rhythm of many others—one of the better illustrations of how delicately balanced are the bonds between members in groups of all kinds.

For the individual, most of the trauma of role conflict comes from his efforts to reduce these disruptions of relationships. The greater our involvement in the group, the more imperative it is that we mend our fences with our associates. (Of course, role conflict will not be a serious problem in our casual group memberships, where ego involvement is slight.) The attempt to restore normal relationships does, however, have one side effect that is all to our good: It is one of the better methods of increasing our sensitivity to our impact on others. It forces us into introspective activities productive of better self-knowledge.

A perfectly obvious truism should still be noted—the more memberships we have, the more certain it is that role conflicts will result. The probability is greatest when we are operating at Maslow's level of social needs. The need for belonging develops early in life and tends to become stabilized at a high level in early maturity. The more we interact, the greater the chances for dissonant vectors to enter the picture. As a result of role conflicts, our social needs are *less* satisfied than before, and we perceive threat in an extensive part of our emotional life. When membership in an important group is endangered by a role conflict, the reaction is reflexive, swift, and powerful.

The individual who is elaborating at the social level to compensate for lack of satisfaction of ego needs may also be in for trouble. The more he "joins," the greater the probability of role conflict. When it appears, his ego needs remain unsatisfied, and his social needs are less satisfied than they were.

Specific methods of reducing role conflicts will be considered later in this chapter, but we should mention here that, in general, this situation requires a certain sequence of activity. Once the problem is recognized, the person involved must make some quick, incisive judgments. How deep is the conflict? How seriously is it affecting his overall performance? Are there noticeable mental, emotional, and physical effects which are bothersome? How about his relationships with his peers (and the leaders) in both groups concerned? If the answers to these questions indicate a serious situation, the individual must decide which group is more meaningful to him. Is one of deeper significance than the other, or are they nearly equal? If one clearly is much more important, the quicker and easier way to resolve the role conflict will be to drop the other. But, if the two groups are about equally significant, the individual will search for a means of reducing the conflict to manageable proportions. This can sometimes be done through a reevaluation and reprioritization of group objectives. A slight subordination of one group's demands in most cases is all that is needed to bring peace.

This penalty of multigroup membership is common to social living. Everyone will experience it at some time, and probably more than once. If we are prepared for this eventuality, our reaction to it will be lessened, and final solution will be easier to come by. Some of our major problems with youth today are arising because neither the family nor the school is accepting reasonable responsibility for this part of education. We throw our children into an environment that will inevitably engender role conflicts with little or no forewarning and with even less training in how to cope with them. No wonder young people are resentful when they realize what is happening to them. They quite naturally blame us—the older generation.

The Conflict Neurosis

The introduction of a serious role conflict into anyone's life makes him a prime target for a neurosis. The inability to juggle two roles into a semblance of harmony produces strains which quickly cause anxiety and escape efforts. The first reaction, after the individual in question has determined that the roles are not compatible, is to run away from the causal situation. It's the old theory of "Don't look now, and maybe it will go away." "It" doesn't. The longer a man is subjected to a role conflict, the greater will be the tension and the threat to ultimate mental health.

When it is discovered that escape from the conflict is not possible, the next reaction is lowered efficiency in all group activities. Goal-task production suffers; quality of work is lowered; both incoming and outgoing communications are garbled; interpersonal reactions become abrasive.

As soon as this growing inefficiency is recognized, the tension is again increased. The vicious circle that is established stretches our normal life completely out of shape and leaves us progressively worse off.

Remember, this is a case of two group memberships, both of which are necessary to the individual. Role conflicts do not appear (or are at least minimal) when one group is of minor importance, with little ego-involvement. If, however, the two groups are of about equal importance, our every effort will go toward saving satisfactory memberships in both; we see the loss of either as a major threat to our security and successful living.

The neurotic finds it impossible to reconcile all aspects of his existence into a harmonious and viable whole. This discovery makes him more and more ill at ease. Not only is his emotional and mental health involved, but there may be a serious physical reaction. In the extreme case, he drifts into hypochondria and can become nearly nonfunctional physically.

There is one curious little sidelight to the general matter of neuroticism. It is demonstrable that many of the world's most creative people have been highly neurotic, but this does not necessarily mean that their personal lives have not been easy or smooth. Still, as individuals, all of us hope to achieve harmony in our daily living. We seek the type of adjustment to all the forces acting upon us which will keep us mentally healthy at all times and so preclude the appearance of a neurosis.

The neurotic's powers of judgment are seriously affected by his condition. Values shift or are distorted. Basic principles which have always appeared unshakeable change. Peers are perceived differently—they seem to change as the neurotic's thinking changes. All this, most certainly, is severely threatening. But, since each of us has his own method of reacting to threat—or perhaps a series of reactions—it is not possible to lay out broad generalities of predictable reaction patterns.

From the group dynamics viewpoint, one member's serious role conflict may disrupt the whole group, depending upon the position and influence of the individual concerned. If he happens to be the group leader, the result can be shattering for the entire membership. His atypical behavior will become more and more obvious as the conflict progresses and will be viewed as especially alarming because of the significance always attached to his actions and reactions. If the leader's role conflict results in an actual neurosis, the prognosis for the group will not be good. For, regardless of its cause in a single individual, neuroticism is infectious.

It is, in fact, often the leader who is responsible for neuroticism among a group. An especially competitive leader is not above deliberately setting his group's objectives directly against those of another group as a contest of sheer power. In the ensuing battle, members who also have membership in the other group will be caught in the middle. They will get little sympathy from this kind of leader, who will consider their problem a test of their group loyalty—which, of course, it really is.

When role conflict is so deep-seated as to produce a neurotic behavior pattern in members of two groups, some fundamental choices and decisions have to be made. In the ultimate analysis, as we have seen, the only way out may be severance from one of the groups. If, on the other hand, the individual concerned either cannot or will not give up one of his memberships, he must make some other basic readjustments if he is to restore his effectiveness in both groups. His values must be changed; his conceptualization of each group and his role in it must be restructured; and his behavior must be altered to put him back into consonance with the rest of the members—for their relationships will have suffered while he was having his problems.

One other point should be considered. It is often the fault of the subject that he finds himself in this predicament in the first place. Our choice of group memberships, if carefully examined in advance, will warn us of troubles ahead. We have only to compare group objectives and group norms to see when we are setting up an equivocal situation by joining two particular groups. Our planning should be sophisticated and thoughtful enough to avoid some of the traps in which we involve ourselves by blind joining. Better not to get into trouble at all than to have to extricate ourselves after we do.

The Harmonics of Objectives

The basic cause of role conflict is, of course, group objectives which are going in different directions. This means that in order to conform to the norms of one group and gain its objectives, we cannot play a proper role in the second group because of nonconformity to *its* norms and objectives. The greatest of care should be observed before taking membership to insure that the new objectives will not be in dissonance with those of any other major group in our life. This is easier to do than we make it seem. A little preplanning and looking at the obvious should tell us the story. Our problem lies in haphazard joining for whimsical reasons, such as the pressures of friends or the overt popularity of a given group. Neither of these should be germane in causing us to seek membership.

We must design our group memberships so that their

goals reinforce each other and are in complete harmony. When this is done, it actually makes multigroup living easier, it enriches our lives, and it gives us a much broader base for self-actualization. Fundamentally, there should be only two reasons for joining any group: to help emphasize a strength or to shore up a weakness. Memberships provide the best possible opportunities for development—if they are properly and thoughtfully chosen. Moreover, the benefits which accrue from membership in one group may often be carried into our activities in another.

A conscious attempt on our part to increase the harmony among the objectives of our various groups is one of the better mental disciplines. The demands made on our judgment in this process will sharpen it—or, if not, will show up its essential weakness.

A source of help that is often neglected is the possibility of enlisting the advice and wisdom of our peers before choosing new group memberships. A search among our fellows will many times turn up experience that can be invaluable in helping us make decisions. The trouble is that in too many cases we fail to take advantage of it. Yet we like ourselves to be asked for advice, and so do our peers. This is the universal compliment—to have others turn to us for help. By the same token, we must stand ready to share our own experiences whenever others ask us sincerely to do so. The mutuality of this obligation has the sacredness of a contract and is implicit in all our group living.

One other point should be crystal clear. The leaders of every group have an unalterable obligation to communicate the group's objectives fully and openly so that prospective members will make no errors in joining. Therein lies the fundamental evil of a group which maintains hidden agendas. The members are being lied to, as are those who may inquire about joining. Leaders are not excused from their obligation even if they are the dupes of higher authority. If they are truly leaders, they should be alert enough to spot hidden agendas, even if they cannot at first identify them. This particular responsibility of leadership should be carried to the sticking point. If a leader discovers that he has been lied to by his superiors and, therefore, has made misrepresentations to his people, it is a perfectly valid reason for his leaving the group. He can only gain stature with his followers by a public admission that he had been used. What he is admitting is that he has been only a nominal leader.

The blending of our group memberships is analogous to the activity of a good cook. The major memberships constitute the entrée and other main dishes; the minor groups are the garnishes and the condiments. Every cook knows that there are certain incompatible combinations which he would never use, while there are other foods which are always thought of together.

The harmonizing of objectives in our group memberships is a skill. Like any other, it improves with practice of the right sort, and it furnishes us with one of the better opportunities for self-expression and mental and emotional growth. The more critical we become of our group memberships, especially in this matter of their objectives, the more we may expect in satisfaction and personal development. Essentially, we can disregard those rare individuals who apparently have a perfect life with no effort or thought on their part. Such people do exist, but they are the product of the mathematics of probability. Whenever you assemble 4 billion human beings on our small earth, you may be sure that a few of these biological "sports" will show up. We are, of course, speaking of the Marilyn Monroes and the

Albert Einsteins of every generation. The point is that we, as individuals, should be completely undisturbed that we are not in this category.

Our job is clear and relatively simple. Since our society is so organized that we cannot be successful members of it without belonging to many groups, we must choose these groups with great care, getting from each a fragment of a mosaic out of which we will build our life. Each membership must make a definitive contribution to our well-being or be ruthlessly exorcised. This follows from the simple necessity of conserving our energy. The choosing of new memberships thus assumes paramount importance among our definitive activities. The results of this effort will, in effect, determine our success or failure in life.

If this chapter seems to belabor this point mightily, it is only because of its supreme importance—another fact for the data memory bank that is not emphasized in our formal education. We are bombarded with indiscriminate, pressurized offers to "join," but it is seldom that we are urged to exercise comparative judgment before choosing to do so. We do have to do that ourselves.

The Classic Conflict—Company Versus Union

It matters little for the international union president (an executive who receives an executive's pay) to protest that the ultimate objectives of the union and the company are the same. This may be so, but the working objectives of the local union in the plant are seldom in consonance with those of the plant manager. If they were, there would obviously be no real justification for the union. The local union officials—for reasons of sheer self-protection and the perpetuation of their group—must find points of conflict with the company viewpoint in order to justify their own existence. Moreover, it is their duty as leaders to carry on an active campaign to keep their membership strongly behind them in any conflict.

Company management, if it is at all alert, will at the same time be waging a battle for the minds of its employees, whose cooperation is essential to the achievement of the company's goals. Management must not remain inactive and so lose the war by default. Acting in opposition, the two forces—management and union—put the employee in an untenable position. To him it appears quite impossible to be a good company employee and a good union member simultaneously. His personal feelings are highly involved because of the importance of these groups in his life. His job, in most cases, ranks among his top two or three group memberships, and he has been thoroughly conditioned to believe that his union membership is essential to the protection of both his physiological and his safety needs. If he is a good company man, he will have small loyalty toward the union. If he values his union membership, he will not be allowed to express many sentiments favorable to the company.

There could be no more perfect design for role conflict. In fact, there are few other situations in life that even approach this variance of objectives. The individual's reaction will be a personal one, but there are some general aspects of it which are worthy of note.

This dilemma will affect the entire life of the person involved. His work environment will be colored by it; his social contacts—controlled, in a measure, by both company and union—will be influenced; his family will perceive the effects of his personal conflict. If our man is "average," he will feel a strong pull to be *both* a good company employee and a good union member. He knows that his economic future is linked with the success of his company's ventures; but, at the same time, the tiniest of doubts will persist as to the complete probity of the company officials. In the back of his mind, he will acknowledge that the union protects him from "them."

What follows is the severest test of our subject's ability to adapt. He must, for the greater part of his adult life, carry on a dual role that is troublesome to his entire psyche. He must first decide in which milieu he has the better chance for advancement. If he casts his lot on the side of the company, he will be forced to "play it cool" in his union relationships, at least while he is not sure of successful recognition from the company. If he decides in favor of the union, he must play a cagey game in his company contacts. Total ruin will result if he is tagged as "anti-company." With this thin line to walk, his work is cut out for him for a long time to come. Both sides will be inexorable in their scrutiny of his actions and his attitudes, and both will be hypercritical of any observed deviance from norms. His job is to balance these antithetical forces with the least possible harm to himself and his career.

It is inevitable that the cumulation of these opposing forces will result from time to time in a crisis situation. Small items are magnified beyond all belief; minor irritations become major grievances; repressions demand release in the form of action. *The result is the strike.* At this point comes the moment of truth for our subject. Although his actions may be prescribed by the strictest of rituals, his thoughts are still his own. Even while "on the bricks," he just may be formulating a decision which will push him toward the side of the company. Contrariwise, he may be fiercely critical of the position adopted by the company during the confrontation. Should they make a major gaffe, they will have lost this employee irrevocably, and he will forever be a militant unionist.

The only way to resolve this situation is to decide eventually for one side or the other. The two are not coequal, nor can they ever be. At some point, every worker must shade his allegiance in the direction of either the one or the other—there is no other way to relieve the intolerable role conflict under which he has been living. Naturally, it is not necessary that a strike occur for this decision to be made. A normally active mind will occupy itself with this problem in its less severe stages, well before it becomes acute.

Once the decision has been made, the course of action is quite clear. There will be a period of disengagement with the losing side; at the same time, increased activity will be noted in the other camp. The change, to be most successful, will be slow enough that it is not obtrusive and does not alarm the enemy to the point of attack. Finally, the leader of the other group will count the lost member out, but there is a good chance of an amicable severance.

Some people live an entire lifetime without making the definitive decision. Unhappy their lot, for their personal conflict knows no remission.

The Search for Leadership

One of the deeper reactions during role conflict is the fear that the leader, in one or both of the groups involved, is inadequate. Whether or not this is the case, if the person concerned thinks it is so, it is—for him, at least. The reason for his personal quandary is loss of faith in the efficacy of his group membership in satisfying his personal expectations. The role of the leader in this situation of doubt is one of counselor, interpreter, and general resource person. If he is not functioning for the subject in these ways, the latter has every cause to feel that he is being short-changed by his group leadership, this is true even when the leader is unaware of the follower's dilemma—usually because of a breakdown in upward communication. The leader should not be expected to be psychic in this matter and can only help when he has been apprised of the problem.

But, as we have said, this is beside the point. The subject is in trouble; he is looking for help from his leader; it is apparently not forthcoming. When this happens, because of the general state of anxiety induced by his role conflict, he actively reacts to what he perceives as a dangerous lack in his environment. His first reaction is to become sharply and vocally critical of his leadership. This has a greater or lesser effect on the rest of the members according to the personal influence of the subject. If he is a prestigious member, the entire group will become involved as the result of his troubles. There will be widespread dissatisfaction with the group's leaders, but with no substantive evidence to back up the charges.

A small percentage of malcontents in the American public first precipitated a situation which made it bad politics, and therefore impossible, for President Johnson to run for re-election. Both "hawks" and "doves" are classic examples of people suffering from role conflict. In this case, the function of the small group of protesters against the war in Vietnam was to crystallize the thinking of a majority of the American people. Oddly enough, the results of that thinking ran through the entire spectrum regarding the methodology proposed for disengagement from an unpopular war. The only common basis for agreement was the fact that nobody liked the war.

It is a paradox that, should both leaders respond to a cue from the subject, there would be no easing of the role conflict; the responses would only reinforce the different roles demanded by the two groups. Thus, in one sense, the search for leadership is a hopeless cause. At the final reading, role conflict will be resolved by the victim.

Interestingly, the impetus given by a sufferer from role conflict to a search for leadership may be highly contagious. That is, once the signal is given, others may clamber joyously onto the bandwagon out of many other basic motivations. The position of the leader is insecure per se; he is the goal of many attacks for many reasons.

When role conflict precipitates it, much good can actually come from a universalized search for leadership by the group. Periodically, it is healthy for the group to reassess the effectiveness of its leadership. This is what keeps it lean and in fighting trim. The fact that role conflict serves as an original stimulus is only coincidental.

From the other viewpoint, group leaders should be highly sensitive in their reaction once they know that a member has a role conflict. This is one of the most critical times in the membership of that individual. He needs support, understanding, interpretation, and positive counseling from someone. The father image is rampant and must be personified.

At this point, it may be pardonable to generalize for a moment about the search for leadership. As noted, role conflict is only one of many reasons group members use for appraising those to whom they give allegiance. The universal unease which in its many aspects almost monopolizes the modern scene has its basis in a feeling of insecurity about our leaders. An old wives' tale has it that leadership will appear when circumstances demand it. However, we are seeing the living proof that this is not true. Never before in our history has there been a situation more demanding of great leadership than that which faces us now. But one man is no longer capable of carrying the load of so large and complex a society as ours; there must be great leadership at many levels; and its paucity is of deep concern to all behavioral scientists. Our frantic, unsuccessful efforts to find it reveal the deepness of our concern. Since it appears nonexistent—at least in sufficient numbers and depth—our insecurity is escalated into hysteria; we thrash around aimlessly, dangerously.

What we are forgetting, as individuals and as a nation, is that leadership is capable of development from rudimentary beginnings. We have no reason to expect it to appear phoenixlike from the ashes of the last debacle. It is our responsibility to discover potential leadership, to encourage it, to test its wings, and to develop it to its fullest capability. Once we have this up as a priority agenda, we can expect results where before there was only frustration and anxiety. Incidentally, strong capable leadership at all echelons of our group organizations will greatly reduce role conflict because it will do a better job of role definition and thereby prevent our drifting into a never-never land fecund in competing objectives. Our job as group members is to keep up the search inexorably until we get competent and viable leadership.

Ineffective Followership

The major, and most obtrusive, effect of role conflict is ineffective followership. The victim is almost certainly less effective in both his groups because of the anxiety associated with his condition and the feeling of uncertainty about his personal image. If there is anything on earth that we want to be sure of, it is how we fit into the scheme of things.

As personal uncertainty continues, it becomes more and

more the focus of the individual's preoccupation. In the end, it drives everything else from his mind. It therefore follows that his performance as a group member will suffer. It becomes next to impossible for him to concentrate sufficiently on his daily tasks to do a good job with them. Production and quality are double victims of this lack of attention. The alert leader will probe the area of role conflict quickly when he is seeking the reason for a sudden change in performance level in one of his people. What makes it hard to diagnose such a situation is that the victim himself is often unaware of the real nature of his problem. Because it is such a threat to our basic security, the mind is apt to suppress recognition of role conflict at the conscious level. Red-herring "reasons" will be volunteered by the dozen in attempted rationalization.

The second prime symptom of role conflict in a man's followership pattern is a deterioration in his communication. Immersed as he is in his own problems, he neither sends a strong signal nor readily interprets the messages he receives. This is a dangerous irritant in both his regular group activities and to the peers and leaders with whom he deals. Nothing is more mysterious, and therefore more frustrating, than a sudden drying up of communication with a member who has previously been effective in this area. The pure fact of the matter is that he has nothing to communicate but his own sense of urgency and disturbance. Nobody in his right mind is going to tell either his peers or his leader that he is a crazy mixed-up kid.

This problem can develop into a general worsening of interpersonal relationships. A drying up of communication is always interpreted by others as a change for the worse. We revert almost to the position of strangers with those who once were intimates; they don't know what we're thinking—therefore, we are aliens and enemies. And, because we really are refusing to recognize what our problem is, we tend to assume the worst about our own condition. We are mentally waiting in the doctor's office for a diagnosis of obscure symptoms.

Needless to say, our greatest confusion is in the area of goal determination. When we are forced to recognize that the goals of two of our favorite groups are directly opposed, we are in big trouble. The more we struggle to evade the final admission, the greater will be our trauma. In fact, any attempt by our leaders to force us into goal-determination activity will meet with our stiffest resistance. We don't want to face an open and direct comparison of one group's goals when we suspect they are out of phase with those of another group to which we belong. Trying to operate in one group, let alone two, where the goals are indeterminate is like being the navigator on a ship in a pea-soup fog.

In role conflict, also, there is a strong tendency to resist any formal measurement of achievement. We know at the gut level that our performance is below par, but any attempt on another's part to bring this into focus will only irritate us.

It should be emphasized that this mental state is not necessarily one of deliberate negativism. It is a purely automatic defense mechanism that, for the most part, is beyond our direct control.

It is clearly evident that the victim of role conflict puts himself in jeopardy in both of his groups through his ineffective followership. His status, his interpersonal relationships, his leadership potential, and even his very membership are on the line. The principal evidence, so far as the rest of the members are concerned, is his lowered efficiency as a co-worker. No one will tolerate for long a fellow who doesn't carry his share of the load. This is especially true when there is no clear signal as to what his trouble is. For the obviously sick or handicapped brother, patience can be long-lasting; when, however, a man is apparently "goldbricking," tempers will rise and open conflict may result.

About this time, the grave threat of losing both group memberships will usually force the subject to admit openly what is troubling him. At least, he will be more likely to admit it to himself, which is of prime importance. Once the trouble is out in the open, there is always a better chance for successful resolution of the dilemma. The cycle can then begin whereby the conflict is resolved, starting with an evaluative comparison of the importance of the two groups in the subject's hierarchy. From this comparison to an examination of the groups' objectives is a short step, but not necessarily an easy one. The hard work still lies ahead—choosing which of the two groups is the ascendant one and deciding what to do about the other. Will it be necessary to sacrifice one group, or can some sort of viable compromise be arrived at to permit continuation of membership in both groups?

Our deepest pride is involved in our effectiveness in groups. It is here that we make or break our self-image. To know that we are losing effectivity in one or even two of our more valued groups is a problem of the first magnitude. The only answer is, of course, to push to a resolution of the conflict in an acceptable fashion and hope that both memberships will be salvaged. If they cannot, the one remaining will have gained in importance to us.

The Repair of Perspective

Even if the victim of role conflict is successful in reducing it, there will be some residual damage to his ability to maintain effective group membership, principally in the area of personal perspective. His whole value system has undergone a severe shock in the dissonance between the groups. He starts to question fundamentals which once seemed unalterable.

This kind of trauma always needs time for its treatment. We must fall back, reassess, reevaluate. Our role conflict arose in the first place from the presence of incompatible norms, which were in turn established to protect and insure achievement of dissimilar goals. Once perceived, these incompatible norms forced us to choose, in most cases, between two memberships, both of which were valuable to us. Whether the reduction of the role conflict was accomplished by severance from one of the groups or by a restructuring of comparative values, the result will be approximately the same—the tilting of our general frame of reference for a significant part of our life.

The process of repair will begin at the foundation level, and the first step is a reprioritization of our most basic beliefs. The new hierarchy of values resulting from this exercise must then be set alongside the structure of our memberships and examined for compatibility. Moreover, because of the difficult time just past, we will be suspicious of all relationships, less willing to accept them at face value. Some of the more difficult readjustments will take place in our peer relationships. Our fellow members will have remarked about the change in us during the time of role conflict; so not only will we have to remold our own thinking, but we also will face the rebuilding of our image in the eyes of the rest of the group. Once again, we are faced with a process that is quite time consuming. When our exposed self has apparently suffered a drastic change, those about us will be reluctant to accept us back into the fold without a lengthy new probationary period.

Role conflict is a maturation aid for the adult who will use it as such. The trauma involved will be worth it if, as a result, we emerge with strengthened values and a better-based hierarchy of principles.

We become so inured to being a member of many groups that we forget that certain inescapable (and most important) parts of our life can never be anything except solo efforts. The process of growing up and maturing is one of them. If there is an essential and mortal weakness in a society structured so heavily along group-membership lines, it is the possibility that an individual can be carried along by his groups and fail to become adult. The more complex and "civilized" the society, the greater the number of cocoons which fail to hatch. Such persons remain parasites on their environment until some basic shock either makes or breaks them. Role conflict is a perfect example of this—at least for the normal individual.

The good part of this cycle is the last. Once the conflict has been resolved and values restructured, and perspective repaired, the "new" individual who emerges will be a much better group member wherever he finds himself. He will regain and perhaps improve his old effectiveness in all groups. He will be more responsive to his leaders, more sensitive to their cues. His interpersonal relationships will be strengthened by the fire, old friendships reinforced, and rewarding new friendships made easier. There will be gains in many aspects of his personality.

The other half of the picture has to do with the effect of this "new" member's experience on the rest of the group. The ultimate result will be increased strength. Although they may relegate him to a sort of limbo while they are reexamining him, once they have again accepted him his membership will be on firmer grounds than before.

We should remember at all times that perspective is a highly individual matter. Depending on the endowments of each person, it will be narrowly circumscribed or as broad as the whole horizon. Each of us finds the level of his ability to perceive, understand, and conceptualize. The meaning of my existence to me is totally different than of yours to you. This is as it should be. Were the world to look alike to all its residents, we should have a gray environment indeed.

* * *

Perhaps, like sulphur and molasses in our grandfather's time, role conflict has a therapeutic place in our mental and emotional lives. We are lesser persons if we have never undergone its trauma and the readjustments it brings. Role conflict has its origin in our perfectly natural effort to live the full and complete life. The mole who retires to his dark burrow will never experience it, nor can he know the growth which is its natural offspring.

The lesson is clear and simple. When our maneuverings and gropings to fill every nook and cranny of existence with new and different experiences momentarily backfire on us, we have a chance to emerge from our difficulties as a bigger and better person, more valuable to all of our groups, and a wiser and more satisfied "me."

Nearly every person alive will at some time be in role conflict. This occurs whenever objectives (and norms) of two major groups are incompatible. Role conflict is the penalty of multigroup membership. It is quite possible for the subject to become neurotic over role conflict, especially if its reduction appears to be impossible without severance from one of the groups.

Our personal objectives must be harmonious if our mental health is to be preserved. The classic role conflict situation (the one that affects more people than any other) is that arising between the company and the union. At the local level, it is often extremely difficult to be a good company man and a good union member simultaneously. Some workers go through their entire working lifetime living with this role conflict.

When role conflict is present, our search for leadership is intensified. Both as symptom and cause, ineffective followership accompanies role conflict. We become a "sick," atypical group member, with resultant complications in our group interactions.

The major aftermath of a role conflict which has been reduced or resolved is a time of repairing personal perspective. Reevaluation is necessary of the subject's most basic objectives. As a result of passing through a role conflict and emerging from it successfully, most people grow, develop, and mature. Although highly traumatic, its end result may be salutary.

Chapter 11

The Deviant

$\mathcal{B}$ECAUSE of man's infinite capacity for variability, it is seldom possible to find a group in which there is total conformity to all norms. One or more members will observe certain norms to a greater or lesser degree than standards specify. The matter of deviance is of great importance to both leaders and members, since it represents a major internal threat to group security. Once established, group objectives must be rigidly adhered to or the group is in trouble.

What Leads to Deviance?

There can be endless causes for deviance in the group, but the most common reasons can be categorized since they spring from fundamental psychological reasons.

Many deviants manifest atypical group behavior as a sign of their rejection of group leadership. Whether this stems from mistrust of the leader as an individual or from rivalry for that leadership is immaterial. Once the follower has decided that he cannot follow the present leader, his first reaction will be to disobey that leader's dictates. Indications of this deviance may be exquisitely subtle or blatantly challenging. The whole spectrum of rebellion will be shown, depending upon the comparative strength of the follower and the leader. In any event, this challenge to leadership cannot go unanswered. If the leader is strong, the group will ordinarily make the first move. The leader himself may never even have to get involved if group countermeasures are quick and strong enough. However, if he does, the confrontation becomes open and extremely personal in nature. This situation is then settled on a one-to-one basis.

Deviance may be caused by an attempt to seize leadership even though the deviant may have nothing personal against the present leader. The man who has a strong drive to take over will make the try, no matter who the incumbent is. This attempted coup d'état will be quite traumatic to the group. Not only the leader but the members will perceive it as a challenge to the fundamental security of the group and will respond accordingly. This is not to say (in large groups especially) that the deviant may not have a few followers among the membership. The splinter group that forms around him is thought of and treated as an individual by the rest of the membership. A deviant operating under this motivation will challenge the group norms on the basis of change for change's sake. He couldn't care less which individual tenet he attempts to upset. His actions constitute a power play, pure and simple.

The creative person may also become a deviant. He is inclined to have little or no reverence for tradition as such. The fact that a method has worked well for a long time is not germane. His interest is in the mystery and challenge of the new. How would it be if—? What would happen when—? In the last analysis, creativity has a strong element of extra legality. If the innovation is great enough, the legal code probably does not provide for this contingency; it will be either legalized or demolished by the governing members, but after the fact. The innovator also is usually a strong crusader for his ideas, giving little peace to those around him until his creation has been tried. The highly creative member of a group can aid materially in its growth and development—or be the principal cause of its untimely demise. Often, however, he will not be interested in the continuing job of the leader. He is too busy seeking other innovations to be an administrator.

Another type of deviant is the one-time-only rebel. His record of conformity is probably near perfect, but for some reason he finds it impossible to accept one particular group norm. This member is likely to be the most recalcitrant deviant in any group, not amenable to any group sanction. Depending upon how important the norm is in the group's hierarchy, his punishment will be light, strong, onerous, or even the most severe—expulsion from the group. In most cases, this type of deviance is evidence of conflict between the norm and a basic principle of the member. It is impossible to forecast the circumstances in which this conflict will arise, but it is a safe bet that it will happen with fair frequency.

Yet another reason for deviance is sheer boredom. All of us, at various times in our existence, suddenly may become fed up with things as they are and demand a change in routine as the only possible remedy for our dissatisfaction. The timing for this feeling, too, is unpredictable. But, when it occurs, the member will choose a norm—any norm—and challenge it as a protest against his mental state. Because this type of deviance does occur at random, its effect will be heightened by its unexpectedness. Quite a flurry of activity will follow its appearance, but the deviant probably will not resist too strongly or for too long the sanctions imposed by the group. Once his safety valve has been opened, his pressure will subside fairly quickly.

These suggestions by no means exhaust the list of causes for deviance. In fact, there are limitless reasons why members may choose to fight city hall. At some point, they will consider it important to run counter to the herd as an expression of their own sacred individuality. In the last analysis, it is a method of asserting "myness" to our peers and leaders.

Deviance and Group Cohesiveness

The deviant is responsible for more than a little of the cohesiveness of his group. His failure to observe one or more of the norms is seen as a positive threat to the group's existence. The normal first reaction of other members is to draw closer together in mutual support against this threat. Ordinarily, this heightened cohesiveness will persist as long as the deviance is in evidence. In the presence of deviance, cohesiveness will increase faster and be of greater magnitude than it would at the first perception of an outside threat. The latter is frightening, but *internal* threat is terrifying.

The physical and emotional alert triggered by this heightened togetherness will spill over into greater general group activity, and groups with high cohesiveness will achieve their major objectives more quickly. At the same time, interpersonal relationships among the rest of the membership are likely to be smoother than normal. Small personal differences will be submerged by the reaction to the threat. Attempted communication with group leadership is a part of this general reaction. Members turn to the father image for reassurance and guidance in this painful situation.

Alert leadership will seize the opportunity to reinforce group objectives and norms. Full advantage should be taken of the example of nonconformity and the dangers it can conjure up. This period of close rapport can be useful to a skilled leader.

There is another possibility which should be considered. If the deviance persists and moderate sanctions are not successful in hazing the deviant back into conformity, cohesiveness may suffer as successively more severe sanctions are applied. Somewhere along the line, personal regard for the deviant will obtrude into the thinking of at least some of the members. His closer friends will begin to question whether his sin is worthy of all the punishment. The fine unanimity of the early period of the deviance will disappear in a cloud of differences. Once again, the sensitivity of the leadership must be called into play. This is a time for decision. Positive reinforcement of the norm under attack must be given and splinter groups must be broken up. The crisis involves the group as a whole rather than the individual members. Definitive action must be undertaken to suppress the deviance and heal the rift in group solidarity. Any one or several members are expendable in this crisis situation.

In general, group cohesiveness is the product of many vectors. Its magnitude and positive or negative direction of movement will be the result of all of them. The effect of deviance will, in almost every case, be a sharp emphatic thrust.

What is the situation of the deviant himself in this general picture? He will be getting the first intimations of the disfavor of the group. His reaction may be fright or anger, depending upon his personal makeup. If he is frightened by the apparent anger of his peers and friends, he will be a likely candidate for return to conformity. If angered, his deviance, which may have begun whimsically, will now be set in concrete, and he may pursue it to the bitter end.

A reconsideration of the causes of deviance might be in order at this point. The person who is so much an individual that he cannot conform to any established pattern is not the major problem. His atypicality will be universally expressed in all his memberships. As soon as the pattern becomes evident the news will spread, and his potential for threat to any of his groups will be proportionately reduced. The real threat is the one-time deviant, whose behavior will be recognized as alarmingly against his pattern. He will elicit the greatest action from the group and the deepest concern from its leadership because he has been a model member for the greater part of his group history. Remember also that his principles are involved, and thus his reclamation will be the most difficult. By stubbornly setting his head and refusing to knuckle under to increasingly severe sanctions, he will cause correspondingly deeper concern within the group.

The entire matter of deviance is inextricably bound to individual differences. Each of us in our own time will be a deviant in one or more of our groups, and every one of us will at some time feel the lash of group disfavor. Our only assuagement will be the knowledge that we have contributed to the perpetuation of the group in two ways: by heightening cohesiveness and by forcing a reexamination of one or more group norms. The ultimate result of deviance can be a better and stronger group and a deeper understanding of group objectives.

The Deviant and Assumed Leadership

A not unusual cause of deviance is the assumption of group leadership. If the deviant aspires to leadership, he must at some time make his move or forget his hopes. The deviance then takes the form of a challenge to battle the entrenched leadership. We must remember that the man who seeks leadership is usually strongly motivated. The position at the head of the pack is overpoweringly attractive to him, and he will spend a lifetime, if necessary, to get there.

If a member assumes leadership in a group, he will inevitably embroil every other member in the ensuing fight. There is no such thing as effective neutrality in this arena. Even if a member wants to remain neutral, he will not be allowed to do so. The issue is too critical and too important to the future of the group for anyone to be passive. Forcing the membership to make a choice can have a therapeutic effect, if it is not done too often. Either the present leader will be reinforced, or he will have to vacate his position. In either case, there will be no doubt as to the effective leadership of the winner of the struggle.

The power play, traumatic as it is to all parties, is an interesting phenomenon with a recognizable life cycle of its own. Its birth is usually signaled by an act of deviance, as already mentioned. Its childhood and youth are symbolized by preliminary skirmishing and choosing up sides by the membership. Maturity to old age encompasses the actual battle between the pretender and the incumbent. And the power play dies when the decision is reached.

A fascinating variant of deviance and assumed leadership occurs in the upper echelons of formal groups and is totally masked and hidden from the members lower in the group. To the initiate, cues are perfectly readable. An innocuous-looking memo, a new organization chart, the transfer (in or out) of a key manager, and especially the clever use of rumor and the grapevine clearly signal the battle of the gods. For the most part, a power play at this level will not have a drastic effect on the line soldier. Only the members of middle management may suffer the fate of the innocent bystander. Basically, there is no difference between this deviance and the assumption of leadership at any level.

The reactions of the membership to this conflict situation will run the gamut. Aside from the inescapable need to make a choice between the combatants, there will be a normal distribution of personal feelings about the entire situation. Some will be minimally involved and will bear an air of detachment about the fight. Others will be truly concerned but will make an effort to keep the situation from interfering with their normal group activities. A few will become totally immersed in the donnybrook, to the exclusion of any other constructive activity.

We should not ignore either the position or the reactions of the established leader. His initial response to the threat will be typical of his personal makeup. Ordinarily, a leader will display an aggressive reaction, which can take many forms. Watchful waiting can be so filled with repressed action as to be most threatening. Once the nominal leader has "read" his enemy, he will follow, again, a course typical of his own makeup. He may ambush, attack frontally, or circle and come in on the flank. His titular leadership gives him many advantages. He has the organization, the operation, and the history—and habit—of group loyalty going for him. The challenger carries the burden of proof. He must show that the established leader is truly short in his delivery of promised results and that group objectives are not being achieved on schedule. He must also prove beyond a reasonable doubt that the group objectives themselves are improperly drawn or unrealistic. All this amounts to an admission that the challenger will have to be demonstrably superior to the incumbent to have a fighting chance of unseating him. From his vantage point, the nominal leader has by far the better chance of emerging the victor.

In the meantime, what is the situation of the group as a whole? Its members have been subjected to an unexpected and unusual trauma. They may be faced with hitherto unfelt doubts about the status quo. At least some uncertainty will be introduced as to the leader they have been following. If the leader proves to be "wrong," what becomes of the basic goals of the group? Should the group exist at all? What will happen to members' personal careers as a result of this unwanted interference? Adjustment to this sort of situation is difficult in the extreme. In fact, the average member will *not* adjust to it, but will demand a clear-cut definition and resolution of the dilemma before resuming any sort of normal personal operation.

This may be the most difficult sort of deviance for the group to handle. Fundamental values are at stake; the existence of the group is threatened. Still the deviance is valuable, and not the least of its value lies in the impetus given to personal maturation in this trial by fire. When we have survived such a struggle, we have a retrospective reference point for the judgment of many other factors of group existence. Things have a way of falling into place as they are put up against this master template. Other decisions downstream are made easier as a result of this experience.

Sanctions Against the Deviant

In the thinking of the group membership one fact is unalterable—the deviant must be punished. His defiance of the basis of group structure (the norm) is intolerable. Perhaps the term "punishment" is not strictly accurate. The intent is only to get the deviant back into line and restore the complete integrity of the group.

Sanctions can be applied in several ways. The leader may apply them as a recognized part of his general duties. Some leaders will go to great lengths to avoid doing so, since they feel that their very position already interferes with their group relationships without the addition of this extra hazard. So such leaders try to shift to the general membership the responsibility for applying group sanctions. It is harder for a person to be angry at a whole group than at one or two individual members.

The group that has this responsibility may also react in a similar manner. Many groups, especially semiformal ones, set up formal disciplinary committees. To further dilute the opprobrium, membership in the disciplinary committee is frequently rotated at relatively short intervals, so that no member will come to be permanently associated with this unpopular subgroup.

In a comfortable majority of cases, group sanctions will be applied spontaneously by the entire group, acting as a sort of committee of the whole. In this way, no one or two people can ever be saddled with the hatred of the deviant. The group acting in concert to force the deviant back into line represents a common example of social pressure in its purest form. It takes an extraordinary personality to withstand this force. In most cases, the deviant will collapse quickly and return to the fold.

Groups have a way of agreeing upon a specific sanction rather swiftly, but they are amazingly sensitive when tailoring the sanction to the size and import of the dereliction. This lifesaving ability means that many deviants are salvaged and returned to conformity and good membership who would otherwise have been lost. Another variable enters the picture when the deviant does not succumb to social pressure but continues in his infraction of the rule. To the group, he is compounding the threat. The severity of sanction is escalated at once and continued to the point of no return. Expulsion from the group, the ultimate sanction, will be caused more rapidly by persistence in deviance than by random disregard of several norms.

The reaction of the deviant to the application of sanctions will be conditioned by several variables. The first variable is obviously the reason for his deviance. Is he making a deliberate run at the authority of the nominal leader? Is his nonconformity the result of conflict between the norm and his own basic principle? Is his failure to observe this norm only a safety-valve reaction? Or is this behavior a childish attempt to get the attention of the group?

When the deviant acts out of deep ego involvement over a principle, we can expect his resistance to social sanction to be stiffest. At the other extreme, if he is merely seeking attention he will be satisfied when he does get enough attention of the group for them to punish him. In either event, this is the random type of deviant. The compulsive deviant will pay little attention to either the kind or severity of the sanction imposed. He is the truly atypical member of society, and no templates have been drawn to fit his pattern. This antisocial being can never really be a member of any group; he is a member only by chance, and he will detach himself and float away in a short time. However, when his motivation is deep he can become one of the real change agents of our society.

In terms of group dynamics, the entire matter of deviance is abnormal. Yet it is also the one white hope for the future of our society. Deviance is the only cause of progress in any society.

Deviance is a symptom of dissatisfaction with the status

quo and, in the extreme case, an indication of systemic disease within the group. The leader must quickly diagnose which of these two possibilities is the real reason for a particular deviance. Naturally, the sick group is a strong indictment of the leader. In any event, the leader is deeply concerned, and his reaction will be protective of himself, his position, and the situation of the group. There just may be little or no direct communication from the leader to his membership about deviance. He may feel it is better to perpetuate the fiction that all is well than to publicly admit to shortcomings in the functioning of the group. The membership, if it is normal, will understand the reason for the leader's reticence and will forgive him for it.

Picking Up the Slack

As the group becomes preoccupied with the deviance in its midst, the attention of the entire group is centered first on the deviant and then upon the effort to apply an appropriate sanction. This concentration on an unusual group process results in a severe falling off of productive activity. Actual constructive work done toward goal achievement becomes perilously minimal. Quality suffers greatly. It is possible for this condition to continue for some time and even escalate, since the leader is as involved as the rest of the members, if not more so.

The length of this diversion will be governed by the amount of time necessary to reduce the deviance. Of course, like any other new thing, the involvement with the deviance and the sanction invoked will dissipate somewhat as time passes. The gatekeeper of the group will eventually sound the alarm and remind the membership that group life must go on. This is ordinarily the turning point, and a gradually accelerating return to normality will ensue. In most cases, the group will be back to full-bore activity by the time definitive disposition has been arrived at for the deviant.

A parallel activity always accompanies this cycle. When group members become deviant their own regular work will suffer badly, leaving a hole in total productivity which has to be made up from some other source. (This process amounts to the closing of ranks after casualties occur in a battle.) As a result, working partnerships are disrupted. Any group will pair itself off into smaller work parties, either naturally or under orders from group leaders. These working relationships, if they succeed at all, become comfortable with the membership. Any disturbance of them is an irritant that will affect production as well as tempers. Closing up the group to cover for a deviant is made even more difficult by the fact that no one knows immediately whether the defection is temporary or permanent. Thus the creation of new working partnerships is delayed during this uncertain period. Why bother to get used to a new partner if the old one will be returning in a short time?

Picking up the slack in the group is also made harder because of damage to communication channels. They are so clogged with messages about the deviant or the sanction imposed on him that routine messages are blocked. This is especially true in the vertical lines between the membership and its leader—in other words, the channels necessary for the accomplishment of the group's regular work. This communication block appears quickly after the deviance and will persist during the latter's life span. In a sense, it is as if the group were oblivious of regular work procedures.

The most deeply troubled members will be the friends and working partners of the deviant—*especially if they have not joined in his deviance*. Their position is like that of the family of a criminal. Feeling themselves the objects of attack and disapproval (whether they actually are or not), their only possible reaction is a defensive one. They feel compelled to explain their position even when the rest of the members don't really demand it. This compulsion will seriously affect the attitudes, productivity, and general effectiveness of these members. Of course, if they have formed a splinter group and joined in the deviance, their treatment by and their posture toward the rest of the group will be different. But they will have known this in advance and will have prepared themselves at least in part.

The group will react to deviance as one individual. It feels a generalized malaise, with a concomitant loss of total effectivity. Related symptoms are troublesome and can often retard the group's recovery from the original illness.

The group leader is under great stress during periods of major deviance. Few other situations are as dangerous to the leader and the group as is this one. The leader's understanding of the problems must be complete and totally clear or he will rush into an inappropriate action.

The readjustment of all members to pick up the slack can have some surprising results. The heavier pressure may result in the discovery of abilities hitherto unsuspected. Some people never disclose their true potential unless challenged. By the same token, some members will crack and deteriorate when the trauma becomes this great. Some who have seemed to be solid citizens will be found wanting.

This period calls for some of the best teamwork possible from the group. Its existence is threatened internally in at least two ways: by the actions of the deviant member or members and by a resultant failure to achieve objectives because of decreased work effort or lowered quality. How well everyone rises to this challenge will be a real measure of the group's worth. Picking up the slack must be recognized as a regular part of group process, since rare indeed is the group which never has a deviant. In fact, the more important and meaningful the group, the more certain it is that some members will eventually challenge the status quo.

Group Reappraisal

One effect of deviance within a group is a good one: reappraisal. No matter what the basic cause of deviance, the group will have reason to question its objectives, its norms, and its leadership. If norms are properly drawn, they will totally support the group's objectives. If not, either norms or objectives should be altered to bring them together. It will more often be the norm rather than the objective that meets with the disfavor of the deviant. That is to say, he will verbalize his disagreement around the norm rather than the objective, since a single norm is much easier to attack than the intellectual concept that group objectives often are.

Group reappraisal must be done by all members, either individually or collectively. This important situation requires a consensus about the present status of the group and what change is to be made. Quite often, the deviant is the first to have noticed that the group is getting out of step with the rest of the world—that is, its objectives or norms are becoming anachronistic. If this is the case, the group will of course want to get itself back into harmony with its environment. The periodicity of these efforts at introspection cannot be specified exactly. Groups may go about their business for a long time and then suddenly have several occasions calling for reappraisal within a few days or weeks. However, deviance often is one of the signals that a significant change in objectives or norms may be needed.

The leader himself may be the cause of deviance. If this is so, all aspects of his performance must be measured objectively. This is obviously next to impossible in the formal group, but semiformal and informal groups, which have direct control over the tenure of the leader, can go through this exercise whenever desirable.

To be functional, reappraisal should not stop with one or two areas of activity. A complete job should be done, covering every aspect of group process. A major housecleaning of this sort is time consuming and usually not well received by the membership, since it brings to a halt other activities. The knowledge that its result will be salutary should overcome these objections: Even if no changes are necessary, it will have been worthwhile to learn that everything is shipshape.

Although it is true that all members must be involved in a reappraisal, it is not necessary that each individual member in a large group reinvent the wheel. The reappraisal process can be put on an organized basis by parceling out responsibility for various aspects of the exercise. It then is incumbent on those who are spearheading the activity to communicate thoroughly and completely with every member. Results of a group reappraisal are too important to let any member be incompletely or incorrectly informed as to the outcome. Once the members know that a survey is to be made, they are quickly involved and will demand complete knowledge of the general outcome. Although the work is put out in pieces, there is a committee-of-the-whole aspect about reappraisal which should be carefully fostered. It is one of the many cases where the group is treated as if it were an individual.

If a group is normally healthy and doing a fair-to-good job of attaining its goals on schedule, reappraisal will fall into the category of preventive therapy. Close introspection will bring to light potential trouble before it has time to develop. This is particularly true in respect to keeping the group in harmony with its surroundings. Ordinarily, the expertise of a good leader makes him a little more alert to potential trouble than the members are.

In few cases is the deviant aware of the group reaction to his defiance. His course seems perfectly logical to him (unless he is directly challenging established authority), and he will be surprised—even shocked—if he learns what a furor he has caused. The whole relationship between the deviant and the rest of the group undergoes dramatic change in a short time after his nonconformity has been recognized. He may well be the last member to become aware of this change. One of the immediate reactions of the rest of the members will be a tendency to stop talking to the deviant simply because, in most cases, they don't know what to say. Until they have sorted out facts, actions, attitudes, and apparent results, they find it hard to communicate with the deviant on any normal plane. For something of the same reason, the deviant will stop talking to the other members as soon as he senses their attitude toward him. This kind of reaction is nearly universal: It can indicate uncertainty, pique, fear, or dislike. In any event, for the moment the deviant and the rest of the group have no effective interaction. This makes reappraisal more difficult, because no one knows what the central figure in the controversy is thinking. Fortunately, this silent period usually does not last long. Some or all of the members will begin to approach the deviant in order to get him back into conformity. With this as a point of entry, often fuller communication is set up on a continuing basis. *Every* member of the group, including the deviant, must have a part in this forced process of reappraisal.

The Deviant and Group Objectives

The trauma that the deviant's actions arouse will have a strong effect on the objectives of his group. Most of this effect will be ancillary to the deviant's own activity; it is rare that he will consciously attack the structure of objectives. His nonconformity will simply center the attention of the group on its norms and objectives.

At this point, it might be productive to look at the *function* of objectives. First, they are the instrument around which the group is structured. They define its purpose and comprise the charter under which it operates. Second, objectives impose a time constraint, a control function which is extremely important in determining group effectiveness.

The deviant is a major force within the group working against its ideals. In more cases than not, he is a strong personality who recognizes fewer constraints on his operations than do most members. He is prepared to challenge an objective just as he will challenge the actions of a peer if they are contrary to his wishes. This challenging attitude will at first meet with strong opposition from the members; but, if he persists, their thinking may also begin to shift. If they take a long, hard look, they may find the objectives dysfunctional in one or more areas. The deviant can thus become a de facto leader by shifting the focus of objectives in a new direction. This "unleadership" activity can proceed for some time before it is recognized by the membership. On the other hand, the deviant does consciously assume the posture of leadership on those occasions when his deeper principles are involved by actively trying to force a restructuring of objectives according to his wishes. The group reaction to either of these situations follows a fairly predictable pattern. Initially, strong resistance is generated, but, once the group has had a chance to think, a point of decision will be reached. Either conflict with the deviant will be intensified, with a parallel strengthening of the norms and objectives under attack, or some alterations will be made. The deviant's role is not so much one of clear-cut leadership as it is that of a catalyst. His behavior will automatically produce a reaction from the group, but in a majority of situations he will not have any real control over this. Most of the time, especially at first, he will be the target of group action.

Any normal group must be continually aware that its objectives are subject to change at any time. This is a function of a changing external environment and internal changes in values as the members develop. Acceptance of this fact is one of the essentials of sophisticated membership. The group whose objectives have become static or rigid is old and moribund no matter what its chronological age. Thus the appearance of deviance is often a blessing in disguise.

General alertness (one of whose manifestations is deviance) will cause interest in what the deviant considers mistakes in time control measures. His whole agitation is often directed toward realigning the group's time schedule. This can mean success or failure in competition with others. When we speak of a "sense of timing," we mean just that—an intuitive appraisal of the fitness of a work schedule. In formal groups, this ordinarily has to do with production and delivery schedules. Customer wishes may or may not be the sole determinants of a factory's pace. In informal or semiformal groups timing may be of just as great importance, but it may often involve events other than physical production. It is in such cases that a deviant's acute sense of timing can be of inestimable value.

The deviant is a catalyst who can cause the rest of the members to sharpen their own perception of objectives and of the timing involved in successful achievement. Sharpened perceptions can result even when the deviant is unsuccessful in pushing through his changes. The fact that the membership was aroused enough to think through their feelings and to determine their present wishes is highly salutary. Thus, although he will often lose personally because of his actions, the deviant is actually performing a real service by making the members question basic verities.

The mechanism of deviance is unpredictable and difficult to control when it does occur. We can be sure of one thing —deviance is a phenomenon which will not be long absent from any normal group. Its periodicity is not symmetrical, but we may be sure that it will appear.

The Deviant and Progress

Change is threatening to most people: It represents the new, unknown, and therefore dangerous situation which immediately mobilizes characteristic defensive reactions. Many people are suspicious of a change even where the advantage is open and obvious. They fear some hidden "catch" which will vitiate the good and result in a net loss.

The deviant is at a disadvantage in trying to introduce innovation simply because he *is* a nonconformist. His unique position among his peers makes all his actions suspect. The other members are looking for a hidden agenda, and, of course, there may well be one. Since habitual deviants are strongly individualistic, it is entirely possible that their intent is the exploitation of others. The only hope of the deviant for selling his proposal is to have the fire of the zealot and the persistence of a stubborn man. For long periods of time, a deviant must be impervious to his own feelings and sensitivity. He needs the ability to balance the short-term upset against the long-term gain for both himself and the membership.

A good leader will always possess a modicum of the makeup of the deviant. He cannot be totally conformist and function as a leader. With this in mind, it is also obvious that the leader has advantages in effecting change over the deviant who is a follower. Most leaders, however, will temper their deviance under the exigencies of other pressures of leadership. They know that the progress of the group will be a function of their ability to absorb and rationalize change.

In most societies, progress is not a spiral staircase, but a series of short rises followed by a leveling off at plateaus. Historically, change and progress are much easier to accomplish in a young culture, where the drag of accumulated tradition is less onerous than in an older civilization. We have only to note the greater difficulty of making a significant change in the British culture than in the American to establish this fact.

This may sound as if change and progress could be equated on an absolute basis. Nothing could be further from the truth. Change can be accomplished simply by rearranging existing elements; progress entails a recognizable and quantifiable inherent *advantage*. The gain has to be net. Once again, it should be emphasized that the deviant's existence in the group is in itself a stimulus to the necessary introspection, since he is an atypical member. The fact that he is there makes others examine his differences from themselves.

Progress is a rich and heady food; an overdose of it can produce mental and spiritual indigestion. This is why a period of readjustment should be allowed after every incremental advance. Advantages come to people in categories of time saving, increased wealth, or greater personal satisfaction. Any of these three produces an imbalance in the individual sufficient to make him fall back and reconnoiter. He is looking at a new and strange terrain.

Not all deviants propose innovation from selfish motives. It is incontestable that some unique characters do have the ultimate good of their fellows in mind as they campaign for change. They meet the same resistance as do their more Machiavellian brothers; their only advantage is the purity of their motivation.

There is incontrovertible growth and development in a group which has accepted a progressive change. It will be operating thereafter at a higher level with all the concomitant advantages of broader perspective and greater vision. This is an integral part of growth and maturation. It would be hard to measure the exact contribution of the deviant to group progress. Innovation as such is sterile unless all concerned perceive the advantages they can derive from it. One of the more discouraging aspects of any deviant's existence is to crusade for change after change, see them grudgingly accepted, and realize with a thud that there is no appreciation of the gains involved. Actually, the *true* deviant couldn't care less. He is not actually people-centered; he is moved by the idea of change for the sake of change. His personal kicks come from forcing his will on his peers; he is not concerned with their reaction.

Progress, like so many other concepts, is a relative thing. In our immediate surroundings, we accept as commonplace things that would have been astounding to our fathers. The difference must be exponential for us to recognize progress. This imposes self-limiting constraints upon the activity and influence of the deviant in any society. What would have been monumental a century ago would not cause a ripple on today's scene. What we are saying is that deviance itself must be more pronounced and more innovative in order to make its mark on the modern scene. Perhaps this is for the best. Man has a limited ability to ingest, digest, and assimilate large chunks of progress.

* * *

A deviant is an obtrusive nonconformist. His presence in the group is that of the fox in the chicken coop. The causes of deviance run across an entire spectrum of reasons, from violation of personal principle to rebellion against established leadership to a "safety valve" release of personal pressures.

The appearance of deviance will immediately sharply increase group cohesiveness. This effect will continue until the deviance has been reduced or until personal feelings for the deviant begin to intrude into the consciousness of his friends and peers. One of the more salient causes of deviance is an assumption of leadership—a direct challenge to the incumbent which cannot go unanswered.

Sanctions against the deviant will be nicely calculated against the magnitude of the offense. They will range from practical nonrecognition of the offense to expulsion from the group. The removal of the deviant from the working membership results in the need to pick up the slack. This becomes a joint project of the membership not subject to much influence from established leadership. But an unfailing result of significant deviance is a reappraisal of the status of the group. This includes objectives and norms, as well as a caustic look at the contribution of every individual member. We cannot fail to observe the effect of the deviant on group objectives, either calculated or random.

Chapter 12

The Isolate

T_{HE} isolate is not simply the extreme extension of the deviant. There are many subtle forces at work within the group, in the member, and in the outside environment, which combine to cause one situation or the other. There are observable differences in the ways in which the membership regard and react to the deviant and the isolate. These two also respond differently. True, the same individual may progress (or *regress*) from deviance to isolation. When this happens, there are some significant changes in his mental and emotional states. Neither condition is typical of general group membership, and it should be remembered that every different position, treatment by the group, and personal perception will be unique.

The Deviant Versus the Isolate

The deviant is still a member of the group, although his status may have suffered and his position be quite perilous. The isolate, although still physically present, can no longer claim membership. The rest of the members have counted him out and restructured their activities without him.

The sin of the deviant is, at least for the moment, much less grievous than that of the isolate. The deviant is guilty of a gross misdemeanor, whereas the isolate has committed a felony. Although it could be argued that this is a difference in degree rather than kind, the treatment given the two offenders contradicts this position.

The deviant's attitude toward the group is different from that of the isolate, because he knows that his estrangement is probably temporary. With the expectation of reentry into a state of grace, his hostilities (if indeed there are any) are less than those of the isolate. *This point is crucial.* If something real or perceived in the environment generates hostility in the deviant, the prognosis is rapid development toward eventual isolation. For this reason, the perceptiveness of the leader is especially critical at this point. If he sees the possibility of escalation and is aware of factors in the environment which could aggravate the deviant, he has a better than even chance of salvaging this member. His ability to foresee the stumbling block and lead his group safely around it will be a good test of his control over the membership.

The deviant naturally has much more freedom of action within the group than does the isolate. The latter is, in effect, restricted from any of his normal activities, at least insofar as they have impact on others. His remaining degree of freedom is therapeutic for the deviant and in some cases may be sufficient to keep him from slipping over the edge into isolation. This fact has been recognized for years by psychiatrists and psychoanalysts, as evidenced by their free and frequent use of action per se as treatment. Any normal individual is aware of how much his frustration and anxiety are heightened in a crisis situation if he is unable to take any kind of action. Our adrenal glands prepare us for action; it is not their fault if we fail to burn up the secretion they pour into our blood.

The deviant, since his mind is in less turmoil than is that of the isolate, is better able to evaluate his position and make plans for return to full group membership. Actually, the isolate's hands are tied; he is unable to make any effort at reparation. His capsule was burnt up prior to reentry. But, even if he could do something, his judgment would be likely to lead him astray.

The deviant can count on considerable aid and comfort from his friends within the group. They may not sympathize with his actions or his position, but they are still his friends and will be more than likely to come to his aid at the time of showdown. The isolate has forfeited all the rights of friendship. It would be ridiculous to suggest that his friends would in every case deny him *outside this group*, but their hands are tied so far as his membership here is concerned. By group action, he has been removed from friendship considerations.

We should not overlook the reverse action—how the two atypical members affect the rest. The deviant will cause concern in other members, but this concern does not reach the boiling point. Others have made value judgments about the heinousness of his crime and have returned a verdict in his favor. Not so with the one to be lopped off. His sin is mortal, and purgatory will not be enough. The actions of the deviant will ordinarily not seriously affect the work output of the rest of the membership; actions which lead to isolation of a member cause so much upset that the effectivity of all will suffer. Personal regard for the deviant will not be likely to undergo permanent change. The isolate will no longer be deemed worthy of consideration or evaluation.

Thus the group dynamics are obviously quite different in the two situations. In one sense, deviance and isolation should not really be juxtaposed—to do so is to foster a misleading mental set. The situations are different and separate. The fact that the same individual may be concerned in both is not germane, any more than it is germane that a man who once had influenza now has cancer.

Reasons for Isolation

In a sense, a group has only one reason for isolating one of its members—the deliberate and continued flouting of a major norm. This sort of direct challenge to the normative authority of the group must be answered; it endangers group integrity too much to be countenanced for a moment. It is entirely analogous to the quarantine we used to practice when people had certain kinds of communicable disease. The reasoning is that removing the cause of major deviance will at least keep other members free of infection. This may or may not be so; a single exposure to an idea may be all that is necessary for a member to "catch" it.

So far as the group is concerned, this is a completely valid reason for either sealing off or cutting out the guilty one. However, it must be recognized that other intervening variables also result in the isolation of a member. His personality may prove to be unacceptable to the various members. Personal dislike, if violent enough and widespread enough, will result in group severance. It is a cruel fact of life that all of us depend upon our impact on others for much of the success or failure we achieve during our lifetime. Sterling worth hidden beneath a repelling exterior is of little value. This last concept opens the door to the entire spectrum of subjective evaluation. It is sad that almost every person's status is largely controlled by factors in no way indicative of his real value. We are judged, accepted or rejected, and rewarded or penalized on the basis of our personality rather than our character and our comeliness rather than our essential being. This is sad, but it is no less true. If we face up to this reality, we can protect ourselves by acquiring expertise in group dynamics.

The vagaries of the group can go so far as to fasten on one idiosyncrasy and make it the cause for isolation. The man who stubbornly hangs on to an offensive mannerism does so at his peril. But part of the blame must be laid at the door of the offender; isolation for this reason is never consummated without repeated warnings.

We have been neglecting the role of the leader in isolation. A direct, unresolved confrontation between a member and his leader is quite likely to lead to isolation—at least, if the leader enjoys even moderate popularity with his people. It is *not* true that the knight in shining armor will in every case slay the dragon. That animal has some good built-in protective devices.

Deliberate isolation, as will be discussed later, is yet another matter.

A cogent reason for isolation of any member is his injudicious choice of time and object of challenge. This may or may not be conscious on his part. The best that can be said for this situation is that the victim of group action is lacking in sensitivity if he allows himself to be maneuvered into a losing gambit. Almost every group will recognize and respect the member's fundamental principle. This does not necessarily mean that one cannot be isolated because of a principle—remember Martin Luther, priest of the Roman Catholic Church. Isolation may occur, but it will be the result of much longer and more thorough consideration by the membership. So far as that goes, the question remains: What is anyone doing in a group that is subversive to his principle? If not the subject of isolation, he should remove himself from this situation. The trouble is, all of us are prone to let inertia take over and postpone corrective action until it is too late. This is just as true of the group as it is of the individual. Once more, this points up the necessity for discriminative choice of group memberships.

In rare instances, isolation will stem from misunderstanding of cues given by the "sinner." In these days, communication is so complicated and subjected to so much filtering that total misreading is not impossible. The culprit sends one signal, while an entirely different one is received and decoded. The resulting isolation is all the more difficult to rescind because all concerned have clean consciences. Their motives are impeccable; the fault must lie with the other party.

The entire process of isolation is ritualistic in the extreme. One is reminded of the days of chivalry—the passing of a challenge, its acceptance, and the resulting brawl, with serious results to both parties in most instances. It is only regrettable that the motives of all parties are not as pure as those of the "Knight Parfait."

From any vantage point, isolation is serious to both the group and its victim. That one member can have sufficient influence to threaten the existence of the entire group is hard to believe, but the membership does believe this and acts accordingly. The effects of isolation on the member are obviously traumatic in the extreme.

It is not easy to affix blame for the reaction of the

members to what they perceive as a distinct threat. Their concern is naturally for the integrity and continued existence of the group; anything less would be unforgivable. Buried somewhere in the stubble of this harvest is a lesson for all of us. We owe it to ourselves and to our group to be perceptive, mature, and deliberative as we face the prospect of terminating the membership of *anyone* who once was accepted in full faith and credence. Anything less than this posture is a denial of every duty we have to the group.

Group Reactions to the Isolate

It would be a mistake to assume that member attitudes toward an isolate are uniform. There is, of course, one item of commonality: All agree that his offense is of such magnitude that expulsion from the group is the only proper punishment. Aside from this, individual reactions cover a wide range.

Long before the formal expulsion, most members will have stopped communicating with the isolate. He will no longer know the results either of group deliberation or of individual thinking. No comments will come his way to help him gain his goals and objectives. Communication which he volunteers will be received in such a manner as to make it impossible for him to know the reaction to it.

Whatever contribution the isolate is still making to group activities will receive no evaluation as to quality or quantity. He can determine his personal effectiveness only by his own observation and analysis; and he will be the first to realize the sketchiness of this kind of judgment. This lack of any real cues from the other members is one of the more significant factors contributing to his alienation from the group. If he has any personal pride at all under these circumstances, he is prone to want to leave. Few of us have any interest in remaining in a group where we are obviously unwanted. The acceleration of the separation process thus receives impetus from both the isolate and the membership. Almost anything that either side does during this time reinforces the tendency toward separation.

The amount of personal animosity shown by the other members will vary widely. This is conditioned by two factors. The first is the personal popularity of the isolate and the number of close friends he has among the membership. The second factor is the personal commitment of the other members. The greater their involvement, the greater the possibility that the actions of the isolate will have aroused their anger. Some members may be stimulated to attack the isolate in ways above and beyond severance. Some years ago, it was not uncommon to tar and feather a victim just prior to his physical expulsion from a community. Most of our personal feelings have their roots in some facet of our group living. Our strongest likes and dislikes of individuals will usually have a group association.

The psychology of isolation is by its nature atypical. As the actions of the member continue toward an obvious denouement, members' personal feelings will range from deep anger to gray neutrality to great regret. If group solidarity remains intact, all reactions will be negative. If there are members who retain positive feelings or who believe the offense is not worthy of separation, the stage is set for a splinter group movement and the disruption of the group. Schisms of this sort have historically occurred in the church.

There is one member reaction that is worthy of further examination. It is entirely possible that the isolate become the focus of many of our unreduced hostilities. It is easy

The Isolate

to charge this scapegoat with responsibility for things that have been bothering us for a long time. His eventual burden of guilt will be magnified out of all recognition if this tendency is allowed to proliferate. In times of stress, it is human to abandon logic and let pure emotion take over. As a result, the poor isolate gets the blame for many things with which he had no connection and thus becomes deeply embittered, further reducing the possibility of a reconciliation.

At this point, it might be fitting to recapitulate the group process that leads to isolation. The deviance can be minor at the outset; the critical factor is the refusal of the member to return to conformity. The steady increase in pressure from escalating sanctions will have a sharply divisive effect in itself. The cleavage is increased by the rigidity of the deviant and by the mounting severity of his punishment. There comes a point of no return, and if the deviant ignores this, his group membership is forfeit. Because of the threat to group solidarity, all members will feel some emotional involvement. We can never face danger in a purely objective frame of mind. At the very least, fear or anger will be aroused. Most human beings will have stronger reactions under the impetus of either of these emotions. Strangely enough, the isolate is likely to show the least amount of emotional upset, especially if he is a consistent nonconformist with less than average involvement in his group living. The last of the great individualists will always find it harder to enjoy smooth group relationships than will the average citizen.

Severance of a member has ramifications in other aspects of group life. The emotional upset strains interpersonal relationships among the other members, and intense preoccupation with the trouble at hand reduces general group effectiveness. Leader-follower relationships will be examined much more minutely than is generally common. The leader will be particularly concerned—more for the group than for any given individual member.

Group Sanctions Against the Isolate

Nowhere is there a better illustration of the two theories of punishment than the isolation of a group member. Under a mental set thousands of years old, there are still many who feel that punishment for a sin is in effect exacting revenge for the error. We are familiar with the God of justice portrayed in the Old Testament. The philosophy of "an eye for an eye" was the attitude behind Mosaic law. The Theory X man subscribes completely to this thinking. He is morally certain that all are guilty of willfully breaking rules; he is delighted with an opportunity to punish a deviant under the professed belief that this punitive action will be a deterrent to others. Actually, deep down he doesn't *really* believe it will deter them. The Theory X man is quick to apply sanctions and slow to remove them.

The Theory Y man thinks in terms of corrective action rather than punishment. He would rather not apply discipline unless it is therapeutic and helps to prevent a recurrence of the offense. The complete polarization of a group with some members from each school of thought is easy to see. The conflict over whether sanctions should be applied at all, given moderate emphasis, or exerted to the fullest brings new vectors into the group which will have serious effects on interpersonal relationships. At this point, the safety and continued existence of the group will again depend on the sensitivity and expertise of the leader. He must recognize this polarization of thinking the moment it occurs and then turn to with every power at his command to reconcile these differences. Strong leadership when a member is about to be isolated is a must.

It should not be inferred from this that a Theory Y man would never agree to isolate a deviant. When he would acquiesce, he would be thinking of the welfare of the group as opposed to that of an individual. Mr. Y's frame of reference is much broader than is Mr. X's, and he will more often think in terms of possible effect on the entire membership.

Another major determinant of the duration and severity of sanctions is the attitude and posture of the deviant. The members will be cognizant of the many personal reasons which can cause deviance. In their thinking, some of these are much more acceptable reasons than others. Nearly everyone will respect a fundamental principle as a cause for deviance. It is probable that their concern for the group will make the members think in terms of a sanction, but in this case most of them will wish to temper the sanction to the exact point which would cause the deviant to conform. If, on the other hand, they read his deviance as intransigence, they will throw the book at the offender. The type and frequency of cues given by the deviant apropos his failure to observe a norm will be carefully weighed by his peers before they make their decision. Should they think he is deliberately challenging them, their action will be quicker and more definitive. If the deviant carries on an active campaign of proselytizing during his period of aberrant behavior, this unforgivable sin ordinarily will result in his immediate isolation. His physical demeanor will influence the judgment rendered by his peers. A group will be slower to isolate a member who maintains a friendly attitude, whereas an unfriendly or sullen deportment will draw their wrath as quickly as any other single action.

We must remember the staggering number of possible communication loops as a group increases in size. The sheer size and complexity of the communicative process in a modern business enterprise is beyond our ability to comprehend. In such a group, the process of isolating a member becomes quite cumbersome. The delay may give the deviant a false sense of security which will allow him to continue his defiance far beyond the point where he could recant and rejoin the group if he so desired. He will have established his pattern of behavior so indelibly that his peers will not take him back.

Isolation is one extreme in the spectrum of deviance. All its qualities are magnified and intensified in the thinking of the members. Predictable actions will also be extreme, whatever form they take. Personal rejection of the isolate will be the least common denominator of member reaction. Accompanying side effects will not be unknown—such as punitive action taken against the close friends of the isolate, even though they had no part in his behavior. Group process is at fever heat, and atypical interactions abound. Permanent changes in group alignment are quite common in the aftermath of the trauma associated with the expulsion of a member. It is safe to say that the group will never be the same after this event.

The confrontations that precede and lead to expulsion will involve the entire membership in some degree. This event so deeply affects the entire group that none can escape without some mark. In many cases the structure will be permanently altered, with the formation of new informal groups and the dissolution of some older ones. This is a natural fallout of differences in opinion during the happening. As might be suspected, it can have a significant impact on group productivity and objectives.

The Isolate and Leadership Reaction

Thus far we have considered only casually the reaction of the leader to isolation of a member. Actually, his involvement and feelings are likely to be deeper than most members' since he has the most responsibility. First and foremost, he must be sensitive to the possibilities of harm to the group as a whole. Historically, thousands of groups have been fatally disrupted by the projected isolation of a member. The leader will be deeply aware of the emotional overtones of all members. He will know how judgment can be warped when objectivity has been lost. His fears may cause him to overreact either in defense of the deviant or against him. The big danger lies in the chance that his hyperactivity will aggravate a situation and blow it up even larger than it would otherwise have been.

If for any reason the leader has been partially insulated from group reactions and fails to notice the disturbance as it builds, his position will be much worse. He will have lost the early opportunity to curb the deviance through his personal influence and to salvage a good member. Timeliness in meeting and grappling with deviance is of the utmost importance. All doctors know that many lives are saved each year by preventive medicine—recognizing early symptoms and treating them before the patients become desperately ill. The wise leader will work mightily to keep to the middle course between the extremes. He will want to detect the earliest faint signs of serious deviance but not jump on it so hard as to make it worse.

The leader is a human being; he will have personal feelings about the deviance just as will all the members. His most understandable reaction toward the deviant's actions will be anger and deep disturbance. He will be lucky indeed not to transfer this anger to the deviant, since the future of the group may be riding on the leader's actions. A leader can exert all his influence toward hastening the isolation so that the crisis will come to a quick conclusion and there will be a better chance for healing the wounds.

The opposite can also happen. If the leader perceives the deviant in his former status as a good member, he may go all out to save him—even to the point of taking on the entire group and fighting its considered decision to sever the sinner. This is begging for civil war. Nothing short of a miracle can prevent the complete polarization of the membership as a result of this leadership posture. Some will go along with the leader, either out of loyalty to him or in the hope of self-betterment. The other members will resent what they consider a disloyal act of the leader and will redouble their efforts to bring the deviant to justice. This leadership stance will rarely succeed. If it does, success is a sign of exceptional leadership or of extreme original popularity of the deviant.

The leader is bound to feel a certain amount of ambivalence about the isolate and the other members. He does have a vested interest in the success of the group; he also has a personal responsibility to the individual concerned. It is difficult to reconcile these two vectors without damage to someone. The victim may easily be the leader as well as the isolate. We must remember that the group is stronger than any individual in it, including the leader. If there is ever a time for the exercise of all the leader's powers of conciliation and for his best judgment, this is it.

One reaction should be immediately forthcoming from the leader at the first sign of deviance: He *must* determine the cause and significance. Is this the revolt of one man, or is it the precursor of a movement within the group against established norms and objectives? Need he be concerned about a possible reorientation—even a complete restructuring of the group? Is his leadership seriously out of step with the thinking of the membership? All these questions are implicit in any deviant action. The leader may need disinterested counsel in answering these questions. His own ego involvement is too great for an objective approach to the problems. However, no successful leader is without his special resource persons to whom he can turn in time of trouble. The most important thing of all is for him to be aware of the time and circumstances which require his turning to them.

There is another potential leadership reaction to deviance—extending unwarranted guilt by association to the immediate friends and peers of the deviant. When we find a defect in any individual, it is quite natural to suspect the motives of his close associates. This is perhaps the most sensitive and critical area in the process. Personal loyalties can carry friends beyond the depth of their individual convictions, with a concomitant distortion of the seriousness of the revolt. In other words, friends may go along for the ride with no real involvement of their own principles. This is naturally a source of great confusion to the leader. He must have complete and direct communication before making up his mind about the involvement (or lack of it) of these people. Yet his own survival of the crisis will depend largely upon the validity of his decisions in this area.

Deliberate Isolation

The group's cutting one of its members out punitively does not cover the whole spectrum of isolation.

Occasionally, a member cuts *himself* off from group contacts deliberately. These cases are rare but certainly not unheard of.

One example of the deliberate isolate is the antisocial member of a formal work group who is there purely because he must earn a living for himself. He is not interested in interacting with others and will, in fact, avoid it whenever possible. It is hard for him to make even the contacts necessary to do his job. In unavoidable contacts he is ill at ease, taciturn, and at times surly. He will cause trouble for others on the job by withholding necessary information. Needless to say, this sort of behavior will soon build the desired wall about him. Other members will gladly cooperate with him to insure his isolation.

Another reason for deliberate isolation is a sudden change in the group's goal orientation that one member finds impossible to accept. He feels hurt and angry at having his perspective forcibly changed, especially if the new configuration should go against some of his deeper principles. In this case, especially if he has been a valued member, the group will make a serious effort to reclaim him to full membership. Some more perceptive members may feel guilty for having put him into this situation of trauma and anxiety by shifting goals. The prognosis for his reclamation is good, especially when there is supportive action from the rest of the membership. This deliberate isolate is more of a pouter than a deep hater and will sooner or later realize the futility of his position and return to conformity.

Another deliberate isolate is the member who wants to "punish" the group for real or fancied mistreatment. "You hurt me, so there! I'm not going to talk to you *ever again!*" This reversion to infantilism is indicative of severe emotional immaturity and should be a cue for group leadership to do a little reassessment of this member, possibly allowing the deliberate isolation to become permanent by group consensus.

There is always the possibility of a significant personality change in the member who seeks isolation after a history of normal membership. Marked changes of this sort are not as rare as we may think. Various vectors can combine to result in a realignment of personal goals or in the formulation of an entirely new image. This metamorphosis may be the result of a sudden shock, a late maturation process, a careful "think-through" of fundamental personal values—you name it, and it can happen. Other members are simply perplexed to see it happen in a group situation that is undergoing no major or climactic change. Normal evolution is present, of course, but the bulk of the membership is taking this in stride, while the one person is showing an entirely new personality to his peers and to his leader. Whatever the reason for the personality change, there will inevitably be drastic effects on his membership in this group and probably on others. Since *he* has changed and the group has not, his only recourse is to isolate himself until he has a chance to sort out his values. He need not make a definite decision to sever permanently, but he should do some personal reassessment before making membership decisions.

A person may isolate himself as the result of pressures exerted on him from *outside* associations. His membership may be offensive to close friends outside the group, and they will turn on the pressure to get him to leave. Such influence produces uneasiness, and he must have time to make comparisons and order his values. One thing is sure: In this case, either the group or his other friendships will be jettisoned.

Deliberate isolation will have a greater effect on the other members than will the isolation they have brought about. The first reaction is one of puzzled frustration. "What's going on here? What's with Tom, anyway?" This is ordinarily followed by a period of feverish attempts to get the isolate back into the mainstream. If this is not successful, resentment and hostility will evolve from their personal feelings of rejection by an old friend. Actually, not too much is gained if the deliberate isolate explains his reasons for withdrawal. As far as the others are concerned, there can be no valid reason for threatening group structure.

As can be seen from all this, the reclamation of a deliberate isolate is a delicate and difficult procedure. Its chances for success are less than even; the man who feels so strongly as to put himself personally beyond the pale is not going to respond quickly to overtures from his peers—or even from his leader. His return to conformity can happen, but it rarely does.

The members at large can be reassured by understanding how atypical this reaction is and how often it is the result of outside influences. Their best bet is to regard it as a statistic—such a thing will occur once in so many thousands of cases; theirs happened to be the group that chance chose for the event. The members are in need of supportive action; their fundamental safety needs are being strongly attacked from the blind side. Again, an enlightened leader is the best source of solace in this situation: His is the duty to explain, to reinforce, and to give comfort to hurt feelings and threatened psyches. This situation calls loudly for maturity, calm consideration of the problem, and reasoned deliberation over a course of action toward an already established objective. *The safety of the group is under attack.*

Healing the Wounds

During the whole process of isolating one of its members, the group is sick. The analogy to illness in the human body is particularly apt. Thus the group, too, must undergo a period of recuperation after its convulsive effort. The first task is to readjust the workload to redistribute the work that the isolate had been doing (that is, if he has physically left the group). There will be many rearrangements of workloads and working partnerships even if a new member is taken into the group to replace the isolate. The new member will never be a carbon copy of the person he is replacing. His different characteristics and attributes will create his own unique spot in the group. Depending upon his personality, the group may be irritated at being reminded of the isolate or beguiled by the process of orienting the new member.

There will be some repair work to be done on interpersonal relationships. Early in the process leading to the expulsion of a member, and perhaps even near its climax, there will have been sharp differences of opinion about the status of the deviant soon to become an isolate. These personal polarizations are abrasive, and care must be taken to keep them from leading to permanent enmities.

The heightened cohesiveness exhibited by the group as a defense mechanism will have disappeared, and an opposite reaction may set in. In some cases, this would seem to be therapeutic. It gives a chance for a little quiet contemplation and reassessment of personal values, an essential after the trauma just undergone. To many, the expulsion of an isolate may mean that the entire group is disintegrating. At any rate, it does increase the fears of all members for group integrity. Convalescence is the time for restructuring and reevaluating the group as a whole.

The signal to the leader is loud and clear. He must be the major force in rebuilding the group and setting it back on course. The best method is to work members as hard as they can stand. The inevitable losses in productivity and quality must be made up for, and the leader may well decide that this is an excellent time for retraining and for consideration of objectives. The members will probably be mentally ready for this kind of exercise. They will recognize that activity will take their minds off the big problems they have been facing, and their receptivity will be high. So a period of solid advancement and growth can result, indirectly, from the isolation of a member. Other leadership activities are also called for in this situation. The leader will be valuable to many members on a person-to-person basis as they bring their individual contacts back into shape. His guidance and counseling will never be more welcome or more eagerly accepted. The leader, if his deportment is proper, can gain significantly in stature and influence during this time. From his own viewpoint, it is a time for personal development and growth. If he is diligent in following up on the cues given him, he will learn many new facts about his people. No matter how fine the relationship has been, it should now be strengthened and improved.

A residual unwillingness will be evident for some time on the expulsion of another member. The revulsion of feeling against the upset will be great enough to increase the tolerance of deviance—even if a new deviant is flouting the same norm that merited isolation in the past. A deviant appearing at this particular time will be treated more tolerantly than he would have been before the other incident—and than he will be a little later.

* * *

"Groupiness," as distinguished from cohesiveness, will be increased as the end product of this entire cycle. The better knowledge of how other members think, the insight into their value sets and the nuances of their feelings, will be shared by all sentient members. Thus the net result of isolation will almost always be a gain. This last statement should *not* be interpreted as cynical. In a large percentage of cases the isolate does not care too deeply about his membership, or he would not put it on the block in the first place. To use a medical simile, the broken bone, when healed, is stronger than it was before the fracture.

In this segment, we have intensively looked at group process. We should not underestimate the changes occurring in individual members in this trial by fire. We already said the leader should grow and mature from this event; likewise, every member will add to his maturation during this time.

The two preceding chapters have dealt with the Siamese twins of group life—the two situations most threatening (internally) to structure and solidarity, yet with the potential of eventually strengthening the group and making it a more viable entity. Let us now turn to the two remaining areas of group living: group effectiveness and the group dynamics of the family. In many aspects, these cover the entire spectrum of social living. We live and work in groups so as to be stronger and more effective. From time immemorial the family has been the basic structural unit of any society, and it will remain so from here on out no matter what superficial changes it may undergo.

The differences between the deviant and the isolate are more than one of degree; there are also differences in kind. The reasons for isolation go deeper than any consideration of the fractured norm or the threatened objective. Many are purely personal on the part of the member concerned.

Group reactions to the isolate can run a surprisingly wide gamut. Many arise from personal value structures; these are as variable as the individuals involved. The sanctions imposed previous to the final one of isolation will show a continuing line of increasing severity. Always implicit is a waiting period to see whether the deviant will recant and rejoin the group. The reactions of the leader to the isolate are understandably sharper and more definitive than those of the members. He feels much more personally the threat to group safety and continuity.

There are significant numbers of cases of deliberate isolation. This is almost without exception the acknowledgement of an atypical group membership. We might call this spurious membership.

The process of recovery of the group from a bout of isolation is as stylized as is the individual's convalescence from a serious illness. Happily, once done, the group will probably be stronger than ever before.

Chapter 13

Group Effectiveness

A GROUP must be effective in order to justify its existence. Effectiveness is achieved when the objectives are reached quickly and with economy of effort. There are several signs by which we recognize group effectiveness—or the lack of it.

When Is a Group Effective?

This operational definition of group effectiveness should not obscure the vital details of this state. The first step toward achieving group effectiveness is to make sure that goals and objectives are realistic and attainable. Many a group has been chartered, only to founder and die because its goals were too idealistic and completely out of reach despite the best efforts of leadership and membership. This sensitivity to viable goals is an acquired characteristic that can be markedly improved through training. There must also be a constant and consistent reassessment of goals under the direction of the leader. It is his responsibility to be aware of what is going on both inside and outside the group and to balance these forces by immediate modification of objectives if the situation demands it.

Another primary attribute of an effective group is a high degree of cooperation. There will be a general understanding and acceptance of the need to help each other arrive at common goals. If one man could do the trick, there would be no need for a group. The members of an effective group understand that cooperation often means going more than half way. At some time, everyone will need that little extra help from his peers if he is to get his job done. The art of eliciting cooperation can be a fine tool in the hands of an expert; it is just as essential to give it as to get it.

The effective group is an *alert* one. It will not depend solely upon the leader's sensitivity to the environment. Every member will have to be alert to what he perceives and able to put it into proper perspective. When this happens, we have a much more adaptable and versatile group—one that can be competitive and innovative. We see hundreds of daily illustrations of this in formal groups. The enterprise that is ready to make use of what it sees in its surroundings is the one that will survive and prosper. Innovation has saved the life of many a business whose environment was totally hostile.

Group effectiveness is directly proportionate to the willingness of members to work hard, particularly when difficult goals are maintained and reached. Of course, this is the situation Professor Herzberg has in mind when he says that the work itself is our best motivator. Man's capacity for hard work over long periods of time is grossly underestimated by most of us when the goals are hard to reach but attractive. The harder they are to reach, the greater the feeling of accomplishment when we do get there. Hard work must be habitual to a member who values his group and wants to make both it and himself a success.

The twin consideration that goes along with intense group activity is concern for the quality of the work. Mountainous production of rubbish will not prevent the death of the group. Naturally, different objectives will require different levels of quality. None of us expects the same quality in a cheap product as in an expensive one.

The effective group will be harder on itself in judging its work and its progress. Self-criticism will become a way of life, but it will be criticism with a purpose and with the expectation of progress as a result. Discriminating judgment becomes a fine art; fine shades of difference will be examined for meaning and often will have an immediate effect on goals if trends are discovered in these subtle differences.

One of the beneficial fallouts of group effectiveness is esprit de corps. Members come to consider themselves professionals in their field and have professional pride in their accomplishments. This spirit can have strange effects. It can spur people to undreamed-of efforts; it can refine product quality to impeccable standards; it can withstand pressures from outside and can roll with the punches. This has an upward influence as well. An effective group is more likely to show great development in its leadership than a weak one. It is an egg and chicken argument as to whether the leader has more influence on the group's effectiveness or whether an effective group will cause its leader to become more proficient.

Group effectiveness, although it is discussed here as a *combination* of characteristics, can be cultivated and strengthened by planned effort. Leaders and members together can so order their actions and efforts as to increase effectiveness measurably over time. The largest single factors are an awareness of its desirability and a conducive mental set. In effect, group effectiveness can be considered a major objective, with a measured amount of general group effort directed toward its achievement. But there are some major stumbling blocks in the way, as there are for any worthwhile goal.

The Synergy of the Group

A combination of two drugs is often more effective in treating a disease than is either one alone. The same thing happens in groups. Such an effect is called *synergy*. It is in recognition of the fact that the group is greater than the sum of its individual members that most groups are formed —to achieve goals that could never be reached by unilateral activity.

There are several benefits to be had from this property of group action. One is that the individual does not have to knock himself out to see progress and achievement. He can pace his own contribution so as to save his strength and get more enjoyment from other aspects of living. As we become more sophisticated at living in groups, we are able to free ourselves from the tyranny of tasks and enrich our lives in other directions. We have only to compare our increasing life span to the short span common in the days when most men supported themselves and their families by their individual efforts to see how cooperative group living has helped us.

Synergy allows us to be much more ambitious in setting our goals and expanding the architecture of our enterprises. We do things routinely now which man had only dreamed of before he discovered the utility of working together cooperatively. Grand Coulee Dam remained only a dream until six major contracting companies pooled their expertise and made its completion possible. No one of the six organizations could have come close to doing the job alone. This multiple escalation of our potential through groups is the foundation of American industrial greatness.

When conditions are right, synergy occurs in group meetings. Better results sometimes come from attacking a problem jointly. This concept has been popularized in recent years under the name "brainstorming." It is possible to create a climate in which the ideas of one member can be built upon by others; the final product may be finer than the contribution of any one individual. There are, however, some tricky aspects to this procedure. A fine line must be drawn between the process of discarding ideas and the point at which discriminative judgment must enter. Too rapid judgments will effectively kill creativity; too deliberate judgments can allow ill-considered projects to get started, thus wasting time and effort. Group conceptualization must be learned and practiced carefully if it is to be a worthwhile tool. The process will change markedly as the mixture of the membership is altered; not all members will interact effectively in this kind of exercise.

Synergy can remove some of the time pressures under which the group usually operates. The time required to reach goals is significantly lessened. Of course, there is a certain irony in the fact that many of our time constraints are imposed upon us by our increasing multigroup memberships.

It is much harder to decide whether the group exerts a synergistic effect on the process of decision making. In the first place, we can never know whether the decision reached by an individual would be the same as that of the group. So we have no real basis on which to judge quality of the final decision. Also, in many cases group participation will slow down decision making, rather than speed it up.

Synergy is *not* responsible for all of a group's effectiveness, but it certainly is its heart. It therefore is the responsibility of both members and leader to maintain a climate favorable to it. Many factors contribute to this; individual sensitivity is high on the list of importance. Interactions between members are strongly supportive or highly destructive of synergy, depending upon their quality. Group planning, if done with discrimination, can greatly increase synergy. Esprit de corps is always a determinant, as are the quality and strength of general leadership. For example, if the leader is highly charismatic, this is a plus. Norms will have their influence for good or ill.

By this time it is apparent that a certain pattern of group living can lead directly toward greater effectiveness. We do have the freedom to choose our actions within the group so that synergy results. Perhaps this latitude is more important to us *as individuals* than personal freedom now that so much of our living is done within groups. The deference of our personal wishes to the needs of the group can in actuality benefit us—provided, of course, that the group makes the right decisions and retains a high degree of effectiveness. All this should not be construed as advocating the destruction of the individual. Such is the complexity of the human being that in a great many areas the group can never satisfy our needs. We must retain our personal uniqueness at any cost; the human beehive is not our life goal and never could be. This preservation of self is the most important aspect of our life, and it must be pursued with unflagging vigor so long as we live. Paradoxically, however, this pursuit is often best and easiest done through the vehicle of the group.

Cohesiveness and Group Effectiveness

It would seem to be self-evident that an effective group has to be cohesive. The ability to reach its goals quickly and with economy of effort implies a close relationship among the members, at least in its working aspects.

However, *it should not be assumed that a cohesive group is always effective.* Effectiveness is much more than simple togetherness.

Cohesiveness also means better than average communication. If the members share what is in their minds, it is much easier to plan and execute work projects. The greater the communication, the greater the understanding and, ordinarily, the greater the accomplishment.

Cohesiveness is more of a positive factor for group effectiveness if its origin is internal than if it arises from an external threat. The latter situation may actually result in a lowering of group effectiveness, since total absorption with the external threat makes effective progress toward goals more difficult. The more highly organized and efficient the membership has been, the greater the likelihood of stalling out during the distraction of outside threat. Internal threat will also heighten cohesiveness, but its stultifying effect on productivity will be shorter and less pronounced. The leader has better control over the internal threat situation, and the response of the members will be sharper and quicker.

Cohesiveness and its accompanying close relationships among peers will mean more permissiveness as to individual work methods, with a resultant higher *personal* efficiency. The man who is allowed to choose his own working methods is of course more comfortable than the man who has them imposed upon him. He will work more easily, with greater output of a high-quality product.

When bonds are strong between members, the tendency is to give and receive help freely. Less embarrassment will be noticed about discussing personal shortcomings in working methods and how to remedy them. A free interchange on this subject can only improve effectiveness sooner or later. The strengthening of these positive valences is not usually a calculated thing; it is the spontaneous result of the relationships between members. Leader and members can *try* to produce a climate favorable to this configuration, but individual occurrences will seldom be the result of planning.

It should be no surprise to discover that a lessening of cohesiveness—for any reason—will have a deleterious impact on effectiveness. All the benefits previously mentioned will disappear as the bonds holding the group together become weaker. In fact, the net loss may be greater than the previous gains. As individuals, we tend to exaggerate our personal feelings when the group is in trouble, with a resultant acceleration of losses in effectiveness. Everyday living does not go in a straight line; we have our ups and downs both in our personal lives and in our group memberships. To insure our maximum personal maturity, we should be on guard against a downward reaction while cohesiveness is lessening. Each can make his own contribution to braking the runaway train before it crashes. Sensitivity is the key word here. We often sense a change in cohesiveness before we can actually document it. Thus we can forestall disaster by paying attention to our prescient sensations.

Let us reexamine one of our basic tenets—that complex relationships grow up within our various groups. We have noted how success or failure is directly tied to the nature and strength of our personal interactions with our peers and our leaders. This concept should hold no threat for us if our attitudes are sound and we are ready to respond. The limits of these interactions, in both complexity and number, are still under our personal control, for we are free to choose our group memberships. The danger point is reached the moment we have any sense of oppression or frustration because of too many group demands or duties. This is the signal for us to stop expanding our memberships—perhaps even to sever some of them. Far better to be a successful member of a few groups than to thrash helplessly in a mass of unsatisfactory, half-achieved relationships.

A wide distribution of cohesiveness is quite natural within our various groups. Our most important ones should have the tightest bonds. If this is not the case, we are in trouble in our social living and should take a long, hard look at the structure of our memberships. The mature person will thus increase his chance for happiness or, at least, for serenity. We are truly mature when we can make peace with our environment and learn to live with it. The increasing incidence of mental illness should be a warning that this kind of solid adjustment to our social world is not easy to achieve. Knowledge, adequate planning, and hard, concentrated effort must be directed toward maturity as a specific personal goal. A portion of our efforts should go toward increasing group cohesiveness and, thus, effectiveness. We have no time for wheel spinning.

Leadership and Group Effectiveness

As is true in so many other aspects of cooperative living, the leader has a great influence on his people's effectiveness. He has control over several of the components of effectiveness and, by careful planning and adroit distribution of the work, can enhance general effectiveness spectacularly. For example, if he knows his people well, he can create work partnerships and small group relationships which will be demonstrably superior to chance combinations of the membership.

Obviously, the leader will have a direct influence on morale and its effect on group cohesiveness. As already noted, the highly cohesive group is ordinarily a more effective one. However, as was learned early from the Hawthorne study,* not too much faith should be placed in working conditions per se, since intervening variables can vitiate the push given by the physical environment alone. Of course, the same can be said of any other individual factor that has an influence on group effectiveness.

Group effectiveness has a way of centering about two or three members, as do productivity, quality control, morale —or any other building block of group activity. It is up to the leader to locate these people and then concentrate much of his effort on them. This selectivity represents pure conservation of his energy.

Our operational definition included the matter of both time and efficiency in reaching objectives. Only the leader has direct personal responsibility for cumulative efficiency. The leader thus becomes the most critical factor in effectiveness. Obviously, he has to solicit and win the cooperation of the members.

The leader's influence on quality is at least as important as any other aspect of the total picture. It is his clear duty to be as rigorous as necessary to maintain the desired level of quality. This is true even if at times it means a slowdown in production and perhaps a missed deadline. Lowered quality can, over a period of time, completely ruin the effectiveness of any group. Once minimum standards have been set, they must be maintained at all cost.

The leader makes another signal contribution to group effectiveness by keeping a watchful eye out for promising innovations and shortcuts as developed by the membership. On the work scene, a vast majority of improvements in production, process, and quality come from the line— specifically, from the people who actually make and work

* See the Glossary.

with the product. Their willingness to come forth with these ideas is a direct measure of the mass rapport the leader is able to develop. These ideas will be brought forward for no reward other than simple recognition from peers and leadership. Remember that recognition operates at the ego and self-actualization levels of need. In fact, modest to average monetary rewards without accompanying publicity do not significantly stimulate the inventive genius of the membership. This fact is often lost sight of by industrial management, to their later disappointment and chagrin. It is therefore doubly necessary that the immediate group leader remain on the qui vive for cues (mostly nonverbal) which alert him to constructive and inventive ideation.

It might not be amiss here to repeat that the leader's duty is to give every aid he can to the total efficiency of the group. Group effectiveness is the sum of individual effort signaled by reaching the objectives in the easiest possible way. A good case could be made for the premise that this is the heaviest part of the leader's responsibility. He is the grand lubricator of the gears in his job.

The leader is spending time and effort with his people in a way that will most positively accentuate his value to them, individually and collectively. Everyone benefits when the group is effective, because of the rewards and publicity attendant upon this achievement. If the leader is identified as having had a real part in making the group effective, he insures his own recognition and success as well. Success breeds success; it can become a habit just as anything else can.

Personally, this leader can also increase the esteem in which he is held, depending upon his manner and deportment. This is no place for braggadocio. If the members get the slightest suspicion that he is assuming the major credit for group success as a personal achievement on his part, he is lost. We all love the winning coach—just so long as he gives full credit to the *team* for the championship trophies on the shelf. He must exhibit pride in his boys rather than in himself.

The leader's last major contribution to group effectiveness is in supplying the mechanics for its continuation. His is the job of analyzing the surroundings for changes which could affect operations. He must maintain a running analysis on the morale of both group and individuals, making whatever changes are mandatory to keep the machine at its operating peak.

The Informal Group and Effectiveness

The informal group is either the best friend or the worst enemy of the larger group's effectiveness. Many members never fully realize the power of these small but often strategically placed groups. If a group is formed of, say, staff members to various key leaders in a formal group, the members have access to immense power, and it is not at all outside the realm of possibility that they usurp much of this power for their own use. Some of the fundamental goals can be blocked, often without the leadership's ever being aware of the cause of the failure. Since the informal group is not hampered by cumbersome preset controls, it can move faster than the parent organization and will have much direct power over effectiveness. Such a "palace revolution" can totally wreck an enterprise unless the plot is discovered quickly and emergency action is taken.

The informal group also has communicative processes that are much smoother and less cumbersome than those of the formal organization. While the latter is sending everything through channels, a small group may effect a virtual takeover. It is obvious that the subversive type of informal group (subversive, that is, with respect to the objectives of the formal organization) will be fairly common during a union's bargaining with the company. The wise supervisor, aware of how this situation can develop, will be doing his best to woo the leadership of informal groups within his area, so that eventually he can get them to come his way. In fact, if he does enlist the support of small group memberships here and there, he will have multiplied his power and prestige as a leader many times. This will assuredly contribute to group effectiveness. There will be fewer grievances and better company–union relationships as a reflection of the harmony between the line supervisor and the small groups.

A curious reversal of this situation is not unknown. There are times when an informal group becomes impatient with what it considers bungling leadership and decides to take the situation in its own hands. When this happens, spectacular results can be seen. Using their influence on their peers to the fullest extent, the members of this group can engineer changes in goals, production norms, and even controls so that the achievement of objectives is expedited greatly. It goes without saying that this requires cooperation of a high degree. If it is forthcoming, group effectiveness can be increased greatly.

Another possibility for a group that is too large for complete homogeneity is for an informal group to assume the task of monitoring progress toward goals and become the control par excellence. Its purposes are to measure, communicate, and, where necessary, needle and push. This role of a group conscience is not conducive to popularity, but it does increase effectiveness.

Another action which can be performed by an informal

group is the actual disciplining of recalcitrant members—thus saving these members the embarrassment attendant upon formal punishment by the leader. An informal group can haze the deviant back into line without anyone's losing face. This means that a misdemeanor on the part of one or two members will do much less harm to group effectiveness.

It is obvious from the foregoing that informal group actions either for or against the formal leadership result from attitudinal slants of the members. They are reducing their own frustrations and anxiety by undertaking these positive (or negative) actions. The formal leader should be alert for such groups friendly to him and use them fully toward betterment of group effectiveness.

The total influence of the informal group on the effectiveness of the parent organization is major. It may also be decisive. Because of their disproportionate influence on the other members, informal groups that assume a leadership role can negate the intents of a membership many times their own size. This is not necessarily all bad. It can mean that the overall efficiency of the parent group will be enhanced by short-circuiting the time-consuming total group consensus—assuming, of course, that the rest of the members have given this small percentage of their total the authority to "do business" for them. We know from our own experience how often this does happen. The proxy vote is by far the commonest method of doing business in industry.

The informal group can also release the total energies of the membership for undivided effort at achieving the desired goals. The man who can single-mindedly pursue his major objective without distraction will get a lot more done, and the quality of his work is quite likely to be better as well. The threat of group neurosis or psychosis under multiple pressures will be significantly reduced by the safety-valve

effect of the informal group's taking over the worry function.
This unofficial organization and the division of labor resulting from it can come from above or below. The first to perceive the need will be the initiator. If there is consonance of major objectives, the other party will immediately acquiesce; if the objectives are polarized, trouble will ensue. As has already been said, the final effect can be completely positive or completely negative, depending upon the agreement or lack of it between the informal group and the nominal leadership of the larger organization.

Blockage

So far as it concerns the effectiveness of a group, blocking is a two-sided coin. For example, when the group is directing its blocking against an external situation, effectiveness is improved. In order to block, the group must act as an entity with all the necessary communication, cooperation, and unanimity of goals. In striving to evade or avoid a perceived external threat, the membership is aware that concerted action of some sort is a prime necessity. This preconditioning will produce a mental set favorable to blockage. Since blockage is a passive reaction, it can be maintained for a considerable time without producing excessive anxiety. In a sense, it is almost a period of dormancy or rest. The dangers inherent in attempting to block externally are quite apparent. Since no aggressive action is involved, the group may be misread by the enemy, who will then attack what he thinks is weakness. Even though he may be badly mistaken, it is possible for blockage to precipitate violence which otherwise might have been avoided.
Should this eventuality occur, the internal result of this

sort of blockage will boost the effectiveness of the group in the manner already outlined. In addition, the time of relative calm will provide an opportunity to think through plans and methodology leading to efficient operation. This is especially true for the leader. Again on the positive side, the process which led to the decision to block can be nothing but reinforcing to the basic goals of the group. This comes as a side effect, rather than the product of deliberate cerebration on the subject. There may even be an element of surprise in the discovery that objectives seem more real and demonstrably right.

So far as group process is concerned, blockage as an external weapon is just another tool in the eyes of the members. They will be less likely to become emotionally involved—as they do when blockage is being used to thwart the leader in one of his major objectives. It is therefore easier for the positive effects of external blockage to accrue. Many members are never aware of the ambivalence of this group action.

Blocking becomes highly dangerous to group effectiveness when used internally. In fact, the objective of internal blockage is negative. It is the group's desire to defeat one or more of the principal goals of the leader—or sometimes of leaders higher up in the hierarchy than the immediate manager. When the members are strongly united against one stated desire of their leader, they have one of two courses open to them: blockage (passive resistance) or aggression (in this case, another name for open revolt). Blockage is usually perceived by the individual member as a less dangerous method of resistance. He can see himself surviving implication in blockage, whereas if he joins in aggression he either wins all or loses all, including his group membership. From the time of its first use, passive resistance has been terribly difficult for leaders to combat because of the difficulty in placing individual blame and delineating a real crime, even when the entire membership is involved.

However, internal blockage will sap the lifeblood of any group when allowed to continue for any considerable time. There is an immediate impact on all aspects of effectiveness, and they continue to feel the heat so long as blockage is continued. One of the commoner forms of blockage in the formal group is the slowdown. Its effect on productivity is cumulative. For each day it continues, the end result will be grimmer in regard to meeting delivery deadlines and satisfying the customer.

Any way we look at it, the attitude which produces internal blockage is a negative one and will carry over into all the member's group activities. If he feels strongly enough about one of the leader's objectives to fight it in this manner, he will also think negatively about the rest of his job. Overall efficiency is bound to suffer, sometimes as the result of conscious thought on his part. Negativism by association is as recognizable a human characteristic as is guilt by association. If one of the leader's most sought-after goals is inimical, the remainder will be suspect as well and will suffer while this mental set prevails. We would be more than human were we able to compartmentalize our thinking to the extent of preventing a similar negative effect from spreading to other parts of the group activity.

The group's future after internal blockage is dubious and is usually a function of the time element involved. If blockage is short-lived, recovery can be swift and complete; if it is lengthy, or if a stalemate is reached between the membership and the leader, the group's existence is in jeopardy.

The need is for quick and functional communication between leader and members to reach some sort of working agreement. The longer this is delayed, the harder it is to achieve. If we miss the first two or three chances for talking it out, we are in serious danger of letting loss of face force us into a fatal situation. The first time your friend fails to recognize you when he passes is of course a coincidence; if it happens two or three times running, some hard efforts must be made to repair the psychological damage.

Group Perspective

No group will be able to claim great effectiveness unless both the individuals and the membership at large have a good perspective. It is logical to expect effective performance to be partially the result of comparisons made with artificial standards or observed performances of other groups. Ideally, each member will have his own base of comparison against his output and will govern his planning accordingly. But there must be a cooperative group action to agree upon group standards as a separate entity from the sum of individual standards. Once more, the knowledge that the group is more than the sum of its individual members is basic to any real understanding of how it operates.

It goes without saying that such an operation will demand rigorous controls to make certain that activities are aimed at the target and productive enough to reach it. These controls will become a built-in part of the normative activity. Usually, the controls will be monitored by the leader as a part of his job. In his sensitive position, he will be able to make necessary adjustments and redistribution of effort more quickly than could any other member. It would be a serious blunder to keep harping on production and fail to mention quality considerations in group perspective. The essential difference between raw production and quality production obviously involves value judgments. There can be no arguing with the number of units put out by the group; there can be many and violent differences about the quality of those units. It is therefore urgent to reach a consensus on quality standards. It is not necessary that these be totally congruent with the quality ideals of a given member. It *is* necessary that he agree with group quality standards.

The ability to make fine discriminations is one of the attributes that must be considered in our frantic search for an adequate description of intelligence. Implicit in the word "perspective" is the matter of discriminative judgment. We are forced to decide that one thing is better than another, that one situation is more likely to produce successful activity than another, and that what we see in our surroundings should govern our choice of action. One thing is certain: This is a trainable characteristic. The group which eventually becomes noticeably effective may start with poor discrimination, but, as ability in this area grows, the eventual outcome will be effectiveness. There is much good sense in the motto of the industrial engineer: "Work smarter— not harder."

A proper perspective will not necessarily be verbalized in the group's objectives. More probably, it will be approached and realized indirectly, as the result of many kinds of activity. The leader will no doubt have perspective in his consciousness from time to time, but the members will be too busy with other things to dwell on it—*until they become sophisticated in the examination of group process*. After this occurs, the examination of the state of group perspective will become a regular part of the agenda in looking at process.

The implications of broad perspective and its relation to

personal growth and development are obvious. The immature individual has tunnel vision and a narrow viewpoint; the man who stands tall will have a broader horizon.

This brings up the matter of the semantic difficulties which may occur when people talk about development. Individual concepts of its nature will cover an immensely wide area. One will be thinking of the strengthening of weaknesses; another will be concentrating on capitalizing and improving existing strengths. One man's pictorialization will be symmetrical—the well-rounded individual—while his peer will think in terms of a solid, unshakable pyramid personality.

This difference in conceptualization has been the basis for many of the difficulties lying in the way of developmental programs for any group. We fail to communicate because we use identical terms to mean different things. It is no wonder we have become confused and disoriented in this field, and it is high time that some general ground rules be developed. A serious effort should be made to correlate the meaning of development on a generalized basis, so that our developmental activities can be coordinated.

If we recognize perspective as a part of both individual and group development, it is then possible to build it into our overall planning. This becomes a part of the individual's responsibility to himself and the leader's duty to the group. We must consciously stretch our viewpoint to include more and more of our surroundings as we progress. The correlation between a broad perspective and improved group effectiveness is obvious.

* * *

A group is effective when it achieves its objectives quickly and economically. It is a truism that an effective group is a mature one. In fact, the relationship is such that effectiveness and maturity can be measured against each other.

An attribute of the group's effectiveness is the synergistic effect of its activity. We are saying that the group is more powerful than the sum of its individual members. Herein lies one of the principal advantages of pooled effort.

The cohesive group is the effective one. The greater breadth and depth of communication can only have a positive impact on its effectiveness. The leader increases effectiveness in direct proportion to his strengths and sensitivity. In every aspect of his planning, effectiveness will loom as an objective.

The informal group can have positive or negative influence on effectiveness. The same can be said of blockage, depending on whether it is external or internal in direction.

One major contributor toward high effectiveness is a broad individual and group perspective. There must be bases for comparison in order to set standards.

Chapter 14

Group Dynamics and the Family

Much of what we have discussed in these pages has been in the context of the formal group since this group is so important in our lives and we spend so much time in it. The remaining emphasis has been distributed between the informal and the semiformal groups, which are also vital to a well-rounded life. However, one specific group far transcends any of these in influence on our beginnings, our early growth, and our final emergence as a responsible adult. No other group has the same measure of importance to our entire life as does the family.

The Family as a Social Group

Every society of which we have any record has recognized in one way or another the impact the family has on its members. Most civilizations make of it the basic building block and venerate it as such. Even those twisted ideologies which have attempted to destroy the effect of the family have, by their actions, only reinforced its hold over its members.

There are three possible methods of organizing our thinking about familial relationships. We can think of it (1) emotionally (love—or hate); (2) socially, as a basis for organization of our group living; or (3) in terms of religious orientation, as some societies do, with the family an actual subject of worship.

The trend in America was established early and remained clean-cut until recent days. Our verbalization about the family was expected to be in terms of the deepest involvement of love. The conforming American knew it would be suicidal to impute anything less than the loftiest of feelings toward his family, either as a unit or as a collection of individuals. It would be interesting to try to decide whether this was a symptom or a cause. Did America develop into a nation of the middle class because this was a basic belief, or is the belief simply a reflection of our fundamental reactions?

It would be patently absurd to assume that all Americans hold their family ties in equal veneration. There is just as wide a distribution of this characteristic as there is of any other. The point is that the median of our emotional regard for family is high.

One or two generations ago, thanks to its immobility the American family held its place as the center of life much more firmly than it does now. Families on farms went for weeks and months without social contacts with outsiders. In the towns and cities, longer working hours and lack of transportation had, in effect, the same result. Now that we have been freed from physical restraint by universally available methods of transportation, the scene has changed significantly. Today's children and young people spend much more of their time away from the family than did their parents or grandparents. Of course, much of that time is spent in the environs of their friends' families, so that in one sense they are still under a familial influence. We have not felt the pressures of these intervening variables for a sufficient time to make a proper evaluation of them as yet. Is there really a *basic* change in the American attitude toward the family, or is it superficial? If there is a fundamental change, in what direction will it lead our society? Is the permissiveness noted in many modern families to be deplored deeply, as some do, or is it a healthy attitude which will result in a more self-reliant adult?

Our concern for these problem questions should be grave. If our reactions to the family are on an emotional level, we then have some unsolved maturation problems in other necessary categories of our growth. At some point we must cease to react emotionally and begin to act rationally. According to what developmental psychologists now tell us, the family is the logical vehicle for this evolution so far as the chronology of our growth is concerned.

The second attitude (toward family as a social binder) is well illustrated by British and French history. Without for one moment denigrating whatever affection the Englishman or Frenchman may have for his family, we must recognize he has a concurrent consideration: The family is sacred as such because it holds society together. Certain parts of his personal behavior pattern may seem to deny this principle, but when the final confrontation is made he knows there is no choice—family must come first. In modern times, even an English king recognized this and, in the long run, was honored by his nation for his resultant actions.

The third posture (wherein family becomes an object of worship) is recognized in Chinese and Japanese societies.

The individual, as a result, becomes totally subservient to the needs and welfare of the family. Whether a family is patriarchal or matriarchal, the elders are venerated blindly; their power of decision making is absolute and for the most part unquestioned. In the case of the Chinese especially, this lack of regard for the individual and his needs made the Communist takeover much easier than it ever could be in a society centered about the cult of the individual. In a sense, the state becomes a superfamily, and unquestioning obedience comes easily in this situation.

Considered in these frames of reference, it is easy to see how some of the national traits have developed in the societies mentioned. In one way or another, the family is primary in our physical, intellectual, and spiritual development. Our ethnic and national mores are transmitted for the most part though this vehicle. First principles are determined by its thrust; our thinking is patterned according to its dictates. Other vectors must be strong indeed to change the resultant configuration. These can arise, but the battle will be a notable one, with the odds favoring the family most of the way.

Family Leadership

By definition, the family is an informal group. This means that the leadership in the family will rotate, and normally this is what happens. In the average family, the father is deferred to in such matters as finance, long-range planning, method of earning a livelihood, and the other decisions classified as major. The mother, on the other hand, is the unquestioned leader in the everyday activities associated with raising the family. Her judgment prevails in the details by which we live: the choice of our family menus, determining the hour of bedtime, teaching manners and mores—all the things that make our family unit distinctive and give it the character by which we remember it.

These generalizations are of course not universally the case. There are families which live under the dictatorship of one parent to the total exclusion of judgmental choices on the part of the other. It amounts to a parenthood of one—a neurotic structure that is likely to breed children of questionable mental health.

In the "normal" family, further sharing of leadership will develop as the children grow and their separate personalities begin to emerge. One of the children may assume influence in the matter of family recreation; another will be able to sway his peers in matters of dress; a third may be given leadership in choice of family friends and socialization. This type of arrangement, which we noted as a characteristic of informal groups, helps greatly in the well-rounded development of the siblings. Responsibility for one facet of family life will hasten maturation noticeably. Strengthening of leadership attributes in one area will usually result in stronger followership in others. Nowhere is the necessity of give-and-take more clearly demonstrated than in family living.

One intervening variable should not be overlooked in any consideration of family leadership: the unusually heavy emotional involvement of the members. In most of our other groups, any strong feeling about the leadership (if such exists at all) will not have the strength and depth of our feeling for our family. This means that our reaction to family leadership will be quicker and stronger than our followership elsewhere, whether our emotion is love or hatred for the family leader involved. Little as we like to admit it, there are families in which one member develops an abiding hatred for another. Such a situation will have deep effects on our adult lives and can cause odd warping of personalities. Our subconscious efforts to adjust and compensate for this "unnatural" state will produce actions for which we can find no conscious motivation.

The family circle is the first training spot for leadership activity that most of us meet. The methods we develop in the family for influencing others and the results of these methods will determine how we approach our first leadership attempts in other groups. To most, the first discovery that strangers will not follow us because of emotional involvement is disturbing. For most people, the effects of several quick failures at attempted leadership will be hard to overcome. A natural and frequently observed reaction is for that person to withdraw and avoid other leadership situations for some time thereafter.

However, not every assumption of leadership within the family will be successful either. If there are several children, sibling rivalries can produce some titanic struggles for the leader's spot, thus providing all concerned with a much more natural leadership preparation for what they will meet in life outside the family. The family can be just as much a jungle as the city streets.

The training received in the family for leadership will never be duplicated again. There is more latitude in the family than is to be found in other groups. Methodology can be evaluated quickly, since the time span involved is usually short. If one method fails, another can be substituted at once, with a direct comparison available soon enough to be viable. Moreover, we have definitive feedback from the other members to reinforce our own observations.

There is another implication of leadership training in the family: Each member has an excellent opportunity to judge leadership styles and activities in others and make value judgments which will have a deep effect on his response to leadership in adult life. In today's society this is of urgent importance, for we have enough mobility now to move—in most cases—if we find the climate in one group insupportable. The feelings and attitudes we take with us from our family life are strong determinants of our behavior in groups for the rest of our days.

The value of family leadership in character building can hardly be overestimated. We get our first taste of responsibility and duty to others here; we come under fire by criticism; we are forced to make decisions and then carry them out. Although tempered by love in most cases, the lumps we take from other members of the family when we make a bad decision will influence us from then on. As a learning situation, this is difficult to equal later.

One observation is clear: The family can never be stronger than the leadership displayed and practiced within it. (The effects on adult life of weak leadership within the family are discussed later.) Indications are that this one facet of our national picture is more critical than anyone had ever before thought it to be.

Family Deviance

The deviant in the family can never hide. The closeness of the relationship, as well as the physical proximity, makes it impossible for any deviation from the norm to go unobserved. There are many more norms in an average family than its members would tolerate in an outside formal or semiformal group. The authoritarian atmosphere that surrounds the family while the children are young demands close controls all the way. The rules and regulations set forth by the father and mother for family operation are often regarded as onerous by the children, but they know they must follow the rules to stay out of trouble. Moreover, let one child break a family rule, and any siblings in the area will automatically sound an alarm vociferous enough to catch a parent's ear.

Reasons for deviance in the family will in the main be the same as those anywhere else. Most frequently met are attempts to avoid an unpleasant duty or to gain an advantage in position over other members. ("If I can connive to evade my dishdrying chores, I can get outside to play earlier than my brothers.")

There is one intervening variable in the family situation which changes the picture: the emotion present in all familial interactions. Each of us has a tendency to be much more deeply shocked by deviance in a member of our family than we would be by the same action in an outsider. A feeling of protectiveness toward those we love is a universal human trait. We find it hard to see a family member persist in actions which our value judgments tell us are wrong. Our affection spurs us to immediate action much more vigorous than we would display in similar situations in other groups. Our fear for a brother or sister may make us react much more violently than we normally would. Carried to an extreme, this attitude of overprotectiveness can be harmful to family unity and general development.

The method by which a family faces up to deviance is revelatory of its leadership philosophy and character. We hear much these days of parental unwillingness to take a stand against the breaking of norms. The euphemism for this is "permissiveness." For more than a generation, we have been inundated with a flood of propaganda purporting to prove that it is harmful to the development of a child for a parent to be severe or repressive of antisocial acts. As we shall see, this is one explanation for the generation gap we hear so much about these days. Suffice it to say here that most children feel terribly insecure in the absence of strong parental authority. What this does to their developing characters and personalities we are only just now beginning to discover.

The major issue, of course, is to determine the fine line between being too strict and too permissive. From the standpoint of mental hygiene, if a choice must be made between two evils it would be better to err on the side of strictness. Although it will not be popular with the children, this allows for a healthy structuring of relationships from which sound character will develop.

Family deviance often has its origin in sibling rivalry. The urge to get ahead of brother or sister is so strong that it can overcome (at least temporarily) fear of reprisal. There are times when it becomes the most important thing in the world to defy a brother or sister and, thereby, the entire family. In other words, in a significant number of cases the deviance leads directly to the satisfaction of ego needs. The wise parent will make allowances for this situation when recognized and will temper his administration of sanctions. Our need to grow is overpowering at many stages of our personal development.

Friendship influences can account for the otherwise inexplicable appearance of deviant action. An impressionable young son may bring to the dining table—suddenly and unexpectedly—language that horrifies everyone within earshot. A little probing may bring to light the influence of an admired new associate whose training is vastly different and noticeably inferior.

Deviance as such is more threatening to the family than to any other group because of the type of bonding it employs. Since our ties are so much stronger and the meaning so much deeper in this than in other relationships, any attack on the family is especially traumatic. So we can hardly be blamed if our reaction is instantaneous and violent. It goes without saying that the stronger the family ties, the stronger the defense thrown up against any attack upon it.

One predictable effect of family deviance is disrupted communication. We will not talk as freely to the member who is acting strangely. Neither will we respond as freely to his outputs. Our consternation at his odd behavior will make us retreat from his advances until we can evaluate the situation and make some judgments about its seriousness. This will make him react in exactly the same way we did, and a vicious circle is closed. Whether ever verbalized or not, each of us carries the hope that family relationships can be continued throughout life as a talisman against other interpersonal disasters. If everything else goes wrong, we hope we can always fall back on family as the innermost bastion of our defenses.

One aspect must be noted. If there is concerted deviance on the part of several children, we just may see major changes in family norms. Here as elsewhere, an overwhelming majority may force changes upon a reluctant leadership which otherwise would never have permitted them. A generation ago, a miniskirt would have met with formal censure from the law; its universality today gives it the protection of social respectability. Of course, when the majority has been achieved it is no longer deviance!

Family Sanctions

Since there are many norms in a typical family, it follows that there must be many sanctions. This is so. Our earliest memories of family sanctions usually have to do with corporal punishment. The quick slap or the considered spanking furnishes the most effective deterrent to the rambunctious youngster. He soon associates physical pain with the words "no, no." The age at which punishment starts to be less effective than other kinds of sanctions will vary with the individual. Some children of ten or twelve goad their parents to physical reprisal, while others respond to verbal or nonverbal cues without violence at four or five. In a normal household with two children it is not uncommon for one to be deviant to the point of corporal punishment only a few times in his childhood, whereas the second's behavior pattern has a sinusoidal curve whose half-wavelength is about ten days. This child's security needs seem to demand physical punishment to assuage them; this is the only form of attention that is satisfying. Once the trauma of the spanking wears off, a week to ten days of good behavior can be expected, and then the cycle is repeated.

It is hard to make many parents realize how insecure children will feel if their peccadillos are ignored. They want to know the limits of acceptable behavior from their earliest infancy.

The intersibling application of sanctions is one of the commonest ploys of childhood. A youngster can be fiendishly adept at thinking up ways to punish a brother or sister for breaking norms established unilaterally by the first child. The adjustment to this youthful whimsicality is one lesson in social living driven home to each of us. From this activity, we begin to form value judgments concerning norms and sanctions and the flouting of them.

We have so far been considering the haphazard application of sanctions between children on a spontaneous basis. When major deviance appears in one member, the entire group is instantly absorbed in its corrective repression. It is not uncommon for a family conclave to be held to discuss the problem. This meeting may be either in or without the presence of the deviant. In these situations, an attempt is made to tailor the sanction exactly to the size and weight of the deviant action. Solidarity depends upon the return of the deviant to conformity; this is the sole objective of the family's actions. The amount of resistance met will be a function of the attractiveness of the sin and, more particularly, the influence of another person aiding and abetting in the deviance. Never again will we be as vulnerable to friendship pressures as we are in our teens and early twenties. The value systems of some will force them to renounce family ties before "betraying" their friends of the moment. This is of course a temporary aberration.

The fact that our deepest emotions are involved in our family relationships does *not* mean that the mere application of sanctions will at once result in a return to conformity. On the contrary, the same individual's recalcitrance may be much deeper in the family than in other groups. *Because we love our family so deeply, it is doubly hard to admit error and pay the necessary penalty.* If there is a milligram of the martyr in us, it will be aroused by a united family determined to show us the light. It is actually possible that familial deviance will be harder to reduce than any found in outside groups. This means that the family environment is excellent training for our individual reaction to the treatment of deviance in other groups. Anything we meet there will be less traumatic than one of our emotion-packed confrontations with the family.

It is entirely possible that family sanctions will be *too* severe for the error involved. Just as the bowler overcorrects when he misses a strike, so can the family impose sanctions far out of proportion to the severity of the deviance. This will of course prolong the resistance of the offender and make his reclamation more difficult.

The most maddening thing to parents is the universal reaction of children to compare their punishments with those of other children in other families. "But Mary's mother lets her watch the late show." "*All* the other kids get to stay out past midnight. Why do you treat me like a baby?" This is especially hurtful to parental feelings if the remarks happen to be true. This reverse English applied to group pressures is quite often effective in relaxing sanctions, at least in degree.

Of course, the important thing to remember is the absolute necessity of maintaining basic standards of norms (and sanctions when the norms are not observed). Unless discipline has its beginning in earliest childhood, its inculcation later may be next to impossible. Much of our social unrest and grossly deviant behavior against the laxest of norms stems from ignorance of the fundamentals of self-discipline. If it has never been impressed upon us that there are irreducible minimal standards of acceptable behavior, we can hardly be blamed for resenting a sudden repressive action by those about us. We then feel ourselves the objects of discriminatory punishment, and this is never tolerable.

Thus the family is the basic training unit for social behavior and the proving ground for our character and behavior patterns.

The Generation Gap

It is hilarious to observe how every generation discovers to its horror, amazement, and chagrin that the one coming up behind it is not in perfectly synchronous communication with its predecessors. Why should it be? Each of us as an individual has God-given rights to grow up and express ourself as a person. Each of us will hopefully grow and mature further than our parents did. If we do not, our civilization is at least stagnant and probably moribund. Every person, as one of the mileposts of his maturation, must make way for youth without constraint or envy.

Today's young people are noisily vocal in expressing their contempt for The Establishment. Of course, in their immaturity they ignore the fact that The Establishment has guaranteed their right to protest—even against it. No one has come close to showing that the insurgency of this crop of kids is measurably greater than that of any preceding generation. The mass communications media give their tantrums greater visibility, but we, as their fathers and grandfathers, can remember our own hangups, frustrations, and "uptightness." There is a strong argument that this generation's method of revolt is more honest than ours was. At least it is open and straightforward.

One factor commonly overlooked in all our hysteria is the ridiculously small percentage of the total young population involved in open defiance of accepted group norms. Irrespective of the number of students at campuses where violence flares, the youth involved are always a microscopically small percentage of the total. This activist population gets visibility and publicity far beyond what it deserves. It is heartening to note that the recent appearance of a "Crusade for Decency" is apparently a demand for equal time on the part of more sober and well-behaved youth.

From the standpoint of family relationships, the seeds of a generation gap are sown during the first four or five years of our children's lives. If we have not by then established firm habits of open communication, we never will. The child of two is perfectly capable of recognizing withdrawal by his parents—or insincerity in their approaches and answers. The deepest hurt of all is to want to talk to another and be rebuffed time after time for no apparently valid reason. And parents must remember that their own time of greatest need to talk with their offspring will be when the children have acquired new interests and families of their own. To open new channels of communication at that time is a hopeless task; it's hard enough to maintain old and well-traveled ones.

Of course our children will come to have value sets different from ours. Of course they will outgrow and develop beyond the rigid confines of their family. Of course their development and maturation will make them question whether father is always right. If they did not, we could hardly take pride in what we have produced. For each of us the primary question is: How much of the generation gap is my fault? How have I failed to answer my children when they called?

If our familial relationships are sound, let the generation gap appear with all its sounding of tocsins and clashing of arms. For those families that have a solid foundation, there is always the lovers' reconciliation after the confrontation has run its course. It was Mark Twain who said that when he was eighteen, he was amazed at how much his father had learned in the previous four years. Our emotions tend to blind us to nature's irreversible growth pattern. Because our children are individuals and therefore differ from us, we are insulted, anxious, and finally fearful. All our desperate flounderings to regain the dependent child only alienate him further until we realize what is happening to him and see how natural his reactions are after all.

Of course, we are only making a vain attempt at self-deception unless we face up to the one thing that is different in this generation—the widespread use of narcotics of every variety. Physiologists have not even begun to evaluate the real effects of drug addiction on this and future generations. We know that some narcotics produce irreversible distortions of personality as well as terrible physical effects. The specter of chromosome damage hangs over us with no present resolution. The costs in hard dollars can wreck a youngster's economic future before it has even been established. The intangible impact on values and principles can never really be quantified, but it will make itself known in no uncertain manner.

If there has ever been a time for parents to pool their best efforts in an all-out assault on a common enemy, this is it. If we lose this battle, we have lost the war—our children and all their descendants as well. The specious argument that their parents' use of tobacco and liquor can be equated with their use of drugs is not even worthy of an answer, and they know this.

We must beat this enemy. The future of our society depends upon it. And when we do, we can then return to the "normal" problems of maintaining communication with our children at a viable level and praying for the insight to give them understanding with our love. Love no longer has a right to be blind; parents must recognize their children's problems as their own and give them the help they are asking for by whatever means is at their command.

Ambivalence of Family Membership

Our other memberships can come close to tearing us apart as they conflict with our family ties. If we fall within the so-called normal range, our feelings of love for our family make us much more sensitive to the different objectives and norms in other groups. This pulling in two directions can begin at any time after we have taken membership in a group other than our family. Child psychologists find many neuroses among children barely started in school which come from the shock of discovering that the family does not, in every facet of its existence, present a perfect image of society at large. The school, as a grand mixture of many families, comes closer to this mirror of society. When the child discovers that the norms of his classroom differ widely from those of his family, it has a strong effect upon him. In trying to reconcile these opposable norms, he meets role conflict for the first time.

Most of us make a valiant attempt to conform in both groups; this arduous job subjects us to strain which quickly gives rise to anxiety and attempts at evasion of the problem. This often results in a double life. A loving child will go to almost any lengths to keep his family from knowing that, in obeying the norms of another group, he is automatically deviant within his own home. The necessity for "living a lie" in at least one of the groups is traumatic in the extreme. And the longer it continues, the more fear there will be of eventual discovery. How desperately many of us tried to keep from our parents the fact that we had begun to smoke when we went off to college. How many of us were never able to smoke in front of our parents; they knew we did, but we avoided the actual act in their presence and maintained a tacit armed truce.

When familial bonds are strong, the member may attempt to reduce ambivalence by pushing in the other group and crusading to change its norms to conform with those of his family. This action is generally recognized for what it is, and sanctions are applied with special gusto to this deviant for his provincialism. This punishment, because it is severe, will only increase frustration in the deviant and probably will not be too efficacious in making him conform. At the same time, it is common for a member to have the first seed of doubt implanted in his mind about family infallibility. If so many others disagree with his family's way of doing things, what standards will reassure him that his family is correct? He hardly can bring himself to face up to a situation wherein it would be his family which was "odd."

This opposition of norms, once felt, can easily lead to a search for truth by joining other groups in an effort to find reinforcement for the viewpoint of one group or the other. Little as a person relishes the prospect of learning his family is out of step, even this possibly would be preferable to a continuation of his uncertainty, with its attendant pressures. The man who has suffered agonies while suspecting he has a cancer is oddly relieved to find his self-diagnosis confirmed; at least the uncertainty is over.

Within the family, the member who is subjected to ambivalence will be predictably uncertain in his behavior. He is reaching for a balance which at the moment is unattainable. No matter how hard he tries, he cannot completely dispel the unease accompanying the basic role conflict. It is not likely that he will receive much help from other members of either his family or the outside group. If memberships there have achieved a reasonable balance, they will exhibit little empathy for him. In most cases, it will be necessary for him to carry on his own battle to its conclusion. Small wonder that the families themselves are basic causes for many neuroses.

Ambivalence, if it persists for too long a time, will place family ties in jeopardy. Nobody can be expected to go on forever with his anxiety level up to his chin. It is difficult to determine at what point in his maturation he will make the considered judgment that the family will *not* be the center of his universe for his entire lifetime. His first duty is to himself and the development of his personal uniqueness; then comes the realization that somewhere along the line he will become one of the founders of another family. In that situation, he will again be subjected to great pressures to accommodate his long-established habits to his mate's demands. No matter how dominant one of the new pair may be, their family will inevitably bear some of the marks of both parents. It is in this manner that cultures evolve—by combining elements of the families of both parents. The new norms will be different from those familiar to the parents if their relationship is good.

When ties have been strong, residual ambivalence will show in tiebacks to both sets of grandparents. Considerable agility will be required to meet the demands of visiting back and forth and recognizing the sovereignty of the host family's habits. When visiting a grandparent we follow his norms; when grandpa comes to us, he will follow ours. Of course, there is no legislation that can make him *like* our norms.

Ambivalence of family membership is a product of emerging personal uniqueness. If we all were cast in the same mold, the only variation would be flash that could be removed with a blow of the hammer. Since we are not, we should, in a sense, be glad to recognize the appearance of ambivalence as one sign of maturity. Our interfacing with other groups is essential to our existence. The balancing of pressures among all the groups will be a measure of our maturity and our ability to live in social groups.

Life Interpretation as a Family Function

During the early years of a child's life, no function of the family is more important than to explain to him what life is all about. While he is helpless, no other agency can be expected to devote the time, care, or thought to interpreting his environment and giving him a perspective. During this process, it is natural that many of his biases will originate, to follow him for the rest of his life and color all his thinking. Since we interpret our perceptions according to our mental set—that is, we exhibit selective perception—it follows that our world will be largely conditioned by what our family has taught us.

It is true that every family is unique and every member of every family is unique, but, within a grouping of families, there will be interactions and cross-influencing. Thus a small culture grows which we call our community. There will be many common norms, goals, and behavior patterns among the residents of this group of families. This commonality, in turn, tends to broaden and deepen the reinforcement of those items which our family first transmitted to us.

One observation should be interposed here. The *amount* and *direction* of this vector will be dependent upon the intensity and type of the member's feeling for his family. If familial bonds are strong, the imprinting will be heavy; if he tends to seek much of his socialization outside the family from an early age, he will not lean so heavily upon siblings and parents for interpretive values. Naturally, if his feelings toward his family are antipathetic, their influence on his life interpretation will be negative. That is, he will tend to reject the values of his family, even to the point of accepting opposite ones. This spectrum is operant in every population of families on a normal bell curve distribution.

Internally, demands by younger family members for interpretation of what is seen serves as a stimulus to the development of judgmental values among those called upon. It is another iteration of a well-known fact: We learn best and remember longest what we teach to others. The verbalization of interpretive factors will strengthen them in our own consciousness. It is, of course, this fact that makes politicians and religious leaders put so much emphasis on "standing up and being counted." Analysts and psychiatrists carry this a step further and study the self-hypnotic effects which may result from repeated affirmations of fundamental beliefs. Adolph Hitler was a true master of this kind of psychological manipulation.

As can be seen, the interpretation of life received as bits and pieces by one member of a family from all the others will form a mosaic, rather than a smooth surface. This can sometimes lead to compartmentalization, with simultaneous entertainment of mutually exclusive bits of belief. All of us have our little inconsistencies resulting from this effect. Intellectually we may be strongly against superstition, but we feel uncomfortable when a black cat crosses our path. We may be strongly Republican in our general political leanings, but we have no difficulty in voting for a Democratic candidate for alderman who is a personal friend.

The foundation for our mental habits can be traced to this process as well. Methodology of thinking is acquired during the early years; once established, it is quite difficult to alter. Habits of haphazard, logical, or intuitive thought are acquired in our youth, usually from the patterns common to the family. This is a segment of life interpretation—how we think concerning its mysteries and complexities.

When used in its purest sense, this family activity is a great teacher of the fundamentals of cooperative action. One member, because of age, may be mostly a receiver, but he will from time to time make a surprising number of contributions to the family's group perception of life. The fresh, unbiased viewpoint of the child is capable of some extremely sharp and lovely observations—usually at totally unexpected times.

In this general vein, it is interesting to speculate how

many times families and their individual members will actually *synthesize* a viewpoint of life which cannot be entirely substantiated by what they see about them. This is one of the happiest of human characteristics. It makes life much more tolerable for Mr. Average Guy to inject just a tiny bit of fantasy into his conceptualization of his existence. James Thurber expressed it with his own inimitable genius in "The Secret Life of Walter Mitty." This kind of buffer, unless overdone, can make our daily living infinitely more bearable.

Seldom does this function of the family find formal expression. It is an ongoing, day-to-day thing particularly parental, and incidentally resorted to by older siblings. Like the coaching of the subordinate on the job by the boss, it happens as needed, triggered by a younger family member or an older one. If the youngster has a question, he asks it; if the elder sees the baby brother about to misperceive his surroundings, he volunteers corrective advice.

As a learning experience, few equal it. Every element for increased understanding is there—a question, a need to know, and, one hopes, an honest answer from one presumed to have the knowledge. Especially significant are both the receptivity of the learner and the habit formed by repeated incidence of the situation.

As the young family member begins to be more strongly influenced by his peripheral associations, this activity gradually subsides until outside vectors become the stronger. Perhaps, at this point, we could say that the member has "graduated" from the school of the family.

The Family and the Nation

In a sense, everything that has been said in these pages has pointed toward the issue of the family and the nation. Just as the group is more than the sum of the individuals composing it, so is the nation more than the sum of the families composing it. No other factor can come close to the importance of the family in the future of America. Our material wealth, power, influence over the rest of the world—none of these has meaning unless the country has the strength and backup of a solid, enduring family structure.

Our communications media are crammed with alarmist messages about the deterioration of the American family. They tell us that we are spinning ourselves to pieces from the sheer centrifugal force of our transportation devices and that the family as we have known it in the United States will cease to exist in another generation.

This is an arguable premise. All the noise, all the hysteria, all the protest and violence involve such a small percentage of our population as to leave undisturbed our basic solidity and integrity. The purveyors of alarm are masters at distracting our attention from the governing fact: The silent, vast, unheard-from majority of American families still display the virtues that made our country what it is. Most American children still feel that their home is the center of the universe until they become adult. Most of our young people observe the major norms set up by both family and society at large. Most of our offspring are working hard at getting an education in the belief that this is the way to improve their lot in life while making a contribution to society. In fact, sociologists tell us that the numbers of young Americans who are deeply concerned with improving conditions are at record levels.

It is said repeatedly that we have let our concepts of morality and standards of behavior regress. Who are "we"? How many are we, and what percentage of our population do we constitute? Remember how a picture may be distorted by keeping the spotlight on a few in the cast and shrouding the great majority in gloom. True, the incidence of divorce *is* increasing, but the incidence of broken homes is no greater than it was a couple of generations ago when divorce meant automatic social ostracism. A broken family which remains technically together is a hollow mockery indeed and may leave scars far deeper than those that follow a clean break.

The fact that our sons and daughters question us closely as they grow up and demand reasons for our dicta and proposed family norms is good. At least, they are thinking about the nature of right and wrong. If they come to a reasoned decision that a thing is right, it will have more impact on their future behavior than blind obedience to a fiat from Olympus. Their reactions will actually strengthen our own beliefs because we have been forced to defend them in a rational manner.

One fact emerges, however, of which we should be constantly aware. This awakening individualism and the questioning intelligence at its source will complicate the group dynamics of the family. Process becomes much more involved; interactions are sharper and more meaningful; family decisions will have to be on a more cooperative basis than in the past. This is good. It is the living enactment of the philosophy on which our nation was founded; if we carry democratic action into the heart of our lives, our family evolution is going in the right direction.

Parents should not fear the obvious fact that their offspring are better educated and more sophisticated than they were at the same age. This fact is inherent in our structure, and we would be failures unless this happened. The further they surpass us, the more successful we have been in fulfilling our familial responsibilities.

As seen in this light, we could properly expect that the

American family of the generation to come will be *more* solidly founded than in the past. Rational relationships will be more enduring than dictated ones, especially when love is also there. For one thing, we can be realistic in our expectations of our children. Parents who demand the impossible can only expect to be disappointed and to frustrate the offspring.

Another trend we have already noted: The longer time span of at least partial dependency on the family is due to longer and longer educational requirements for the young person to be competitive in adult life. With the standard minimal educational level reaching college graduation and climbing toward the graduate level, the family will remain as the pivotal center of its younger members for just so many years longer.

There is too much basic strength, too much latent promise, in the mainstream of the American people to sell us short in this or the next generation. Of course the job will be harder, but it is a long way this side of the impossible. Our children are doing a better job with their families than we did; theirs will too!

* * *

Throughout recorded history, the family has been the basic social building block, and this is as true today as it ever was. We get our basic training there; we learn our norms; we start to become social beings within its structure.

Family leadership, since it is rotational, reinforces the fact that it is an informal group. A normal family automatically recognizes special strengths in its members and shares the responsibility of leadership.

Family deviance is impossible to hide, and is more traumatic because of the involved emotionalism. For the same reasons, family sanctions are more severe than those imposed on other group memberships.

There has always been a "generation gap." Modern parents actually are in a better position than ever to keep it small, if they work at their duty of free and open communication. It is inevitable that the individual will come to have ambivalent feelings about his family as his involvement increases in other groups. This is a perfectly normal aspect of maturation.

One of the more basic functions of parents and older children is to interpret the meaning of life to the younger children. They expect it and demand it as their right. The care with which this is done will be a large determinant of the mental and emotional health of the growing child. But the family will continue to be the basis for the greatness of the American nation. We have no right at this point to be pessimistic about its future if each of us does his job as a family member.

Conclusion

A REPRISE of what has been discussed in these pages brings to light several salient facts. First, and outstanding, there is nothing esoteric about group dynamics. The interactions between individuals in their group memberships follow some simple and completely understandable principles that are more closely related to common sense than to a mysterious scientific body of knowledge.

Second, it is easy to see from the beginning how important to our success in any field is the manner in which we relate to our fellows. If a general pattern of abrasiveness develops, we are in severe trouble. No one else can ever rectify this situation, since habitual bad relations with many others *must* be centered in *our* method of operation.

Third, success or failure in interpersonal relationships is closely allied to our attitudes and our degree of sensitivity. We wear attitudes like clothing. They are perfectly visible to our peers, and it is a fundamental of human psychology that we tend to respond in kind to what is displayed by another. Our understanding of others is governed by how much we understand of their thoughts, their biases, their attitudes, and their motivation. Viable working relationships can be worked out with people whose goals are quite different from ours, but only if we understand what makes them behave as they do and can make our own mental adjustments to their approach.

Fourth, our comfort in our environment is significantly tied to the number of group memberships we maintain. Too few memberships do not allow us sufficient sphere of activity; too many crush us between the millstones of frantic activity and role conflicts. Our judgments about what groups to join and what to avoid will be a dominant determinant of our personal success in life.

Fifth, any improvement man makes in his environment will be the product of group efforts. Society today is far too complex to be altered in any major way by the efforts of one individual. This has a corollary—we must be mentally prepared for continuing change. Ours is a society of change; we must strive to both cause and manage change if we want a better world in which to live. It is obvious that our value judgments will be constantly in use to determine whether a proposed difference is good or bad. Blind acceptance of change for its own sake is the primrose path to chaos.

Sixth and last, successful group living demands goodwill. We must emulate good leadership in adopting personally the criterion of the best for the most as the benchmark for our actions. If it is good for the group, and our membership in that group is valid, it will be good for us as individuals. And if we are people of goodwill we want both benefits.

Glossary

Adaptation: The ability of an organism to change as a result of a particular stimulus or felt need.

Aggression: An active response to counteract a stimulus which is felt to pose a threat. It implies hostility.

Anxiety: An emotion rather like aggression. Anxiety is a major factor in virtually every form of personality breakdown and is a significant component of the "normal" personality as well. A typical behavior sequence would be: disturbance of equilibrium—impulse to act in a certain way—memory of former punishment—anxiety—inhibition of action tendency.

Assumed leadership: An effort by one or more members of an unstructured group to become the leader. Until confirmed by acceptance of the group, this leadership is "assumed."

Authoritarian: A mental set which causes the person to react in a directive manner in a given situation; in other words, an attempt to act with authority.

Behavior: The sum total of a person's or group's reactions to stimuli. We often speak of behavior patterns as typical to a given kind of stimulus.

Blockage: The group reaction which is intended to foil a

stimulus presented by an outside agent. It protects the integrity of the group.

Closure: A desire to complete an incomplete design, shown for very brief intervals. Anxious persons feel this desire more than relaxed subjects do. It is also implied that sampling of the visual environment, which would have revealed the breaks in the design, is also interfered with by other modalities, particularly visceral ones.

Cognition: A knowledge or, as we more commonly say, a recognition, of something within our environment.

Cohesiveness: The strength of the forces which tend to hold a group together; in essence, the power of the group's common objectives.

Communication: The transmission of a concept or an idea of one person or group to another by any means.

Concept: An idea in its fullest connotation in the mind of an individual.

Conflict: The negative valence which causes a person or group to evade a given stimulus.

Conformity: The acceptance of and adherence to a certain pattern of behavior by an individual or a group.

Consensus: Total agreement on the part of the members of a group concerning a given question.

Deviant: An individual whose behavior varies from norms established by the group.

Displacement: Aggression that is vented, not upon the immediate frustrating agent, but upon some substitute. This is particularly likely if the frustrator (1) is not available or (2) is in a position to inflict severe punishment if attacked. If the frustrator has certain attributes, the "scapegoat" is likely to be chosen because he also possesses them.

Domination: Power of an individual or a group to get acquiescence from other members of the group.

Effective leadership: That leadership which will achieve the goals and objectives set up by the group.

Ego: A Freudian term indicating what we call the conscious self.

Emotions: States that are more complex than feelings and appear to be products of learning rather than of heredity. Emotions can usually be analyzed into a feeling or feelings, plus certain expectancies about the object of the emotion.

Empathy: The ability to understand how another person thinks or feels, not necessarily requiring agreement.

Empirical: Relying on observation or experience, often without due regard for system or theory.

Esteem: The high regard of one or more members of a group for another member.

Expectations: The hopes of achievement held by an individual from a given situation.

Formal group: A group which is established by fiat or superposition from above.

Frustration: The state that results when any behavior sequence is blocked. It is used to describe the situation in which a person wants two incompatible goals and to identify events in which an individual anticipates a given outcome and is disappointed.

Goals: The targets toward which an individual or a group is working.

Group: Two or more individuals with a common objective.

Group dynamics: The study of the actions, interactions, and forces exerted by or upon a group.

Group integrity: The forces which tend to keep a group intact and working toward its goals.

Group pressure: The force exerted by a group upon its members (or outwardly) which tends to achieve the group's objectives.

Halo effect: The result of a tendency to overevaluate a person or a thing because of emotional involvement or similarity of purposes.

Hawthorne study: A famous study conducted by Harvard Business School professors in the 1930's in the Hawthorne Plant of the Western Electric Company. From this study evolved the "human relations" concept of doing business.

Homogeneity: A strong similarity, in many respects, between members of a group.

Hostility: A negative reaction to a given stimulus resulting in aggressive action of some sort.

Identification: The acceptance by an individual of the goals and beliefs of a group; in other words, an orientation to or association with that group.

Imposed leadership: Leadership put upon a group by formal means from above. It can never be effective until accepted by the rank and file.

Individual differences: Dissimilarities between two or more people which make them each unique.

Informal group: Usually a small group which is generated spontaneously by recognition of common objectives or aims.

Inhibition: Any force or combination of forces which tends to reduce or cause to disappear what otherwise would be normal reaction to a stimulus.

Interaction: Reactions between two or more individual members of a group.

Integration: The weaving together into a common structure of diverse elements.

Isolate: Any individual who for any reason is rejected by the members of his group.

Leadership: The ability to cause other individuals to follow one's direction.

Member satisfaction: Realization by group members of partial or complete achievement of the group's goals.

Mental set: The tendency on the part of an individual to react intellectually according to a pattern when faced by a specific stimulus.

Motivation: That force or forces which cause an individual or group to pursue actively a given goal; a goal-seeking drive.

Norms: Accepted standards of behavior by a group under a given stimulus.

Perception: That which an individual receives from any sensory stimuli. See also *Cognition.*

Perceptual defense: A reaction in which people become "blind" to objects that they prefer not to know about; the blocking of perception under conditions usually involving some kind of threat to the person.

Permissiveness: A leadership style which encourages individual freedom of action within the group.

Projection: A defense reaction in which a person projects an inner state, such as an emotion, into the outside world, denying any connection with himself. Thus a hostile, pugnacious person says that others are behaving aggressively and are trying to start a fight with him.

Reinforcement: Any "reward" or force that tends to increase an individual's response to a given stimulus.

Repression: The forgetting of unpleasant experiences even though no serious anxiety is involved.

Response: Any activity or behavior that results from a given stimulus.

Status: The comparative level of esteem occupied by an individual within his group. See also *Esteem*.

Stereotype: The categorization of a concept or a person by an individual or a group. Others tend to see him as a type instead of as he is.

Stimulus: Any force which calls forth a response (behavior) on the part of an individual or a group.

Sensitivity: Awareness of the reactions of others.

Stress: A factor that causes tension of all sorts. A person's efforts to protect an equilibrium or to restore one may encounter either blockage or a negative valence eliciting anxiety. Such situations uniformly involve a mobilization of energy and increase of tension. This tension has extensive physiological repercussions which are important to a personality; they represent the organism's reaction to stress. Some authorities say the stress reaction is the body's nonspecific way of dealing with certain kinds of internal and external agents: fatigue, cold, microbes, pain, and anxiety, for example.

Stress tolerance: After a threat is recognized, the organism's "stage of resistance" in which it can take substantially greater stress without damage than was true initially. The occurrence of moderate damage, so to speak, builds up immunity, and the organism can now tolerate an injury which would formerly have been fatal.

Suggestibility: The tendency of individuals or groups to respond to ideas or hints or to indirect leadership.

Tension: The state of frustration engendered within an individual when he is blocked from achieving a goal.

Toteming: Listing people in the order of their contributions to the organization.

Valence: The power or force reacting upon an individual by a stimulus. This may be either positive or negative in direction.

Variable: A condition which results in a change or a series of changes within specific parameters.

Withdrawal: An unfavorable reaction (negative valence) to a given stimulus on the part of an individual or a group.

Index

achievement
  as motivation, 42–43
  role conflict and, 280
action levels, individual effect on, 173–176
adaptation, 151–153
  in multigroup environment, 252–255
  social change and, 238
affluent society
  new groups in, 156
  physiological needs and, 35–36
aggression
  formal work group and, 246–247
  threat and, 124–127
air pollution, 36
Alcoholics Anonymous, 21
Alexander the Great, 185
ambivalence, in family relationships, 367–370
American family, decline of, 353–354, 374; see also family
American Foundation for Management Research, 46–47
American Psychological Association, 33
anti-Semitism, 172

assumed leadership
  as deviance, 292–295
  see also leadership
athlete, motivation of, 59–60
atypical behavior, 286
  see also behavior
authority
  democracy and, 80
  formal group and, 79–81
authority figure, manager as, 79
behavior
  broad principles of, 15
  Chinese Communists and, 18
  conformity and, 138–141
  culture and, 140
  motivation and, 19
  predictability in, 182
behavioral science, principles of, 15–16
behavioral scientist, impact of, 14, 76
beliefs, reprioritization of, 282
Blake, Robert, 120
blockage
  group effectiveness and, 345–348
  methods of, 122–124

387

blue collar workers, culture and, 140
boredom, deviance and, 288–289
Boy Scouts, norms of, 139–140
brainstorming, 335
British family, status of, 354–355
business career, growth in, 21–22
businessman
   "direct action" type, 52
   stereotypes of, 29

challenge, as incentive, 42
change
   adaptation to, 12, 151–153, 255
   decision making in, 253
   deviance and, 306
   in group goals, 167–170
   leadership qualities and, 161–164
   of personal goals, 141–144
   resistance to, 255
   social, *see* social change
charisma
   group spirit and, 164
   leadership and, 186–189, 217
childhood
   family life interpretation in, 370–371
   friendship groups in, 98
Chinese family, role of, 354–355
churches, as semiformal group, 87–88
Churchill, Sir Winston S., 187
city government, company dominance of, 86
civilization, cyclical nature of, 13
clothing, need for, 35
cohesiveness, 107–110
   vs. effectiveness, 336–339
   see also group cohesiveness
"colleague" syndrome, motivation and, 45
colleges, social control by, 148

college student
   beliefs of, 148
   rebellious attitudes of, 141
committee, management by, 101
communication
   blockage and, 124
   deviance and, 289–290
   followership and, 227, 235
   formal group and, 81–82
   in goal setting, 117–118
   group norms and, 62
   leader–follower relations and, 235
   leadership qualities and, 163
   role conflict and, 279
company, vs. labor union, 272–275
company rules, formal group and, 83
company towns, 86
conflict neurosis, 266–269
conformity
   behavior patterns and, 138–141
   curve of distribution for, 136
   as group fetish, 135–141
   motivation and, 138
consensus, group and, 62–63
convenience informal groups, 99
counterattack, protective, 61
creativity
   group membership and, 158
   of inner-directed person, 216–217
   leadership and, 186
culture, behavior and, 140

decad, Mosaic, 233–234
decision making
   change and, 253
   leadership and, 209
delegation, leadership and, 233
democracy
   authority and, 80

meaning of, 257
demographic variables, anomalies in, 149–150
demotivators, 42–43
developmental goals, group planning and, 59
deviance, 286–308
  assumed leadership and, 291–294
  as catalyst, 304
  constructive approach to, 297–300
  as dissatisfaction with status quo, 297
  ego involvement in, 296
  in family, 358–361
  group cohesiveness and, 289–291
  group objectives and, 303–306
  group reappraisal in, 300–303
  group sanctions and, 290
  individual differences and, 291
  leader as cause of, 301, 306
  leadership conflict and, 287
  as nonconformity, 308
  power play as, 292
  progress and, 305–308
  rebellion as, 287–288
  sanctions against, 294–297
deviant, isolate as, 309–312, 320
dismissals and layoffs, 85
dissatisfiers, 42–43
drive
  goal-seeking and, 25–26
  see also motivation
drivership, vs. leadership, 201
drug addiction, 367
dynamics, defined, 11–12
  see also group dynamics

economic goals
  group motivation and, 55–57
  meshing of, 56

economics, study of, 57
education, family and, 375–376
ego drive, 40
ego involvement
  in deviance, 296
  of group, 69–72
ego needs, 34, 38–40, 66–70
  product identification and, 225–226
ego satisfaction, group motivation and, 179
Eisenhower, Dwight D., 176
emotional maturity, 22
emotional problems, work group and, 248
empathy
  defined, 16–17
  as interpersonal relations, 146
employee, knowledge of by manager, 31–32
employee relations, basis of, 32
enemy, "ignoring" of, 128
environment
  control of, 151, 379
  in interpersonal relationships, 145
Establishment, The
  contempt for, 365
  as semiformal group, 92
esteem, group leadership and, 119
ethical values, 139
  erosion of, 142
  reappraisal of, 155

fads, behavior and, 139
faith, followership and, 217–218
family
  changed personal goals and, 143
  direction for child in, 370–372
  ethical and social values from, 139
  generation gap and, 364–367

INDEX

family (*continued*)
  group dynamics and, 352–377
  as informal group, 355–356
  vs. job, 250–251
  leadership of, 355–356
  leadership training in, 357–358
  life interpretation by, 370–373
  mental habits of, 372–373
  nation and, 373–376
  sibling rivalry in, 360
  as social group, 352–355
family deviance, 358–361
family life, as group dynamics, 18
family membership, ambivalence of, 367–370
family norms, 368–369
family relations, thinking about, 353
family sanctions, 361–364
father image
  leadership and, 192–195
  role conflict and, 277
follower
  communication with, 235
  as front-line soldier, 226–229
  identification of with product, 223–226
followership, 211–236
  impersonal observer and, 230–233
  ineffective, 278–281
  maintenance needs and, 220–223
  Mosaic decad and, 233
  security drive and, 211–214
food, expenditures on, 35
forced choice, goal competition and, 243–245
Ford, Henry, 129, 177
formal group, 77–87
  aggression and hostility in, 247–248
  dismissal from, 85
  fiscal goals of, 82
  goals of, 81–82, 116
  leadership in, 87
  membership of, 85
  norms of, 83
  paternalism and, 83
  permissive atmosphere of, 84
  rigidity in, 86
  selection of, 79
freeway systems, safety and, 36–37
French family, role of, 354
friendship groups, 98, 145
front-line soldier
  follower as, 226–229
  leadership of, 227–228

games
  friendship groups and, 138–139
  motivation in, 59
Gandhi, Mohandes K., 154, 187
Gaulle, Gen. Charles de, 129
Gellerman, Saul W., 42
generation gap, 18, 364–367
goal competition
  forced choice in, 243–244
  group hierarchy and, 249–252
goal identification, 195–198
goal setting, 25–26
  communication in, 117–118
  individual and, 179–180
  role conflict and, 280
goals, personal, 141–144
  see also group objectives
God, personal, 258
Goldwater, Barry, 172
goodwill, need for, 379
Graham, Billy, 187
Great Books courses, 58
group
  acceptance by, 38
  adaptation within, 151–153
  aggression and, 124–127

INDEX

group (*continued*)
  blockage by, 121–122
  cliques and, 67
  as collection of individuals, 179–182
  communications with, 50–51, 62, 127
  "counterattack" by, 61
  defined, 11
  demotivation of, 72–76
  development goals of, 57–59
  disruptive factors in, 165
  economic goals of, 55–57
  effectiveness of, 331–351
  formal, 77–87
  goals of, 55–59, 68; *see also* group objectives
  heterogeneity of, 71
  vs. individual, 49–52, 161–182
  individual characteristics of, 52–54
  informal, 97–106
  internal threat to, 62
  kinds of, 77-106
  life cycle of, 53
  objective of, 55–59, 68–70, 116–118, 153, 303–306
  overcommunication in, 73
  personality and, 50
  personality clashes in, 165
  personal problems as demotivator of, 72–73
  power struggles, in, 63
  proliferation of, 238–239
  properties of, 107–134
  reaction to deviance in, 298–300
  self-perpetuation of, 130–133
  self-protective instinct of, 63–65
  semiformal, 87–97
  strengthening of in threat, 128–129
  synergy of, 334–336
  threat to, 51, 53, 122, 128–129
  "turtle" reaction in, 61
  violence by, 125
  work habits of, 53
group aggression, 124–127
group behavior, atypical, 286
group cohesiveness, 107–110
  deviance and, 289–291
  vs. group effectiveness, 336–339
  vs. groupiness, 328–329
  individual's effect on, 170–173
  threats to, 109
group dynamics
  change and, 13
  defined, 12
  emotional maturity and, 22–23
  human nature and, 13
  family life and, 18, 352–377
  interpersonal relationships and, 19–20
  introspection in, 17
  and prediction of others' actions, 18–19
  reasons for studying, 16–17
  self-confidence through, 22
  self-knowledge and, 16–17
group effectiveness, 331–351
  blockage and, 345–348
  cohesiveness and, 336–339
  defined, 332–333
  leadership and, 339–342
  semantic difficulties in, 350
group goals, modification of, 167–170
  see also goal(s); group objectives; motivation
group hierarchy, 249–252
group identification, with product, 224
groupiness, vs. group cohesiveness, 328–329
group leadership
  change and, 50

group leadership (*continued*)
  counterattack in, 61
  demotivation by, 73
  ego involvement and, 69–70
  formal group and, 87
  group norms and, 112
  informal groups and, 100–101
  as outside stimulus, 51
  personality clashes and, 165
  response to, 120–121
  in semiformal group, 94
  see also leadership
group membership
  advice before choosing, 270
  ego satisfaction and, 179
  exponential curve of, 238–240
  family priorities and, 250–251
  individual and, 156–157
  integration of, 259–260
  isolate and, 311–312
  loss of, 256–258, 317–318
  need for, 91–92
  neurosis and, 267–268
  objective harmonizing in, 271–272
  personal goals and, 141–144
  personal perspective in, 281–282
  severance from, 256–258, 317–318
  status through, 176–177
group morale, 81, 172
group motivation, 49–76
  commonalities for, 54–72
  communication and, 55
  development goals and, 57–60
  economic goals and, 55–57
  ego involvement and, 69–72
  by leader, 196
  power and, 63–66
  status in, 66–69
  see also motivation
group neurosis, 54, 61

group norms
  as behavior standards, 110–113
  contradictory, 139–140
  deviance from, 62
  for informal group, 101–104
  intragroup conflict in, 102–103
  sanctions and, 113–115
  semiformal group, 96
  status and, 150
group objectives
  adaptation and, 153
  determination of, 116–118
  deviance and, 303–306
  ego involvement and, 70
  function of, 303
  individual and, 159
  leader's responsibility and, 270–271
group perpetuation, 130–133
group perspective, 348–351
group protection, 60–61
group reappraisal, in deviance, 300–303
group sanctions, 113–115
  deviance and, 290, 294–297
  in family, 361–363
  against isolate, 318–320
group status, individual and, 176–178
  see also status
group suicide, 132
growth
  adaptation and, 152
  democracy and, 257

habits, group membership and, 157
herd instinct, 221
Herzberg, Frederick, 41–47, 70, 75, 78, 220, 247
hippies
  motivation of, 155–156

INDEX

as subculture, 153–154
Vietnam War and, 155
Hitler, Adolf, 185, 187–188, 198
Hitler Jugend, 64
hobby groups, 98
home, child's regard for, 374
hostility, work problems and, 247–248
housing, need for, 35
Hughes, Howard, 177
human nature
  broad principles of, 15
  change in, 12
  complexity of, 239–240
  constancy of, 13
  good and bad elements in, 31
hygienic factors, 42–43

identity, search for, 38
impersonal observer, in followership, 230–233
individual
  action levels of, 173–176
  adaptation by, 151–153
  goal setting and, 179–180
  group cohesiveness and, 170–173
  group compared to, 49–54, 179–182
  group effects caused by, 161–182
  group objectives and, 167–170
  as impersonal observer, 232
  membership loss of, 256–258, 317–318
  status of, 176–178
  as sum of group memberships, 156–160
informal groups, 97–106
  convenience, 99
  effectiveness of, 342–345
  family as, 355–356
  goals of, 117–118
  leadership in, 99–101
  norms of, 101–104
  rotation of leadership in, 99–100
  sanctions by, 104–105
  self-protective, 99
  work problems and, 248–249
informal social groups, need for, 147
inner-directed person, 214–217
innovation, goal change and, 168–169
insurgency, blockage and, 123
integrated life, group membership and, 259–262
interpersonal relationships
  empathy in, 146
  environment in, 145
  group dynamics and, 19–20
  group membership and, 144–147
  leadership and, 180, 185
isolate
  challenge by, 316–319
  defined, 309
  vs. deviant, 309–312
  group reaction to, 312, 315–318
  group sanctions against, 318–320
  leadership reaction and, 321–323
  as "sinner," 314
isolation, 309–330
  cause of, 312–315, 322–323
  as challenge, 313–314
  deliberate, 323–326
  as deviance, 320
  group process in, 317
  group recovery from, 326–330
  as personality change, 325
  psychology of, 316
  significance of 322–323

job, vs. family, 250–251
  see also work groups
job enrichment, vs. enlargement, 46, 247
job training, 58
Johnson, Lyndon B., 51, 276

Kennedy, Jacqueline, 177
Kennedy, John F., 187
kinetic equilibrium, in multigroup membership, 240–243

labor, manager and, 79–80
labor negotiations, and formal group, 78
labor relations
  group blockage and, 121–122
  group dynamics in, 18
labor union
  vs. company, 272–275
  wealth of, 150
leader
  vs. assumed leadership, 293
  as cause of deviance, 301
  character traits of, 161
  charisma of, 164
  conceptual abilities of, 186
  conspiracy against, 205
  continuity of, 198–199
  decision making by, 185
  as deviant, 306
  duty to self, 208–209
  as father figure, 192–195
  group cohesiveness and, 170–173
  group effectiveness and, 339–342
  and group objectives, 270–271
  vs. impersonal observer, 230–233
  intelligence of, 184
  interpersonal relations of, 185
  isolate and, 321–323
  motivation of, 184, 196
  as parent, 203
  permissive, 191
  personal tours of, 189
  power position of, 198–199
  random sampling of, 190
  recognition of, 184
  responsibilities of, 163, 193–194
  stamina of, 185
  subleader and, 217–219
  Theory X and Theory Y types, 174, 196–197, 201
  undermining of, 204
  value judgment of individuals by, 207
  weaknesses of, 205
leader-follower rapport, 190–191
leadership, 183–210
  acceptance of, 120
  action levels and, 173–176
  assured, 291–294
  avoidance of, 213
  blockage and, 123
  charisma and, 186–189
  complexity of, 206
  continuity of, 132
  decision making and, 209
  delegation and, 233
  deviance and, 287
  vs. drivership, 201
  ego drives and, 40
  ego instinct and, 69–71
  employee separations and, 207–208
  entrenchment of, 132
  environment of, 120–121
  father image in, 192–195
  of front-line soldier, 227–228
  goal competition and, 244–245
  goal identification and, 195–198

INDEX

leadership (*continued*)
  group, 50
  group changes and, 161–164
  group cohesiveness and, 108
  group effectiveness and, 331–333, 339–342
  group sanctions and, 115
  and identification with product, 224–226
  inner-directed vs. outer-directed, 215
  inverted, 204–207
  manipulation vs. self-realization in, 201–204
  mass rapport and, 189–192
  of mob, 124
  need for, 119
  new techniques of, 101
  norms of, 199
  permissive vs. dictatorial, 203
  power drive and, 198–200, 204
  "qualities" of, 183–186
  response to, 118–121
  responsibilities of, 207–210
  rotational, 99–100
  schizoid, 219–221
  search for, 275–278
  styles of, 120
  supervision as, 222
  theory of, 15
  threat of, 128–129
Lewis, John L., 95
Lincoln, Abraham, 187
Lindbergh, Charles A., 187
lodges, membership in, 87
love beads, 154
Luther, Martin, 314

McGregor, Douglas, 28–33, 75, 84
Machiavelli, Niccoló, 64–65
maintenance factors, 220–223
man, as social being, 12
management, participative, 33

manager
  attitudes of, 29–32
  as authority figure, 79
  basic economics and, 57
  knowledge of employees by, 31–32
  labor relations and, 79–80
  management-union conflict and, 273
  permissive attitude in, 32–33
  rotation of, 44
  stereotypes of, 29
managerial grid, concept of, 120
manipulation, leadership as, 201–204
Maslow, Abraham H., 21, 33–41, 57, 67, 75, 82
mass rapport, leadership and, 189–192
matrix organization, 79
membership, *see* group membership
mental habits, family and, 372
mobility, individual changes and, 176–177
mob leadership, 124
money, "chase" for, 221
morale, group cohesiveness and, 81, 172
moral values
  erosion of, 142
  source of, 139
Mosaic decad, 233–234
Mosaic law, 318
Moses, 233
mother, leadership of, 355–356
motivation
  behavior and, 19
  conformity and, 138
  defined, 25–26
  of front-line soldier, 228–229
  group, *see* group motivation
  of hippies, 155–156
  job enrichment and, 46

motivation *(continued)*
  job rotation and, 44
  "law" of, 27–29
  of leader, 184, 196
  leadership and, 184
  need levels and, 33
  performance and, 26–27
  power as, 63–64
  self-knowledge and, 76
  value of, 26–27
  in warfare, 75
  zero state in, 43
Motivation in Management (Vroom), 46–47
Mouton, Jane, 120
multigroup membership, 143, 237–262
  adjustments in, 252–255
  conflicting pressures in, 248–249
  forces in, 240–242
  goal competition and, 243–246
  group hierarchy and, 249–252
  integrated life and, 259–262
  kinetic equilibrium and, 240–243
  necessity for, 243
  penalty of, 263–266
  role conflict and, 264–265
  schizophrenia and, 246–249
  withdrawal symptoms and, 255–258
Myers, F. Scott, 42, 44, 47

Napoleon I, 185
need
  levels of, 33–34
  motivation and, 33
  self-actualization, 21
Nero, 65
neurosis
  of group, 54
  infectious, 268
  role conflict and, 266–269

New York Life Insurance Company, 14
Nixon, Richard M., 51
nonconformists, 136–137
norms
  conformity and, 137
  defined, 111–112
  derivation of, 110
  see also group norms

objectives
  changes in, 167–170
  determination of, 116–118
  harmonics of, 268–272
  see also goal setting; group objectives; personal goals
observer
  as individual, 232
  psychology of, 230–231
obsolescence, planned, 225
Onassis, Aristotle, 177
on-the-job training, 58
organizational structure, matrix type, 235
outer-directed person, 214–217
overcommunication, demotivation through, 73

paternalism, formal group and, 83
peer acceptance, 39
perfectionist, ego needs of, 40
performance, motivation and, 26–27
  see also motivation
personal goals
  changes in, 141–144
  examination of, 144
  family and, 143–144
  see also goal setting; objectives
personality
  beliefs centering on, 258
  integrated, 260

personality change
  group dynamics and, 20–21
  isolation as, 325
personality clashes, in politics, 166
personal problems, demotivation through, 72–73
  group effectiveness and, 348–351
perspective, role conflict and, 282–284
physiological needs, 34–35
picket line, in strike, 125
political activity, social control through, 148
population, statistical, 14
Post Office Department, blockage threat of, 123
power
  meaning of, 64
  measurement of, 200
  as motivator, 63–64
  as narcotic, 199
  norms in, 199
  political approach to, 64–66
  of subcultures, 153–156
  violence and, 65
power drive, of leader, 198–200
power play, as deviance, 292
power struggles, in group, 63
Prince, The (Machiavelli), 64–65
product, identification with, 223–226
productivity, group survival and, 132–133
progress, deviant and, 305–308
protest, goal competition and, 245–246
psychedelic drugs, 155
PTA
  as collection of committees, 166
  as semiformal group, 88, 97

rapport, leader–follower, 190–191
rebellion, as deviance, 287
recognition, as motivation, 43, 46
reliability coefficient, 132
religious needs, 38–39
reputation, group membership and, 158
rigidity, of formal group, 86–87
role conflict, 263–285
  cause of, 269–272
  communication and, 279
  company vs. union in, 272–275
  ineffective followership and, 278–281
  leadership search and, 275–278
  as maturation aid, 282
  multigroup membership and, 265
  neurosis in, 266–269
  perspective and, 281–285
  strike and, 274
Roman Catholic church, as semiformal group, 89
Roosevelt, Franklin D., 187–188

safety needs, 36–37
sanctions, 113–115
  of family, 361–364
  of informal group, 104–105
  see also group sanctions
schizoid leadership, 219–221
schizophrenia, multigroup membership and, 246–249
schools, conformity in, 136
security, search for, 37
security drive
  creativity and, 212–213
  followership and, 211–214
security needs, 82
self-actualization needs, 21, 34, 38–41, 57–58

self-confidence, group dynamics and, 22
self-control, social change and, 239
self-determinism
  individual and, 180–181
  leadership and, 175
self-identity, search for, 38
self-image, role conflict and, 281
self-knowledge, 16–17
  in interpersonal relationships, 146
  need for, 76
self-perception, discontinuity of, 264
self-perpetuation, of group, 60, 130–133
self-protective informal group, 99
self-realization, leadership as, 201–204
semiformal group, 87–97
  blockage and, 122
  control of, 95
  entrenchment in, 95–96
  vs. formal, 90
  form of, 88
  goals of, 92, 116, 168
  leadership in, 94
  long-range goals of, 116
  membership in, 88, 90–91
  norms in, 96–97
  objectives of, 93
  self-determinism in, 91
  snobbery in, 88
  structure of, 89–90
  voluntary membership in, 91–92
sexual needs, 34
sibling rivalry, deviance and, 360–361
slipshod work, 225
Smith, Alfred E., 172

social change
  adaptation and, 238
  self-control and, 239
social conflict, goal competition and, 246
social conscience, 149
social control, through political activity, 148
Socialist party, 155–156
social life, motivation and, 27
social needs, 34, 37–38, 66–67
social organization
  changes in, 237–238
  group hierarchy and, 251–252
  group proliferation and, 239
social psychology, science of, 23
social stratification, 38
socio-economic outlook, group behavior and, 147–151
splinter groups
  of front-line soldiers, 229
  impact of, 164–167
statistical population, generalizations on, 14
status
  conflict over, 178
  degradation and, 177–178
  esteem and, 68
  excessive concentration on, 68–69
  group membership and, 177
  group norms and, 150
  individual vs. group, 176–178
  as motivation, 66–69
  power and, 198
status seeking, 67
strike
  bitterness in, 126
  ending of, 126
  role conflict and, 274–275
  violent mob action in, 125
study groups, 58
subcultures, power of, 153–156

subleader, as leadership trainee, 218–220
supervision, as leadership, 222
supervisor–subordinate relationships, 235
synergy, of group, 334–336

Texas Instruments Incorporated, 42
Theory X
 isolate in, 318
 leader in, 174, 201
 manager in, 28–30, 84
Theory X and Theory Y concept, 28–33
Theory Y
 isolate in, 318
 leader in, 174, 196–197
 manager in, 30–31, 84
 "popularization" of, 32–33
Thomas, Norman, 155–156
threat
 aggressive reaction to, 124–127
 communication and, 127–128
 neutralizing of, 129–130
 retreat from, 127–128
 "turtle" reaction in, 128
Thurber, James, 373
transportation needs, 36–37
"turtle" reaction, to threat, 128
two-factor theory (Herzberg), 41–46, 78, 220, 247

vendor–customer relationship, 56

Vietnam peace talks, 51
Vietnam War
 hippies and, 155
 protests against, 276
violence
 goal competition and, 246
 by group, 125
 power and, 65
Volstead Act, 122
Vroom, Victor H., 46–47

War Between the States, 93
water pollution, 36
Willkie, Wendell, 187
withdrawal symptoms, multigroup membership and, 255–258
women's clubs, 58
workforce, reduction in, 37, 207
work groups
 development of, 58
 informal, 98–99
 trauma caused by, 247–248
working conditions, followership and, 221
working organizations, types of, 78–79
workmanship, pride in, 225
work problems, hostility in, 247
work-rule grievances, 84
work scheduling, timing in, 304
world trade, self-actualization and, 41

zero state, motivation and, 43

About the Author

ELTON T. REEVES is assistant professor of management at the Management Institute, University of Wisconsin, Madison. He was awarded his B.S. from the University of Idaho and his M.A. from the University of Washington, and he has done additional graduate work in industrial psychology at Louisiana State University.

Mr. Reeves has been a high school instructor, high school principal, supervisory rubber chemist at U.S. Rubber Company, pharmaceutical detail man at Lederle Laboratories Division of American Cyanamid Company, industrial relations man for Kaiser Aluminum & Chemical Corporation, corporate training director at Warwick Electronics, Inc., and management development coordinator for The Boeing Company before assuming his present responsibilities.

Mr. Reeves is the author of a number of published articles, of *Management Development for the Line Manager*, and is a member of the American Society for Training and Development.